Chinese–Japanese Relations in the Twenty-first Century

Today Japan is known as an 'economic superpower': its presence is ubiquitous in Asian economic affairs, with a 65 per cent share of the region's GDP. But now in the twenty-first century, China – with its vast population and its huge potential market – is predicted to grow in importance, and some even think it will surpass Japan and become the most significant economic power in Asia. This book examines Chinese–Japanese relations from a number of viewpoints to reveal the history and future of this complex, and crucial, relationship.

Historically, China has significantly influenced Japan, not only theologically and culturally but also within, for example, such disparate fields as state-planning, writing, medicine, mining and irrigation systems. When Japan rapidly proceeded with its industrialisation towards the end of the nineteenth century, its lack of raw materials resulted in a renewed interest in China; and this eventually led to war. Japanese aggression in China left a legacy of bitterness that still informs China's ambivalence towards cooperation with Japan. Today, how the two countries interact will have an impact on peace and security in the region as well as on future economic development in the area.

During the 1990s a major focus has been on the two countries' economic relationship. This book argues that to achieve a deeper understanding of the bilateral relationship there is a need for more interdisciplinary cooperation and analysis. *Chinese–Japanese Relations in the Twenty-first Century* is written by eminent international experts whose broad range of disciplinary viewpoints – from history and sociology, to politics and economics – provide a deeper understanding of one of Asia's most critical relationships.

Marie Söderberg is an Associate Professor at the European Institute of Japanese Studies in Stockholm. She came to Japan in 1977 as a news correspondent, also travelling to China. Her works cover issues of Japanese defence, foreign and aid policy. Her most recent publications are *The Business of Japanese Foreign Aid* and *Japanese Influences and Presences in Asia*.

European Institute of Japanese Studies East Asian Economics & Business Series
Edited by Marie Söderberg
Stockholm School of Economics, Sweden

This series presents cutting-edge research on recent developments in business and economics in East Asia. National, regional and international perspectives are employed to examine this dynamic and fast-moving area.

1. **Chinese Legal Reform**
The case of foreign investment law
Yan Wang

2. **Chinese–Japanese Relations in the Twenty-first Century**
Complementarity and conflict
Edited by Marie Söderberg

Chinese–Japanese Relations in the Twenty-first Century
Complementarity and conflict

Edited by Marie Söderberg

LONDON AND NEW YORK

First published 2002
by Routledge
2 Park Square, Milton Park, Abingdon, Oxfordshire OX14 4RN

Simultaneously published in the USA and Canada
by Routledge
711 Third Avenue, New York, NY 10017

Routledge is an imprint of the Taylor and Francis Group, an informa business

First issued in paperback 2015

Selection and editorial matter © 2002 Marie Söderberg; individual chapters
© the contributors

Typeset in Baskerville by
BOOK NOW Ltd

All rights reserved. No part of this book may be reprinted or reproduced or
utilised in any form or by any electronic, mechanical, or other means, now
known or hereafter invented, including photocopying and recording, or in
any information storage or retrieval system, without permission in writing
from the publishers.

British Library Cataloguing in Publication Data
A catalogue record for this book is available from the British Library

Library of Congress Cataloging-in-Publication Data
Chinese–Japanese relations in the twenty-first century : complementarity and conflict / edited by
Marie Söderberg.
     p.   cm. – (European Institute of Japanese Studies East Asian economics & business
series)
    Includes bibliographical references and index.
    1. China–Relations–Japan. 2. Japan–Relations–China 3. Twenty-first
century–Forecasts. I. Söderberg, Marie. II. Series.

DS740.5.J3 C3995 2001
327.51052′09′051–dc21   2001052014

ISBN 978-0-415-25431-1 (hbk)
ISBN 978-1-138-86307-1 (pbk)

Contents

List of tables and figures	vii
List of contributors	ix
Preface	xi
List of abbreviations	xiii
Note on names	xv

Introduction   1
MARIE SÖDERBERG

1 Mirror for the future or the history card? Understanding the
'history problem'   10
DAQING YANG

2 Sino-Japanese relations in the context of the Beijing–Tokyo–
Washington triangle   32
QUANSHENG ZHAO

3 Engagement Japanese style   52
REINHARD DRIFTE

4 Sino-Japanese relations and ballistic missile defence (BMD)   69
CHRISTOPHER W. HUGHES

5 The Taiwan question: reconciling the irreconcilable   88
PHIL DEANS

6 The background and trend of the partnership   103
JIN XIDE

7 The role of ODA in the relationship   114
MARIE SÖDERBERG

vi *Contents*

8 Economic relations: what can we learn from trade and FDI? 130
   HANNS GÜNTHER HILPERT AND NAKAGANE KATSUJI

9 Japanese firms in China: what problems and difficulties
   are they facing? 154
   HU XINXIN

10 Managing the global–local dilemma: problems in controlling
    Japanese subsidiaries in China 177
    JOCHEN LEGEWIE

    Index 195

Tables and figures

Tables

2.1	Comparisons between US, China and Japan, gross domestic product	34
2.2	Comparisons between US, China and Japan, total trade	34
2.3	Comparisons between US, China and Japan, foreign direct investment	35
2.4	Comparisons between US, China and Japan, GDP per capita	36
2.5	Top trading partners of China, Japan and the US	37
4.1	BMD/TMD systems	71
4.2	Chinese ballistic missile capabilities	75
7.1	Bilateral ODA donors to China by size	120
7.2	Multilateral ODA to China by size	121
7.3	Japanese ODA to China	121
8.1	Japan and China compared	131
8.2	Japan's and China's bilateral trade, 1980–99	133
8.3	China's trade by export destinations and import sources, 1980–99	135
8.4	Japan's trade by export destinations and import sources, 1980–99	136
8.5	Japanese export intensity index, 1980–99	137
8.6	Chinese export intensity index, 1980–99	138
8.7	Foreign investment in China by major source countries, 1983–99	141
8.8	Japanese foreign direct investment to China, 1980–99	142
8.9	Japanese investment in China by industrial sector	144
8.10	Regional dispersion of Japan's investment in China	145
8.11	Investment purposes of Japanese investors by region in 1999	145
8.12	The most promising country for Japanese FDI	151
9.1	Top ten investors in China by the year-end 1999	155
9.2	Japanese-funded firms by region in the PRC	156
9.3	Patterns of Japanese FDI in China, 1995–9	157
9.4	Performance in sales of Japanese firms in China	157
9.5	Profitability of Japanese firms in China	157
9.6	Expected profitability of Japanese firms over FY, 1999–2000	157
9.7	Promising FDI destinations over the medium and long term	158
9.8	Self-evaluation of FDI performance by region	159

viii *Tables and figures*

9.9	Changing self-evaluation of FDI performance in China, 1995–9	159
9.10	Concerns in undertaking FDI in China	160
9.11	Changes in problems for Japanese business in China	161
10.1	Typology of control mechanisms	180
10.2	Use of control mechanisms in subsidiaries of firms from different countries	181

Figure

| 8.1 | Four possible scenarios of Sino-Japanese economic relations | 150 |

Contributors

Daqing Yang is Assistant Professor in History and International Affairs at the George Washington University, US.

Quansheng Zhao is Professor and Director of the Division of Comparative and Regional Studies, School of International Service, American University, US.

Reinhard Drifte holds the Chair of Japanese Studies, Department of Politics, University of Newcastle, UK.

Christopher W. Hughes is Associate Fellow, Asia Programme, Royal Institute of International Affairs, and Senior Research Fellow, Centre for the Study of Globalisation and Regionalisation, University of Warwick, UK.

Phil Deans is Lecturer in Chinese Politics, Department of Political Studies, School of Oriental and African Studies, University of London, UK.

Jin Xide is Professor and Director in the Department of Foreign Relations, Institute of Japanese Studies, Chinese Academy of Social Science, China.

Marie Söderberg is Associate Professor at the European Institute of Japanese Studies, Stockholm School of Economics, Sweden.

Hanns Günther Hilpert works in the Economic Section, German Institute of Japanese Studies, Japan.

Nakagane Katsuji is Professor at the Graduate School of Economics, University of Tokyo, Japan.

Hu Xinxin is Professor at the Institute of Japanese Studies, Chinese Academy of Social Science, China.

Jochen Legewie is Deputy Director of the Economic Section, German Institute of Japanese Studies, Japan.

Preface

The relationship between East Asia's two giant powers, China and Japan, has always been and will always be crucial for understanding the development of Asia. The relationship has undergone considerable changes since the end of the Cold War but what we learn about it is often fragmented into different disciplines or knowledge of specific incidents.

With this background, the European Institute of Japanese Studies at Stockholm School of Economics joined forces with the Swedish Institute of International Studies to organise a cross-disciplinary international workshop about the Chinese–Japanese relationship in the first year of the new millennium. We had not anticipated the great interest in this topic and were overwhelmed by the number of scholars from all over the world who were eager to come all the way to another corner of the globe, northern Europe, to present and discuss their research on this topic. We had to make a strict selection between interested applicants, and finally twenty-five scholars from Asia, the Pacific, North America and Europe met in Stockholm in late August 2000. For three very intense days we listened to presentations and discussed the Chinese–Japanese relationship from a number of different angles.

This book is basically built on a selection of the papers presented at the workshop, incorporating into the original versions the comments we made and the discussions we had during the workshop. Where the contents of different papers overlapped, they have been merged. There were many other equally good papers, which we would have liked to be able to include in this volume but were forced to leave out for reasons of space and slightly differing focus. It is our aspiration that this volume will reflect the interesting discussions we had at the workshop and the many angles and views that must be taken into account in an assessment of the Chinese–Japanese relationship and where it is heading.

We would like to take this opportunity to thank the Japan Foundation as well as the Swedish Institute for the Internationalisation of Higher Education and Research (STINT) for their generous economic support that made this workshop possible. Special thanks go to Ambassador Börje Ljunggren, Swedish Ministry of Foreign Affairs, for his opening remarks, to Linus Hagström, Ph.D. candidate, for academic input and contact making, and Marie Tsujita xii *Preface*

Stephenson and Annika Shelly at the European Institute of Japanese Studies for superb administration.

Dr Anders Mellbourn
Director, Swedish Institute of International Affairs
and
Dr Marie Söderberg
Associate Professor, European Institute of Japanese Studies

Abbreviations

ABM	anti-ballistic missile
APEC	Asia–Pacific Economic Cooperation
ARF	ASEAN Regional Forum
ASEAN	Association of Southeast Asian Nations
AWACS	Airborne Warning and Control System
BM	battlefield management
BMD	ballistic missile defence
BMDO	Ballistic Missile Defence Organisation
CAS	Chinese Academy of Sciences
CASS	Chinese Academy of Social Sciences
CCP	Chinese Communist Party
CITIC	China International Trust and Investment Corporation
CWC	Chemical Weapons Convention
DAC	Development Assistance Committee
DSP	Defence Support Programme
EEZ	exclusive economic zone
EU	European Union
FDI	foreign direct investment
FY	fiscal year
GDP	gross domestic product
GPALS	Global Protection Against Limited Strikes
ICBM	intercontinental ballistic missile
IDA	International Development Association, World Bank
IMC	international management control
IMINT	imagery intelligence
JBIC	Japan Bank of International Cooperation
JDA	Japan Defence Agency
JETRO	Japan External Trade Organisation
JICA	Japan International Cooperation Agency
JIPO	Japan–China Investment Promotion Organisation
JRCC	Japan–ROC Cooperation Committee
KMT	Kuomintang
LDP	Liberal Democratic Party (of Japan)

xiv *Abbreviations*

MIRV	Multiple Independently Targetable Re-entry Vehicles
MITI	Ministry of International Trade and Industry
MNCs	multinational companies
MOF	Ministry of Finance, Japan
MOFA	Ministry of Foreign Affairs, Japan
MOFTEC	Ministry of Foreign Trade and Economic Cooperation, China
MRI	Mitsubishi Research Institute
MSDF	Maritime Self-Defence Force
NAFTA	North Atlantic Free Trade Association
NATO	North Atlantic Treaty Organisation
NGO	non-governmental organisation
NIEs	Newly industrialised economies
Nikkakon	Japan–ROC Dietmembers Consultative Committee or Ni-Ka Kankei Giin Kondankai
NMD	National Missile Defence
NORAD	North American Aerospace Command
NPT	Non-Proliferation Treaty
NTWD	Navy Theatre Wide Defence
ODA	official development assistance
OECF	Overseas Economic Cooperation Fund
OOF	other official flows
PLA	People's Liberation Army
PMO	Prime Minister's Office
PNTR	permanent normal trading relations
PPP	purchasing power parity
PRC	People's Republic of China
RMB	Ren Min Bi, or Yuan
ROC	Republic of China
SAR	synthetic aperture radar
SDI	Strategic Defence Initiative
SDIO	Strategic Defence Initiative Office
SOE	state-owned enterprise
SSC	Security Subcommittee
TECRO	Taipei Economic and Cultural Representative Office
TMD	theatre missile defence
UN	United Nations
UNDP	United Nations Development Programme
UNESCO	United Nations Educational, Scientific, and Cultural Organisation
USSPACECOM	US Space Command
WESTPAC	Western Pacific Missile Architecture
WTO	World Trade Organisation

Note on names

Japanese, Chinese and Korean names are written with the surname first, with the exception of people living in the West, who are better known for writing in English than in their native language.

The Hepburn system is used in transcription from Japanese but with names of persons and places the long vowel is not marked.

Introduction

Marie Söderberg

> China? There lies a sleeping giant. Let him sleep. For when he wakes he will move the world.
>
> (remark made by Napoleon)

The People's Republic of China (hereafter called China) is a country with 1.3 billion people: that is, one-fifth of the world's population. It has a territory of 3.7 million square miles, slightly larger than the United States and 25 times larger than Japan. China is also rich in natural resources. These are all attributes connected with a great power. Had it been a country the size of Korea, Malaysia or Thailand, it would not have drawn such attention and provoked such emotional reactions.

Since the opening up in 1979, China's economy has been growing by more than 10 per cent a year. Other countries in East Asia also experienced explosive economic growth, but they were not of the same size. Today China is the world's seventh largest economy and some predict that it will be the world's second largest within two decades. To accommodate such a society in an age of globalisation presents a challenge to the rest of the world. More than anywhere else it presents a challenge to its Asian neighbours, and especially so to Japan – the 'economic superpower' which has a 65 per cent share of the region's GDP.

During the last decade the Japanese economy has been stagnating. However, the size of it is still four times that of the Chinese, and Japan's income per capita level is 38 times as high as China's. Japan is poor in natural resources as well as territorial space but it is a highly developed society. It has increasingly taken an active part in various multilateral forums and it is the world's largest donor of foreign aid.

The relationship between China and Japan is complex and emotional. It contains aspects both of rivalry and complementarity. Opinion polls in both countries show that there is still a considerable amount of distrust between them. This is why many scholars in both China and Japan, who would be the most naturally placed to study this relationship, still have difficulties in approaching the bilateral relationship in a non-prejudiced way. Although it is sensitive, the topic really needs to be addressed, since it is of crucial importance, not only to the two parties involved, but to the whole of Asia. The way that Japan and China

2 Marie Söderberg

interact is likely to have an impact on stability, peace and security as well as on future economic development in the region.

Besides an abundance of literature in Chinese and Japanese, there are, not surprisingly considering the importance of the topic, also several books in English. These look at the relationship from various aspects. There are several authors that see the relationship either from a Chinese perspective[1] or from a Japanese perspective.[2] History is a common theme[3] and so is security.[4] Territorial issues such as the Diaoyu/Senkaku Islands[5] are also dealt with. In the field of economics there are books of a more general character,[6] those that interpret the different economic development patterns from a culture perspective,[7] and those that approach the relationship from more of a business perspective.[8]

This book is a collection of papers that address the relationship from a variety of angles.[9] It is the development after the end of the Cold War and what has happened in more recent years that is the focus of each chapter. The purpose of this volume is to look at the Chinese–Japanese relationship from various academic perspectives and through an interdisciplinary approach achieve a deeper understanding of the relationship. It is our firm belief that no field of interaction between the two can be studied in isolation but has to be put into the context of the overall relationship. Only then can one grasp what is happening between the two countries. In an academic setting one cannot make any definitive predictions about the future. But in all chapters here the authors, besides giving the background, identify problems, point out possible solutions, and draw on existing trends to foretell the scenarios of the future. To get the widest possible perspective this is done by scholars from a number of countries. Besides Chinese and Japanese academics our contributors are from the US and various parts of Europe. With so many different people working on different perspectives of the relationship it is of course not possible to reach a mutual consensus on its exact course and direction. It is our sincere aspiration, however, that this volume will help the understanding of the relationship and its multi-dimensionality.

If wisely handled, the relationship could be very beneficial for both parties. Japan possesses financial resources and advanced technology. The Chinese have an abundance of natural resources and labour. Cooperation could bring great benefits, but there is always the fear that these would not be equally distributed. There is also a considerable amount of rivalry between Japan and China and an abundance of nationalism in both countries.

This volume focuses on the relationship in the post-Cold-War era, but before presenting the structure of the book we need a short exposé of the historical setting of the relationship.

The history of the relationship

At the end of the sixth century Chinese influences on Japan were substantial. China was one of the most highly developed countries in the world, whereas Japan, in contrast, was a backward island country. To the Chinese emperor,

Japan was just another tributary state, and to Japan, China was most important because of its advanced civilisation. From that period on there was an extensive amount of cultural 'borrowing', not only theologically and culturally, but also within disparate fields such as state planning, legal codes, writing, medicine, and mining and irrigation systems, just to mention a few examples. Traditionally, it has been the Chinese who have who have given various inputs to the development of the Japanese society.

With Western efforts to forcibly open up East Asia in the mid-nineteenth century, the situation changed. China and Japan reacted very differently to Western intrusion. China resisted, failed to modernise and was defeated and divided. In Japan, on the other hand, the intrusion led to a collapse of the traditional order: the centralisation of sovereignty in a new Meiji state that, in place of resistance, started a process of self-strengthening through learning and eventually identifying with the Western state system. The Japanese quickly learned how to build a modern, industrialised society. They also learned how to build up military might and were going to use it to subordinate China. Between 1894 and 1895 Japan fought and won a war with China through which it gained Taiwan. In the Boxer Rebellion of 1900, Japan was on the side of the Westerners. It won a war over Russia in 1905 and in 1910 Korea was annexed. During WWI, it captured some German islands in the North Pacific and took over the German leased territory in China's Shandon province. Through the Versailles Treaty, Japan was elevated to a new status as a great power and started to expand its economy and armed forces to demonstrate its supremacy in China.

In contrast to these aggressive, militaristic trends, there was also a certain amount of sympathy from a number of Japanese towards China. They saw the Chinese struggle for modernisation as a parallel to their own Meiji restoration. Much of their commercial outflow was motivated by the search for raw materials and also, in the 1920s, to help Japanese industries, such as the textile industry, which had reached a stage where high production costs were making it uncompetitive. The huge exodus of Japanese people into China during this period brought with it Japanese intellectual influences, as did the Chinese students who returned home after education in Japan.

A prerequisite for cooperation between the two countries was that Chinese political reforms would deliver a stable environment. They never did, and by the end of the 1920s the combination of a shift in the world economy and a growing extremism in Japan were decisive for the nature of their relationship. The Manchurian 'incident' in 1931 was the start of Japanese aggression, and in 1937 Japan launched a war against China proper. In 1941, Japanese aggression expanded into Southeast Asia and in December of that year Pearl Harbor was attacked.

The Japanese aggression in China left a legacy of bitterness that still pervades Chinese ambivalence towards cooperation with Japan today. The surrender of Japan in 1945 is to many Chinese the most memorable event in the history of the Chinese–Japanese relationship.

After this the relationship changed again. China emerged as a communist

4 *Marie Söderberg*

country in 1949 and Japan became a member of the anti-communist bloc headed by the US. The American containment policy, strengthened by Chinese support of North Korea in the Korean War, isolated China from the Western world for the next two decades. Chinese adoption of Soviet-style long-term central planning also made interaction with market-driven economies like Japan's very difficult. Not surprisingly, from an administrative point of view, Soviet-type economies deal more easily with each other. In fact, the Soviet Union in the 1950s supplied China during its first five-year plan with the capital goods and plants needed. The rupture with the Soviet Union in the 1960s forced the Chinese leadership to look for new partners and Japan was in possession of the heavy industrial equipment China was looking for. The absence of official relations was then sidestepped by the Chinese trading with 'friendly firms' as well as the establishment of some quasi-official channels for trade.[10] The Cultural Revolution that followed slowed the progress in trade and it was not until normalisation of relations in 1972, which came after the sudden US *rapprochement* with China, that trade really took off. In 1978 a ten-year trade agreement was concluded in which Japan committed itself to a long-term import–export programme with China which required a certain amount of private-sector coordination that was and still is unusual for a market economy. This was facilitated by an extensive use of financing from the EXIM Bank (Export Import Bank of Japan). It was also at this time that China decided to accept aid from abroad and Japan immediately became the main donor.

During the 1980s and 1990s the main focus was on the economic side of the relationship. After the Plaza Accord in 1985, when the value of the yen rose considerably, there was a rush by Japanese companies to establish production in China. The bloodshed at Tiananmen Square in 1989 interrupted the economic activities to a certain degree, although Japan was the first country of the G7 to lift sanctions afterwards.

The Chinese economy has been growing rapidly and the potential of the huge Chinese market has drawn considerable attention, not only from Japanese companies but from companies all over the world. Japan's economy, on the other hand, has been stagnant during the 1990s. The shift in balance between the two spills over into other fields as well. The 'Japan passing' that made the headlines when President Clinton went straight to Beijing without making a stop over in Tokyo reveals Japan's feelings about the growing might of its neighbour.

China holds a permanent seat on the UN Security Council, something long sought after in Japan but not specifically supported by its neighbour. In China, on the other hand, they worry about Japanese–US cooperation in the research into theatre missile defence (TMD) and the implications such weapons could have on the Taiwan question. There are a number of 'issues' between the two countries on which they have different views and are of different opinions. Some of them have their roots in history, while others are of more recent origin. The end of the Cold War has changed the structure of the international setting in which Chinese–Japanese relations have been imbedded. The two countries are meeting a number of new challenges in their relationship and it is these that are the topic of this book.

Structure of the book

Even if this volume focuses on the period after the Cold War, one cannot avoid history, as this has recently become a very important topic between China and Japan. The last two decades have seen relations caught in a vicious cycle of disputes over World War II history. Controversies have raged over the alleged revision of Japanese textbooks, Japanese politicians' visits to the Yasukuni Shrine, and Chinese demands for an apology for such Japanese wartime atrocities as the Nanjing Massacre. All of these seem to have contributed in significant measure to the deterioration of mutual feelings, reaching a symbolic low during Chinese President Jiang Zemin's state visit to Japan in 1998.

In Chapter 1, 'Mirror for the future or history card? Understanding the history problem', Daqing Yang brings up these issues, traces the causes of them and proposes some possible solutions. Adopting a state-society approach, Yang considers the history problem to be rooted in the body politic of both China and Japan. He argues that the 'state manipulation' theory, though containing much truth, overlooks the complexities of societal and institutional factors such as victim consciousness, pre-existing cultural assumptions, and worldwide trends. Attributing the problem solely to manipulation of the government on the other side often contributes to the prolonging of the dispute. Should all forms of 'state manipulation' then be abandoned in favour of a completely free flow of ideas and feelings about past conflicts? Yang in his chapter concludes that a genuine reconciliation must be based on an understanding of history that can only take place in democratic societies, after the significant transformation of the body politic in *both* Japan and China. In the short run, however, management by both governments and non-governmental institutions are still needed to steer the often volatile relationship away from rupture and to provide a necessary framework for more honest exchanges.

The second chapter puts the relationship into a global context, since it cannot be understood from the perspectives of the two countries only. Changes in the international system since the end of the Cold War are also affecting Japanese–Chinese relations. In the chapter 'Sino-Japanese relations in the context of the Beijing–Tokyo–Washington triangle', Quansheng Zhao analyses the relationship, concentrating primarily on the external actors at the international level, and more specifically on the most significant one of all, the US.

Since the end of the Cold War, tremendous changes in great-power relations have taken place in East Asia, including the upward development of the United States and China, the downward slide of Japan, and the collapse of the former Soviet Union. The new global structure, which is described by some Chinese observers as *chao duo qiang* – meaning one single superpower [the US] faced with many strong powers – is analysed, as well as the impact it has on the Chinese–Japanese relationship. Quansheng Zhao points out future directions and how Japan will deal with 'the rise of China' within this triangular relationship.

Whether to engage or contain China has been a hot topic since the incident at Tiananmen Square in 1989. Japan's policy of engagement is the topic of the next

6 *Marie Söderberg*

chapter 'Engagement Japanese style' by Reinhard Drifte. This chapter critically examines the assumptions and feasibility of the Japanese policy of engagement whose dualistic character is very often ignored. Japanese engagement intends to steer China towards a peaceful and sustainable path by assisting it with economic policy tools such as trade, investment, technology transfer and foreign aid. At the same time, however, Japan is hedging any Chinese strategic breakout or policy failure through the bilateral military deterrent with the US, as well as the political front-building with other Asian countries. The chapter first looks at Japan's changing security perceptions of China since 1989 and then describes how Japan has been reacting to this perception at various policy levels: that is, unilateral and bilateral as well as multilateral.

The fourth chapter takes up the Japanese agreement to carry out cooperative technological research with the US into ballistic missile defence (BMD). In 'Sino-Japanese relations and ballistic missile defence', Christopher W. Hughes argues that for Japanese policy-makers the pursuit of BMD will make the security relationship with China, which has already become highly complex due to the introduction of the revised Guidelines for US–Japan Defence Cooperation, even more fraught and hazardous. Indeed, it may be the case that BMD, to a far greater extent than the revised Guidelines, contains the potential to bring existing Sino-Japanese, Sino-US, and US–Japanese security tensions to a head, with destabilising effects for each of these bilateral relationships and for regional and global security as a whole.

Hughes makes this argument based on the fact that, even though the revised Guidelines have without doubt raised the security tensions between Japan, China and the US, their cautious framing by Japanese policy-makers has provided Japan, the US, and to some extent China also, with sufficient room for strategic manoeuvre to allow them to alleviate tensions and avoid final conflict if necessary. However, in contrast to the uncomfortable but near tolerable *modus vivendi* offered to all sides by the revised Guidelines, it can be argued that BMD presents Japan with a qualitatively more dangerous challenge. This is because the inherent technological and military logic of BMD dictates that Japan becomes more fully integrated than ever before into US military strategy in East Asia and towards China. Taken to its extreme, and without sufficiently careful management by Japanese policy-makers, Hughes means that the subsequent logic of BMD could undermine Japan's political, diplomatic and strategic freedom and set it on a collision course with China's perceived inviolable security interests.

Since 1995, the Taiwan issue has emerged as an area of significant disagreement and potential conflict between Tokyo and Beijing. In Chapter 5, 'The Taiwan question: reconciling the irreconcilable', Phil Deans gives the background and tells us how Sino-Japanese relations between 1972 and 1995 enjoyed a period of relative stability and broad consensus over the 'Taiwan issue'. The disagreements that occurred between Tokyo and Beijing were concerned with formal issues of status and sovereignty – the mechanisms for handling contact between Taipei and Tokyo, the designation of ROC aircraft, and the legal status of the ROC and its representatives in Japan. The Japanese were able to broaden and deepen their economic relations with Taiwan, while 'political' contacts were facilitated by the activities of pro-Taiwan figures in the ruling LDP, under the broad remit of the principle of s*eikei bunri* (*zhengjing fenli*) the 'separation of politics and economics'. Beijing proved willing to tolerate a considerable degree of contact and exchange between Japan and Taiwan provided that it remained 'informal' and did not relate to issues of ROC/Taiwanese sovereignty. The reason the Taiwan issue has increased in significance since 1995, Phil Deans suggests, was due to changes in the domestic politics in the three countries, rather than any putative shift in the international order.

The most obvious change has been the increased salience of military security issues for the three sides, but Taiwan's changing political institutions, increasing nationalism in the PRC, and the increased influence of pro-Taiwan politicians in Japanese politics have also been factors in the growing importance of Taiwan in Sino-Japanese relations.

In Chapter 6, 'The Background and Trend of the Partnership', Jin Xide considers the relationship between the two countries during the 1990s at the diplomatic level. He divides the development into three stages. The first one covered the years from 1989 to around 1993. At this stage, many changes, including US policy transition and great changes in the political and economic situation in both China and Japan exerted a great influence on Japan's China policy. The second stage was from 1994 to 1996 when Sino-Japanese relations witnessed a series of new characteristics featuring frequent political friction between the two countries. The third stage began in 1997 as a reaction to the constant friction and setbacks of China–Japan relations during the previous period. After a series of negotiations and preparations, in 1998 the two countries signed a third policy document since the establishment of diplomatic relations: a 'friendly cooperative partnership for peace and development'. The direction, content and degree of bilateral and multilateral cooperation have been determined in the declared framework of this partnership. However, the process towards the realisation of it will bring many great challenges as well as good opportunities. It will be much easier to cooperate in some fields, such as economics, than in others, such as regional security.

Foreign aid is an area where considerable change will be seen. In Chapter 7, 'The role of ODA', Marie Söderberg presents some of the suggested policy changes in Japanese aid to China. Official development assistance has recently turned into a source of irritation between the two countries. This is largely due to the changes in Japanese policy on foreign aid. It used to consist mostly of cheap loans for economic infrastructure projects such as roads and railways, for which the recipients were requesting aid. In 1992, however, Japan adopted an ODA charter with a number of conditions attached to its aid. In 1995, when China conducted nuclear tests, part of Japanese grant aid (a small part of total aid) was withheld with reference to the charter. This caused considerable irritation in China. Recently, Japan decided to formulate 'country assistance plans' for its main recipients. A major debate, showing a deep discontent in Japan over present aid to China, developed and the formulation had to be stopped for some time. A

8 *Marie Söderberg*

report from an expert committee appointed by the government suggest radical changes in Japanese foreign aid to China. This change of policy is analysed both from a recipient and a donor perspective. What will happen with the new aid policy at the implementation stage is analysed and so is the future role of ODA in the Chinese–Japanese relationship.

Although Japan has provided a tremendous amount of ODA to China, it is above all trade and FDI that are the driving forces and which stimulate the development and industrialisation in China's outward-oriented strategy. These are focused on in Hanns Günther Hilpert and Nakagane Katsuji's chapter 'Economic relations: what can we learn from trade and FDI?'. They start off by analysing the quantitative dimension and the function of trade and FDI. The results and structures revealed here then lead them into a prognosis for the future development of the economic relationship. In the final section, the analysis is extended from pure economics into the realm of political economy by the presentation and the assessment of four different scenarios. These are positioned in a diagram in which the coordination mechanism (state versus market) forms the vertical axis and the psychological distance (sympathy versus hostility) the horizontal axis. The authors conclude that rivalry and regionalism are unlikely and that the relationship is likely to pass into a phase of competition and cooperation. As the economy of China is developing, the relationship will have to evolve from an area of 'special relations' to one that is characterised by an unprecedented scale of globalisation.

The next chapter takes us from the macro-economic level of the relationship down to the company level. Japan has been one of China's most important economic partners since the opening up of the economy, and a large number of Japanese firms have been established in China. Yet many of the Japanese firms that are actually doing businesses in China are reporting a number of problems: they are not able to make profits, there are frequent policy changes, central/local governments do not behave well, infrastructure is underdeveloped and they have difficulties in communicating with their Chinese counterparts, etc. In Chapter 9, 'Japanese firms in China: what problems and difficulties are they facing?', Hu Xinxin outlines the characteristics and performances of Japanese firms in China. The following questions are discussed: what kind of difficulties are Japanese firms actually facing in China? how do Japanese firms see their Chinese partners and how do the Chinese partners see the Japanese? To provide a concrete answer, the author has conducted a survey by doing interviews with business people as well as the personnel sent by some Japanese governmental or semi-governmental institutions. The results of these interviews are compared with previous surveys conducted in the mid-1980s (in Shenzhen) and the early 1990s (in Amoy and Beijing). The aim of this chapter is to seek an answer to the question: how can the problems that still exist be solved?

One of the keys to a company's success is management and the way it is controlled. This is the topic of Chapter 10, 'Managing the global–local dilemma – problems in controlling Japanese subsidiaries in China' by Jochen Legewie. This chapter compares the characteristics of Japanese international management control (IMC) practised in Japanese firms with those being used by management in other countries such as the US, Germany and Sweden. The management control system that Japanese multinational companies (MNCs) employ to coordinate the activities of their subsidiaries in China is analysed. The focus of the analysis is on the role of Japanese expatriates in this IMC system and their performance. In the process, it offers a comprehensive evaluation of the organisational fit of the Japanese IMC model within the current Chinese business environment. Taking Japanese firms as its subject, the analysis identifies areas of incongruity and explains the underlying reasons for problems with the IMC model. In doing so, this paper argues that the Japanese expatriate-based control system in China (as in many other parts of the world) continues to be characterised by an ethnocentrism that prevents a real internationalisation of overseas operations in the 'transnational' sense.

Notes

1 Allen S. Whiting, *China Eyes Japan*, Berkeley, University of California Press, 1989.
2 Quansheng Zhao, *Japanese Policymaking, the Politics behind Politics, Informal Mechanism and the Making of China Policy*, Oxford and New York, Oxford University Press, 1995.
3 Caroline Rose, *Interpreting History in Sino-Japanese Relations*, London, Routledge, 1999.
4 Greg Austin and Stuart Harris, *Japan and Greater China: Political Economy and Military Power in the Asian Century*, London, C. Hurst, 1999.
5 Unryu Suganumas, *Sovereign Rights and Territorial Space in Sino-Japanese Relations: Irredentism and the Diaoyu/Senkaku Islands*, Hawaii, University of Hawaii Press, 2000.
6 Robert Taylor, *Greater China and Japan, Prospects for an Economic Partnership in East Asia*, London, Routledge, 1996.
7 Kazuo John Fukuda, *Japan and China: the Meeting of Asia's Economic Giants*, New York, International Business Press, 1998.
8 Wei-Bin Zhang, *Japan versus China in the Industrial Race*, New York/Basingstoke, St Martin's Press/Macmillan, 1998.
9 So is Christopher Howe, ed., *China and Japan: History, Trends and Prospects*, Oxford, Oxford University Press, 1996, although ours has a much stronger emphasis on the post Cold War era.
10 Ibid., pp. 1–22.

1 Mirror for the future or the history card?

Understanding the 'history problem'

Daqing Yang

Over the last decade or so, issues related to the history of Japan's military invasion of China more than half a century ago have come to cast a huge cloud over the relations between the two Asian neighbours. The most recent high-level clashes over history issues took place during Chinese President Jiang Zemin's state visit to Japan in late 1998. In his speech at Waseda University in Tokyo, after elaborating on age-old friendly exchanges between the two countries over many centuries, he went on to note that:

> Unfortunately, Japan embarked on the path of militarism at the end of the 19th century. It occupied the Chinese territory of Taiwan after the First Sino-Japanese War. After the Russo–Japanese War of 1905, Japan for a time occupied China's Lushun [Port Arthur] and Dalian. Beginning from the 1930s, Japanese militarism launched full-scale war of aggression against China, causing China to suffer a casualty of 35 million people and property loss exceeding 600 billion US dollars. This war brought about profound national disaster to the Chinese people; it also caused much suffering to the Japanese people.[1]

Jiang repeatedly brought up the history issue in his meetings with his Japanese hosts. In the end, China failed to obtain a written apology, which the Japanese government had made to the visiting Korean President Kim Dae Jung the month before. If anything, Jiang's insistence did much to annoy many Japanese, to a considerable extent due to the unfavourable press coverage in Japan.

Why did the past come back to haunt present China–Japan relations with such a vengeance? Was Beijing's obsession with history a demonstration of its leaders playing the 'history card' against Japan, as many Japanese and Western observers believe? Or was it a legitimate reaction to the resurgence of nationalism in present-day Japan? Was this brawl over history a temporary phenomenon that will dissipate over time? Or do these outbursts reveal deeper structural fault lines in the bilateral relationship that may spell great disaster for the future? What are its implications for arguably the most important bilateral relationship in East Asia? What can be done about it? In this chapter I examine how these issues have been dealt with in political and intellectual circles as well as popular opinion in both China and Japan.[2]

Mirror for the future or the history card? 11

Is there a problem with history?

Put simply, the 'history problem' between China and Japan has developed into a vicious cycle of emotional outbursts over the history of Japanese aggression against China during the half century before and during World War II.[3]

Currently, the Chinese government considers the 'history problem' to be one of the major 'sensitive political issues between China and Japan', followed by issues such as Taiwan, the Diaoyu/Senkaku Islands, US–Japan security relations, and the Kōkaryō Dormitory in Kyoto. According to the Chinese Foreign Ministry:

> The history question of how to understand and deal with [*renshi he duidai*] Japanese militarist aggression in China was already a focal point in the 1972 negotiation over the Chinese–Japanese diplomatic normalization. It was clearly spelt out in the Sino-Japanese Joint Declaration and Sino-Japanese Treaty of Peace and Friendship, and has become the political foundation of China–Japan relations. The Chinese side always advocates 'history not forgotten is a guide to the future', and is willing to look to the future and develop lasting friendship between the two peoples on the basis of respecting history.[4]

A few points are worth noting here. First, the 'history problem', listed by the Foreign Ministry as a category separate from 'war reparations' and 'chemical weapons abandoned by Japan in China', seems to China to be above all an issue of attitude, albeit with real implications. During his Japanese visit, the Foreign Ministry notes, President Jiang 'explicated China's principles and positions in comprehensive, profound, and systematic manners. The Japanese side *for the first time* [emphasis mine] recognised [*chenren*] aggression against China and expressed profound self-reflection and apology [*fanxin he daoqian*], and jointly reaffirmed that correct understanding of and dealing with history is an important basis for developing China–Japan relations'. It goes on to say that during Prime Minister Obuchi's visit to China in July 1999, 'both China and Japan once again reaffirmed the agreement over the history issue reached in 1998. The Japanese side also expressed the willingness to squarely face history [*zhenshi lishi*] on this basis, to join hands (with China) to create the future, and to continue to contribute to peace with concrete actions'. Second, China continues to warn against what it calls 'an extremely small right-wing force in Japan' that 'from time to time denies and whitewashes the history of aggression, and creates disturbances in China–Japan relations'. In language reminiscent of the 1960s, it claims that 'We carried out timely, necessary struggle [*jinxin le biyao douzhen*] against them, and urged the Japanese Government to fulfil the pledges made on the history issue with concrete actions, to strictly restrain the extremely small right-wing forces, and to educate its people with correct views of history'.[5]

Although the history problem has not made it to Gaimushō's (MOFA's) home page, in recent speeches at the Chinese government institutes the then Japanese Ambassador to China Tanino Sakutaro devoted special attention to the subject (followed by the Taiwan question):

12 Daqing Yang

> Regarding the so-called 'history problem': first of all, during a certain period in the past, Japan embarked on the mistaken path of militarism, and caused much harm to the peoples of Asia beginning from China; secondly, concerning this the Japanese Government apologised [*shazai*], and most Japanese did as well [*mōshiwakenaikoto*]. Moreover, it is unmistakable that, upon sincere self-reflections over such mistaken national policies, Japan has chosen the righteous path of peace and prosperity in the postwar period.[6]

Here, the admission of a problematic past was straightforward. The timeframe of 'a certain period' is at best unclear and probably begins with 1931, which suggests an aberration rather than the logical outcome of the Meiji nation-state. (Taking over Taiwan in 1895 and incorporating the Senkaku Islands was thus not covered.) Second, the ambassador finds it difficult to accept that the history problem still exists, let alone any suggestion that Japan has not done enough – whether in terms of apologies or compensations. Ambassador Tanino then goes on to give a lengthy lecture on Japan's rebirth after the war as a result of learning the lessons of history:

> As a result, Japan rejected the path of a military power after the war and pledged in the constitution to renounce the use of force or the threat of use of force as means of solving international conflict, abolished conscription system, and rejected possession of strategic weapons such as long-range offensive missiles, long-range offensive aircraft carriers, and long-range bombers. Moreover, possessing various advanced technologies, Japan does not export any weapons to foreign countries. Its armed forces changed its name to Self-Defense Force; namely, that its mission lies solely in defending the Japanese territories is a fundamental consideration. Moreover, Japan considers the guarantee of its own peace and development in the pace and development of Asia, and strenuously strives to provide economic assistance to Asian countries. As a result, for the past seven years in a row since 1991, the Japanese government has provided the largest foreign economic assistance in the world.[7]

It is quite obvious that both governments recognise that they face a serious problem with history, real or otherwise. It is well known that when Japan and China normalised diplomatic relations in 1972, in return for China agreeing not to ask for reparations, the Japanese side acknowledged that it was 'keenly aware of Japan's responsibility for causing enormous damage in the past to the Chinese people through war and deeply reproaches itself'. After a period of warm relations in the late 1970s, the bilateral relations became subject to periodic downward swings over economic and other issues. The early 1980s marked the beginning of history problems in the relationship: alleged Japanese government whitewashing of textbooks to minimise past aggression, as well as statements to a similar effect by Japanese politicians prompted fierce Chinese (and other Asian governments') condemnation, leading (in most cases) to the resignation of the Japanese officials

Mirror for the future or the history card? 13

involved. Conversely, repeated Chinese protests and demands for Japan's repentance in turn fanned the sense of indignation in Japan over perceived Chinese interference in Japan's domestic affairs.[8] In 1987 the events took a particularly nasty turn. Against the background of bilateral economic problems, the legal dispute over a Kyoto dormitory, and the increase in Japan's defence spending, Chinese leader Deng Xiao-ping brought out the history issues, telling the visiting Komeito delegation that 'Japan is the country most indebted to China'. While China did not ask for reparations in 1972, Deng intimated, it was now dissatisfied with the state of affairs between the two countries. Deng's injection of the history issue into current bilateral relations brought about much consternation in Japan.[9]

In addition to these government-level spats, the brewing conflict over history also took on an increasingly populist turn in both countries: since the mid-1980s Chinese students have staged demonstrations over Japanese actions such as the visit to the Yasukuni Shrine by cabinet members. In the 1990s, Chinese victims of Japanese wartime atrocities in China, including the Nanjing Massacre, bacteriological warfare, sexual slavery of the 'comfort women', and forced labour, began their own lawsuits against the Japanese government or corporations demanding apologies and compensation. Although Japanese courts rejected most of them, the end of the legal battle is not in sight.[10]

What is the impact of the history problem on China–Japan relations? One of the most noticeable casualties seems to be the deterioration in the popular perceptions of each other. Although there are many causes of this phenomenon, repeated clashes over the past is certainly a major factor. Opinion polls in China in the late 1990s indicated a much-heightened public awareness of Japan's past aggression in China, whereas Japanese polls registered an all-time low (since 1972) in their favourable feelings toward China. In a nationwide Chinese survey conducted in 1996, the 1937 Nanjing Massacre topped the list of terms the Chinese would commonly associate with Japan (84 per cent), followed by 'Japan's war aggression to China' (81 per cent). The Japanese national flag, to 96.6 per cent of those Chinese surveyed, reminded them of Japan's war against China. 'Japan's attitude toward the history of aggression' was considered by 93.3 per cent to be the biggest obstacle to developing China–Japan relations (followed by the 'Diaoyu Islands problem' (75.5 per cent) and 'Japanese politicians revising militarism' (74.7 per cent)). Even taking into consideration the methodological bias and timing of the poll, it is quite obvious that the history problem has an immense impact on Chinese perceptions of present-day Japan.[11] Although polls in Japan in general have avoided such bluntly direct questions, the trend is nonetheless clear. If the newspaper editorials and public reaction to Jiang's 1998 visit were any indication, there seemed to be a 'history fatigue' *vis-à-vis* China, if not outright indignation. Japanese TV talk show host Tahara Soichiro, in an on-camera interview last March, bluntly told the Chinese ambassador that the biggest cause for the worsening of Japanese attitudes toward China is China's incessant demands for an apology from Japan.[12]

As many analysts have pointed out, the problem with the history of its past

14 *Daqing Yang*

aggression has become a constraint on Japan's foreign policy, especially in its diplomacy *vis-à-vis* China. After the 1989 Tiananmen Square bloodshed, Japanese Prime Minister Uno Sosuke cited special historical as well as geographical circumstances for not forcefully condemning Beijing's bloody crackdown. As Japanese political scientist Ijiri Hidenori put it, 'The history of the past is not fully settled in Chinese–Japanese relations, thus creating a structure of China on the higher moral ground and Japan on the lower. The friction and conflict that burst out are temporarily contained but not resolved fundamentally, so [the relationship] has not left the vicious cycle that actually increases the source for potential frictions.'[13] On the Chinese side, Japan's seeming intransigence and attempts to justify past aggression further strengthen calls for a stronger China, both economically and militarily. '*Luo hou jiu yao ai da*' (if you are backward, you will be beaten) is commonly offered as the lesson from China's recent history of humiliation and foreign aggression. Moreover, the history problem has spilt over to other contentious political areas with Japan. China attributed the root of the continued separation of Taiwan from the 'motherland' to Japan's military aggression against China in 1895. Chinese activists from Hong Kong readily justified their action in the 'Defend Diaoyu Islands Movement' in terms of recovering territory lost to Japanese aggression.

The history problem is not just a political issue, as it has left its shadow in the economic sphere as well. Calls for the boycotting of Japanese goods to stop Japan's 'economic aggression' will continue to be heard, as long as they bring to mind boycotts in the prewar era that are portrayed in China as patriotic acts. The label of 'Chinese collaborators' (*hanjian*) can be applied to those working for a Japanese company or simply buying a Japanese product. In Japan, China's handling of the history issue is now used to strengthen the argument for reducing ODA to China, as some 1.8 trillion yen of Japanese taxpayers' money since 1978 seems to have done little to cultivate Chinese goodwill, let alone forgiveness for Japan's past wrongs. Japanese commentators are particularly incensed at any Chinese suggestion that the current economic aid is linked to the damages done in the past. After all, as one Japanese Foreign Ministry official put it poignantly, 'the main source of Japan's economic aid to China is the tax paid from their income, with their sweat, by the Japanese of the postwar generation that had absolutely nothing to do with the mistaken policy committed in Japan's relations in China for a time in the Showa era'.[14]

When all these trends are added together, the future scenario for the region looks bleak, if not alarming. In an article in the influential *Foreign Affairs*, Nicholas Kristof, who had reported for *The New York Times* both in China and in Japan, described virulent anti-Japanese sentiment among China's youth and went on to note that 'at the heart of the tension in Asia lies Japan's failure to apologise meaningfully for its wartime brutality'. As he put it, 'the danger remains that Japan will recover its nerve before it fully confronts the past'.[15] This may sound too alarmist. Historical animosities between nations or ethnic groups do not lead to a military conflict in themselves, but they make it more likely under certain circumstances since they can easily serve as convenient justifications for bellicose actions; they will also make such conflict more deadly when it does occur.

Interpreting sources of the 'history problem'

If there seems to be a general consensus that a deep historical fault line exists in East Asia, there is considerable disagreement over whose fault it is. Here I divide the existing explanations into four categories, although they are by no means mutually exclusive.

China plays the history card

Many Japanese and Western observers see the current history problem as primarily the result of the Chinese government's manipulation for political and economic gains. Writing shortly after the 1982 textbook controversy, Chalmers Johnson was among the first to express doubt 'that the Chinese government was truly interested in Japanese school textbooks, but there can be no doubt that it found in the textbook controversy a convenient lever to try to bring the Japanese government to heel, in which it was largely successful'.[16] Journalist Ian Buruma later added some precision to the Chinese motivation:

> the [textbook] controversy came at a good time for the Chinese government. Deng Xiao-ping was being criticised by the army and by rivals in the Communist Party for being soft on the United States and Taiwan. And a Japanese trade delegation had visited Taipei just before the Japanese Prime Minister's planned visit to Beijing. So it was in Deng's interest to embarrass the Japanese, to twist the knife a little.[17]

Nakajima Mineo, a leading China expert in Japan, called this tactic 'the bluff of the weak'. By exposing the old historical wounds, this widely shared view goes, China expected to extract massive yen loans and other concessions and to moderate Japan's criticism of China.[18] Some also see Beijing's use of the history issue as a strategy to drive a wedge between Japan and the US. What else can explain Jiang Zemin's stopover in Pearl Harbor on his way to the US in 1997? The *Economist* put the matter most bluntly shortly after Jiang's visit

> Plainly, and for many years, the Chinese have deployed [the war-guilt issue] as a negotiating weapon, often in association with entirely groundless claims that Japanese militarism is again on the rise. It has no moral value to them nor is the sincerity of the apology of particular relevance. Rather, it is a way of putting Japan on the defensive and extracting concessions from it.[19]

To many outside observers, the Chinese government has not always taken the history problem seriously, and this is an indication that the recent Chinese protest over those old history issues lacks sincerity. For instance, Jiang's insistence on getting an apology in 1998 contrasts sharply with the PRC's magnanimity during the previous decades. When meeting with Japanese Diet members in 1954, Zhou Enlai noted that:

The history of the past sixty years of Sino-Japanese relations was not good. However, it is a thing of the past, and we must turn it into a thing of the past. This is because friendship exists between the peoples of China and Japan. Compared to the history of a few thousand years, the history of sixty years is not worth bringing up. Our times have been unfortunate, because we have only been living in these sixty years. However, our ancestors weren't like this. Moreover, we cannot let such history influence our children and grandchildren.[20]

Moreover, in the late 1970s, Beijing even expressed interest in inviting politicians like Yaji Kazuo and Kishi Nobusuke to visit China. As a former LDP Diet member long involved in Chinese affairs pointed out, China's hospitality toward these right-wing politicians who had not shown any trace of repentance for Japanese aggression in Asia, created an impression that their crimes in the prewar era no longer mattered.[21]

Another often-heard criticism of China is that its government applied double standards when accusing the Japanese government of distorting history. With the greater awareness in Japan of the history education in other Asian countries, itself a result of the 1982 textbook controversy, many Japanese readers found out, to their surprise, that not only did the Chinese government censor their textbooks, they were actually written by a government-appointed committee! Translated Chinese textbooks, together with those from other Asian countries, often demonstrate the bias that even fair-minded Chinese scholars now admit.[22] Proponents of the Chinese manipulation theory also frequently point to what they consider to be deliberate Chinese exaggerations of China's losses in the war. For instance, before the 1980s the Chinese government usually gave the figure of eight million casualties in the War of Resistance against Japan. Now, as Jiang was quoted in his Waseda speech, that figure has reached 35 million. What else explains this seeming inflation but intentional distortion for the purpose of bigger extortion?

The China-plays-history-card interpretation is not so much wrong as it sees only half of the picture. There is some truth to another argument that the Chinese government does not simply (or primarily) use history as a card against Japan, but largely as part of patriotic education for domestic consumption. It is common wisdom that patriotism – often in the form of anti-Japanese-nationalism – is intrinsically linked to the government's legitimacy in China. This should not be too much of a shock, since the post-1949 Chinese national anthem has its origin in the war against the Japanese invasion in the 1930s. By making state manipulation the main culprit, however, this argument tends to overestimate Beijing's role, for better or worse. In the 1980s it was the Chinese students who staged demonstrations over Japanese actions such as the visit to the Yasukuni Shrine by cabinet members. In the 1990s, it was activists outside the government who initiated signature campaigns demanding apologies and compensation from Japan.[23] What we now witness in China is a society-wide phenomenon high-lighting the Japanese aggression in China and China's War of Resistance. Public media such as feature films, TV and magazines are saturated with stories about the war and Japanese atrocities. Not all the above-mentioned developments were ordered from above, even if the government may be said to have fostered the overall atmosphere. Moreover, this government-centred interpretation does not explain why overseas Chinese, including those in Japan, were often more adamant in condemning Japanese militarism and raising issues of reparation.[24]

Revival of Japanese militarism

To most Chinese – both in China and overseas – the fault lies squarely on the Japanese side. In fact, the Chinese government has made it clear that China does not have any responsibility for this problem in bilateral relations. At least one strong support can be mustered for this line of argument in the fact that China is not the only country having problems with Japan over history: Japan faces war-related problems with other countries, not just its neighbours in Asia, but also private citizens in the United States and Europe. Likewise, it was the Korean victims and their support groups who first brought up the issue of the 'comfort women' and pressed ahead with wartime labour legal suits.

A favourite Chinese refrain is 'the revival of militarism in Japan'. In his speech in Beijing, the Japanese ambassador took pointed exception to the Chinese views:

> Recently some people in China claim that Japan is abandoning a purely defensive posture and embarking on the path to military power. However, the basic principle of not becoming a military power enjoys strong support from most Japanese. I firmly believe that any tendency different from this principle will meet opposition from Japanese people and will not be realised. On this issue we always strongly ask for the understanding of the Chinese people. All in all, it will probably take a considerable time for the two countries to overcome the problem of 'history'. While Japan educates its young people resolutely in this area, we sincerely wish to continue to strive for Chinese understanding of how thoroughly peacefully Japanese are living their lives today.[25]

However, as most observers have noted, Japan has been extremely divided over how to look at its own recent past, an internal struggle often exacerbated by external pressures. As Japanese political scientist Ijiri put it, the 1982 textbook controversy was first 'an internal affair in which the leftist media, falsely reported that a textbook had been revised by the Education Ministry in a way that toned down descriptions of Japan's wartime action in China'.[26] Although it is increasingly losing any relevance to Japanese (and even foreign) ears, Chinese warnings against the revival of militarism were echoed by many Japanese progressives and pacifists on the left.

Giving some credence to Chinese claims is a vocal band of hawkish politicians on the right: either as elected officials, or in the government, even cabinet members.[27] If the Chinese government was playing any card at all, it was often

18 Daqing Yang

these Japanese who produced the card. In fact, many non-Chinese observers would agree with Japanese scholar Kotake Kazuaki, who puts the matter succinctly: one of the biggest reasons why historical understanding became a diplomatic problem lies in the character of the LDP regime. Among the conservative LDP members and their supporters, according to Kotake, there is a strong tendency to argue that the postwar reform after Japan's defeat was imposed on Japan, and refusing to recognise its positive value. Therefore, there is a restorationist tendency to praise the prewar system and to deny that Japan was the perpetrator in war.[28] Conservative Diet members openly call for Japanese politicians to pay official tribute to the Yasukuni Shrine, and set up a Historical Research Committee in response to then Prime Minister Hosokawa's statement admitting Japan's war responsibility.[29] After all, five million Japanese and a quarter of Diet members signed a petition opposing the 1995 Diet resolution on the fiftieth anniversary of the end of the war. Many writers have written about Japan's difficulty in coming to terms with its militarist past. Transwar continuity in many aspects of politics, to a large extent thanks to the Cold War environment, made it possible for an indicted class-A war criminal like Kishi Nobusuke to become Prime Minister.[30]

Outside political circles, the intellectual world is also fractured over the evaluation of Japan's war record.[31] A vocal group of academics and public opinion leaders regularly seek to correct what they call 'masochistic tendencies' in educating the younger generation about Japan's wartime excesses. As journalist Ian Buruma put it, 'despite their second-rank intellectual status, the Nanjing Massacre revisionists cannot be dismissed as unsavory crackpots, for unlike those who argue that the Holocaust never happened, they are not confined to an extreme fringe. They have a large audience and are supported by powerful right-wing politicians.' Books by members of one such group, the Institute for Orthodox History, have become national bestsellers.[32] After all, right-wing politicians like Ishihara Shintaro are elected by popular vote, even though not all of his supporters always agree with his nationalist views. Denial of Japan's intention to commit aggression during World War II is simply not limited to the 'extreme small right-wing forces' but has considerable support in the mainstream. Younger generations were taught about Japan's own plight during the war but, until the 1980s, not adequately informed about Japan's war crimes.[33] All of these, coupled with a new sense of pride and confidence (much bruised after the Bubble Economy went bust), have provided fertile soil to produce a resurgence of nationalistic views on Japan's own history.

Bilateral dynamics

To some, the history problem is the result of misunderstanding, reflecting a deeper cultural difference between China and Japan that is camouflaged by the popular idea that the two countries share a common culture. For instance, many Japanese argue that terms like *shinshitsu* (advance into) and *jiken* (incident) are not such benign terms as they sound in Chinese, and hence their use in describing

Mirror for the future or the history card? 19

Japanese action in China does not amount to whitewashing. With apparent sincerity, some Japanese and even Chinese say that cultural misunderstanding has exacerbated the history problem between the two countries. While the Japanese prefer to be ambiguous, they argue the Chinese style is more direct. While Japanese consider that death absolves all traces of guilt, thus making visits to Yasukuni Shrine an innocent expression of respect, China was missing the point altogether.[34] In addition, others attribute some of the problems – including those over history – to 'different social systems'. In a recent speech, Japanese ambassador Tanino also attributed many problems in current Chinese–Japanese relations to the 'lack of understanding of the different institutions and systems of the two countries'.[35]

There is another aspect of the structural causes of the problem with history that some call the 'asymmetrical structure' of China–Japan relations. As political scientist Iriji Hidenori put it, 'the patterns of actions has become more and more "structural" in the way that China meddles in Japan's internal politics, while Japan shows its deep regret for the things that the Chinese complain about'.[36] Another Japanese scholar has concluded that the basic factor affecting the weight of the problem of historical understanding in Sino-Japanese relations is the change of the asymmetrical character of this relationship.[37]

Changes in bilateral relations as well as each country's strategic priorities are perhaps the most important forces in bringing the history problem to the forefront. Before the 1972 normalisation, it was often the Japanese visitors to China who brought up the issues of wartime atrocities such as the Nanjing Massacre. Even though the problem of war reparations was an issue during the negotiations in 1972, and there was already a recognition that the term used in place of an apology by Prime Minister Tanaka Kakuei was inadequate (largely due to an interpretation error), both countries were ready to compromise in order to attend to other more pressing issues, such as dealing with the Soviet threat. The trend continued until the end of 1970s, when the two countries signed a Peace and Friendship Treaty. The fact that history did not become a problem in bilateral relations at this time, however, does not mean that it did not exist, as some argue. In some sense, the relative tranquillity then might have sown the seeds of the trouble today.

By the 1990s, the collapse of the Soviet Union had removed what had been a bonding factor between Japan and China since the early 1970s. Moreover, the overall mutual perception had changed considerably from the previous decade due to many issues not directly related to the history problem. China's own record in the bloodshed in Tiananmen Square in 1989 brought about a very sharp drop in the positive image of China held by the Japanese public.[38] Much of it was also due to a mutually reinforcing dynamic. The talk of the 'China threat', especially after the 1994 World Bank report on Chinese economic prospects, gained currency at a time when Japan was experiencing the worst postwar economic recession. China's increasing military budget, as well as its 1995 nuclear test, contributed to the deterioration of the relationship, as did the strengthening of the US–Japan alliance.[39] Perhaps the most obvious example of the interactive

20   Daqing Yang

dynamics is the Chinese book that caused a sensation in 1997, *China That Can Say No*. Regarded as an indication of rising Chinese nationalism, it was itself a copycat version of *Japan That Can Say No*, a nationalist bestseller in the late 1980s by Japanese author (and current governor of Tokyo) Ishihara Shintaro.

Generation change has also contributed to the escalating history problem. Not only were the majority of both Chinese and Japanese born and educated after the war, as the result of the education they received in their own countries, their memories of the war have become more divergent. Moreover, the bilateral relations in the last decade have suffered especially from the passing of the so-called 'well-diggers' – a small group of individuals on both sides who managed to establish a degree of trust between the two countries. Until the early 1980s, there had been a remarkable continuity of Chinese officials responsible for Japanese affairs. As one observer put it, 'as a result of their long experience and their language competence, they have become thoroughly familiar with the intricacies of Japan's political and economic operations. They have also cultivated shared policy interests as well as deepening personal relationships with their Japanese counterparts in business circles'.[40] This generation shift came at a time when the role of the mass media in bilateral relations as well as channels of popular contacts have increased. There seems to be a greater linkage between domestic and foreign policy in both countries, making the emotional issue of history even more explosive and more difficult to manage.

Scars of war naturally hard to heal

In a sense, the recurring historical problems in the last two decades have little to do with intentions on either side, or even changes in their structural relationship. The history problem has deeper roots in human psychology. Which comes more naturally, amnesia or forgiveness? Does hate simply fade away with time, or will hate persist without proper redress and reconciliation? Is the history issue between Japan and China simply a time bomb that will not go away, but has been merely postponed?

First, to the Chinese side at least, the problem does not just date from the Eight-Year War (certainly not from 1941!), but from 1895 (large indemnity, loss of Taiwan) if not earlier. As the late Arnold Toynbee put it, of all foreign invasions in China in modern times, Japan's was the longest and most extensive.[41] In the restrained language of another British historian, Ian Nish, the half century between 1895 and 1945 was one of 'Japan's unremitting pressure on the heartland of China with only minor interruptions'.[42] On what basis, then, can we expect real pain to fade away when many survivors are still alive, even if other pains might have been laid on top? When Simone de Beauvoir encountered a group of Japanese businessmen in Nanjing during her trip to China in 1956, it was natural for her to immediately conjure up the infamous Japanese massacre of 1937. Yet her Chinese hostess preferred to forget about it.[43] In this sense, perhaps it was the relative silence and mutual avoidance on both sides of the historical issues before the 1980s that were 'unnatural'.

Moreover, one should not forget that mutual ill feelings between China and Japan had existed in the past, even before the war. They also existed on both sides, even if they might have been different in kind or degree. Even taking into consideration the alleged Japanese war atrocities in China, the fact that someone as well informed about Japan as Guo Moruo could in 1938 characterise the Japanese as 'only half civilised' is an indication of a deep-rooted bias. For many Japanese, its struggle with the dual identity of Asia and the West since the beginning of the Meiji era has often resulted in a sense of superiority *vis-à-vis* other Asians.[44] These pre-existing prejudices against the other only made the scars of war more difficult to heal.

Therefore, we end up with a classic case of 'blind men and the elephant': each of the above explanations has some truth. By making state manipulation the main culprit the China-plays-the-history-card interpretation tends to give Beijing too much credit, for better or worse. It does not explain that often overseas Chinese were more adamant in condemning Japanese militarism and raising issues of reparations. It does not explain the activism of Chinese residents in Japan, or the most radical behaviour that came from private Chinese citizens, whether in open threats to kill Japanese in China or alleged cyber attacks on Japanese government websites. Indeed, efforts to demand individual compensation were spearheaded by private citizens. It was Tong Zeng, a Chinese college lecturer, who gathered signatures to petition the Chinese government to demand Japanese reparations. He was recently stripped of his position.[45]

Seeing Japan as the only source of the problem ignores the fact that there have been many significant improvements since the early 1980s, as in the textbook case, as well as greater general awareness of Japan's role as a victimiser in addition to being victimised. To a large extent, the recent surge in nationalistic noises is a backlash against the progress that had been made. An opinion poll conducted by *Nihon Keizai Shimbun* in 1997 revealed that 47.6 per cent agreed that Japan had not clearly or adequately apologised to Asia for the war, compared with 40.4 per cent who thought Japan had done all that was possible.[46] In the Diet, however, members of the ruling LDP as well as the Liberal Party, as one recent study shows, tend to think that Japan has apologised enough.[47] Analysis focusing on one country, while important, can sometimes lead to finger-pointing and further animosity. A thorough understanding of the history problem in China–Japan relations must therefore include the domestic conditions and bilateral dynamics in considering the postwar repercussions of such a major historical monstrosity.

Prescriptions: will pragmatists prevail?

Some comparisons

If the current history problem has multiple causes, then its solution also needs to be pursued in all directions. While there are no doubt many idiosyncrasies in their bilateral relations, the history problem that exists between China and Japan

22 *Daqing Yang*

is also part of a global phenomenon. Whether we speak of the manipulation of the 'victim consciousness' or 'historical amnesia' or historical settlement, the post-Cold-War world is witnessing the onset of the memory wars.[48] As globalisation quickens its pace, some predict a clash of civilisations, or nationalism. Whether or not it was the end of the Cold War that unfroze old issues, the emergence of issues of history in international relations worldwide suggests the need to re-examine the very theory of pragmatic realism. As one observer noted 'Pragmatism, in its true sense, means taking all the facts into account. In practice those who most pride themselves on it leave out vast areas of human feelings and great tides of political psychology'.[49] How to bring about reconciliation and historical justice? Or, in the parlance of political psychologists, how to develop a respectful and 're-humanised' relationship between former adversaries? What are the necessary ingredients and objective conditions? Is it still possible to build shared historical understanding among different ethnic groups, despite the loss of 'that noble dream' of unfettered objectivity?

Fortunately, there have been some relatively successful instances of historical reconciliation. There have been many recent works that explore that between Germany and France or that between Germany and Eastern Europe.[50] After all, some Westerners have claimed that 'Japan and China get along together just about as well or badly as do the Germans and the French'.[51] So if the Germans and the French have worked it out, why are the Chinese and the Japanese unable to do so? Closer to home, Korea and Japan have made some progress in the last year or so. After all, Jiang's 1998 visit has been widely contrasted with the visit by Kim Dae Jung a few months before, when he and Obuchi Keizo seemed to have put the history question behind them. Some have already suggested that Sino-Japanese reconciliation could learn from Franco-German relations in the early postwar era as well as from ongoing Japanese–Korean dialogue.[52]

What can we learn from these 'success stories'? First, reconciliation requires a long process of ground work. Dialogues between Japan and Korea jointly to produce history textbooks go back to the UNESCO initiative in 1956! When the then Korean President Roh Tae Woo visited Japan in 1990, his conciliatory statement over the history issue won uniform Japanese praise, but it was not until Kim Dae Jung's election in 1997 that the relationship entered a new phase. Even with Kim's successful visit to Japan in October 1998 and various ongoing Korean–Japanese joint projects to study history, there are still detractors and it will take years before a truly shared understanding of the past can emerge and take root in both countries.[53]

Leadership, certainly visionary and charismatic leadership, is important. Studies have shown that postwar West German and French leaders resolved from early on to overcome mutual distrust over past conflicts and worked towards close partnership in Europe. The role of West German chancellor Konrad Adenauer and his associates was especially crucial. Here, pragmatic interests are essential since reconciliation does not simply result from religious or moral grounds, although they would be helpful. When two countries can move forward on the history issue, it has a lot to do with pragmatic factors. Korea's

Mirror for the future or the history card? 23

need for assistance from Japan during its economic crisis was reciprocated by Japan's need to avoid isolation in East Asia, especially as it ponders the China factor. Indeed, one Japanese analyst compared the 'history problem' between Japan and Korea as a 'fishbone in the throat', and argued that without taking it out in relations with Korea, Japan could not cope with China's 'history card'. Still, his recommendation that Japan should solve the history issues such as forced labour and 'comfort women' did not go down well with some of the conservatives in Japan.[54] There will always be sceptics. Indeed, not everyone in Japan even considered Kim Dae Jung's 1998 visit an unqualified success.[55]

Looking at the Franco-German and Japanese–Korean cases also raises one question: is democracy (or shared liberal values) a precondition to historical reconciliation? If democracies are said to be the guarantee of lasting peace, are they also the prerequisite for resolving past wrongs? This is perhaps one of the most complex questions of our times, and highly relevant to the China–Japan question: for instance, the *Economist* magazine expressed the view during Jiang's 1998 visit that: 'to treat this Chinese leadership as fitting recipients of an apology would frankly be pretty stomach-churning'.[56] In other words, short of China's communist government being replaced by a democratic regime, Japan would do 'the world and itself a service' by refusing to apologise. Is this the right justification? Would China have done it differently had it been a free market democracy?

In my view, democracy and open society are important ingredients. The impact of the so-called Track-II (non-governmental) dialogue in a non-open society is certainly going to have little real meaning. From a moral perspective, the freedom to criticise one's own government and a willingness to subject one's own record to the same high standard of judgement is a crucial element in overcoming narrow biases. In South Korea, settlement of domestic abuses under the Park and subsequent military regimes, as well as the more recent revelation of brutalities committed by South Korean troops during the Vietnam War, can help lay the foundation for putting Japan's brutal colonial rule in proper perspective. In China, Li Shengzhi, a respected intellectual and a former vice-president of CASS, recently penned a critique of political repression in China, in which he linked the much publicised wartime Japanese brutality with the only partially acknowledged brutal abuses in China after 1949.[57] Without belittling the wrongs of the past, it is nonetheless important to view them ultimately as part of the human experience, instead of demonising one entire nation.

On the other hand, democracy is no panacea. As one Japanese observer points out, even if Japan and China came to possess similar political values (liberalism), historical reconciliation would not take place naturally. In other words, 'sharing political values alone will not lead automatically to reconciliation'.[58] In fact, there is no evidence that a democratic system is enough: one of the few valid points made by nationalists in Japan is that few of the former European colonial powers have apologised adequately, if at all, for their past transgressions in the colonies. Moreover, as we can see from the recent examples in Europe, membership of the

24   *Daqing Yang*

democracy club does not shield a country from problems with its past, whether domestically or externally. Only decades later is Finland finally healing the wound of its own bloody civil war. Austria, which elected Kurt Waldheim as its President and put Joerg Haider's party into the ruling coalition is another reminder. Moreover, past successes suggest that reconciliation did not always have to wait for full democracy: when Willy Brandt made the widely praised gesture of falling to his knees before the memorial to those who died in the Warsaw Ghetto, Poland was still under its communist government. As Ann Phillips has argued, West Germany's accord with Poland laid the basis for a smoother process of reconciliation in the post-communist era (as compared with the Czech Republic).[59] If anything, a liberal democracy should be held to even higher moral standards as an example for others, not lower.

Japan and China

As many have pointed out, the relationship between China and Japan is on the threshold of a new phase, characterised by 'competition and coexistence'. While often a source of friction, the history problem depends on other factors in overall relations – economic, security, and other political issues, such as Taiwan. To prevent the overall relationship from descending into outright rivalry and confrontation, the two countries must take measures to deal with the history problem. Leaving it to its own fate is no solution.

The silver lining is that there have been instances of positive management, even if they may not have produced lasting results. The disposal of the chemical weapons left in China by the former Japanese imperial army, a concrete issue of history, has been handled relatively well and seen by both governments as such. The Japanese government has announced that they will continue to address this issue in good faith, in view of the entering into force of the Chemical Weapons Convention (CWC) in April 1997. According to the Chinese government, 'Japan acknowledges the presence of a large quantity of chemical weapons abandoned in China and adequately recognize the seriousness and urgency of the matter. It has also expressed regret over the continued harm to the Chinese people [caused by these weapons]. Government handling of this matter, though not without problems, has gone generally well, so that this is the only 'history issue' featured on the websites of both Foreign Ministries. Okazaki Hisahiko, a retired diplomat and frequent commentator on foreign affairs in Japan, puts it this way:

> Government has the obligation to maximise national interest and welfare of its people, while diplomacy is to achieve the greatest welfare of the two peoples through the compromise of respective national interests. No government is allowed to sacrifice national interest and people's welfare at any cost by carrying history and other factors. History should be left to historians.[60]

What can historians do? They can perform the critically important psychological task in conflict resolution by reviewing and reinterpreting the most disputed points of their modern history. As one American author noted, 'the importance of searching history for the deeply rooted and often obscure sources of ethnic and sectarian conflict cannot be overemphasised'.[61] In a pioneering article published in 1988, Barry Buzan suggested a resolution of Japan's history issues must depend on three conditions: it must be factually sound, it must be acceptable to the Japanese, and it must be acceptable to other nations. This proposition is still sound today.[62] Historians from Japan and South Korea have been working on such issues for quite some time, but progress has not proved easy.[63] In my view, the starting point for Chinese and Japanese historians to build a cross-national consensus is to recognise the particularistic aspects of Japan's war crimes, while remaining cognisant of its universalistic implications as a human tragedy.[64]

Even though harsh in its criticism of Japan, the Chinese government has always emphasised the importance of Sino-Japanese friendship, even if their words may sometimes sound hollow. Even as dark an era as WWII also had some positive legacies for Japan–China relations. For instance, the story of an 8th Route Army general, PRC Minister of Defence Nie and the little Japanese orphan girl who had been rescued and returned to the Japanese during the war made headlines in both countries and led to a dramatic reunion. So did the stories of many 'abandoned women and children' (*zanryū koji*) that lived with Chinese families (often as Chinese) till the 1970s. These experiences tended to emphasise the decency of common people. Although recent years have seen a sharp increase in publications on wartime Japanese atrocities in China, there are also many historical and artistic works on the activities of those Japanese who were opposed to the war. Jiang's 1998 visit has been cast in a largely negative light in Japan and overseas because of his insistence on a written apology. Yet he also went out of his way to visit Sendai, where the well-known Chinese writer Lu Xun had studied medicine under one Fujino *sensei* almost a century ago. By using a symbol that is familiar to all Chinese school children, Jiang tried to convey a message of genuine friendship between the peoples of Japan and China, but his effort was completely ignored in the media.

For the Chinese public, which by most criteria do not have a very favourable view of Japan, a better understanding of postwar Japan is much needed. This is not surprising. Japan's Prime Minister's Office polls in recent years have indicated that more Japanese feel their country is *not* doing a good job explaining Japanese views to the world. Ambassador Tanino's recent speech in China is one indication that Japan is moving to correct this problem. Not all of his explanations are going to be readily accepted by the Chinese, to be sure. Simply better publicity on the part of Japan is not sufficient to solve the 'perception gap'. The Chinese government and its opinion leaders need to work together with their Japanese counter-parts to facilitate better understanding. In the 1996 survey 85.5 per cent of people in China considered that the 'proper resolution of the

26 Daqing Yang

history problem' would determine future friendly relations between the two countries; many fewer realise that resolution takes joint efforts.

These measures themselves will not revolve the history problem *per se*, but at least they will help prevent the situation from deteriorating. The resolution of the history problem ultimately requires major changes in both countries. As China gradually becomes more open, more radical and nationalistic voices may appear. China may well produce its own Zhirinovsky. Nevertheless, even if greater openness in China in the short run may unleash some more extreme ultra-nationalistic forces, in the long run, greater openness and critical examination of its own history – by a robust intelligentsia and by journalists – will help put past crimes – others and its own – into perspective. This would be a major step towards true reconciliation. Developing healthy national pride is as important for China as it is for Japan. China, with its 1.3 billion population in an age of increasing globalisation and interdependence, still faces enormous challenges in the twenty-first century in pursuing prosperity and strength. At the very least, it is incumbent upon its government and opinion leaders to prevent an arguably understandable anger over historical injustice from foreign aggression from justifying anti-foreign ultra-nationalism that will ultimately damage China's own long-term interests.

On the other side, as Kojima Tomoyuki, a well-known China expert in Japan, wrote in early 1995, in order to build a relationship of mutual trust, Japan should resolve the history issue in various ways. He suggested that in addition to government compensation, business and private volunteers should also join forces to make such compensation.[65] At the grass-roots level, there have been many Japanese who have made trips to China to repair the damage to the famed city wall in Nanjing, to plant trees, and to undertake other activities to make up for wartime excesses in China. Increasing Chinese–Japanese contact – through study, work, visits, and intermarriage – although not always eliminating problems and perhaps in fact creating new ones – do promise better understanding based on real experience rather than a second-hand, one-dimensional view of each other's society.

Many Japanese politicians not traditionally allied with the Chinese position on the history issues have supported efforts to cope with the history question in recent years. For instance, one politician who has thought hard on this issue and proposed remedies is Ozawa Ichiro, LDP-cum-opposition leader and proponent of the 'normal country' vision. Writing in the 1980s, Ozawa recognised that '"History" is not an issue we can avoid'.

> How are we to approach the history issue? We must reflect soberly on our history, examine it in good faith, and apply its lesson to our principles and behavior, our present actions, and our future plans. We can not deny the part aggression has played in our history in Asia. The issue is not that we have never discussed the question of our wartime responsibility, but that we did so only at home: we did not face the Asia-Pacific nations we had invaded.

We have to admit that our government has not made much effort to settle the past. Nor was public feeling sufficiently harsh to prevent the re-emergence of politicians associated with Japan's past aggression. We must be strict with ourselves as we look back on our history, even if we start doing so only today.[66]

There have been some positive actions as well. Following Social Democratic Party Prime Minister Murayama's visit to the Marco Polo Bridge memorial, LDP (and former president of the *Nihon Izokukai*) Hashimoto Ryutaro made the first visit of a Japanese Prime Minister since World War II to the site in northeastern China where Japan's invasion erupted in 1931. Another LDP heavyweight, Nonaka Hiromu, then an acting LDP secretary general, made an unprecedented visit to the Nanjing Massacre Museum in May 1998. However grudgingly these actions may appear, the fact that these visits did take place against apparent internal opposition should not be underestimated.[67] Moreover, there is an indication that some business leaders in Japan have also come to realise the need to settle historical issues from the war era. The recent settlement of the Hanaoka Incident between former Chinese forced labourers and the Japanese construction giant Kajima Corporation is rightfully considered a 'great postwar milestone'. It demonstrates that even though it involved some compromises that did not satisfy everyone, the settlement between former perpetrators and victims can go a long way towards healing the wounds of the past and bringing about closure. So long as the current legal system in Japan cannot adequately address the issue of individual compensation for World-War-II-era victims in a timely fashion, the role of the private sector becomes even more significant.

Conclusion

The history problem has not been invented out of thin air, but has real historical roots; at the same time, it is not just about history. Indeed, that it has emerged as one of the most sensitive issues in China–Japan relations today says more about the current domestic conditions in both countries as well as the dynamics of bilateral relations than about events in the past. If a genuine reconciliation must be based on an understanding of history, significant transformation of the body politic in both Japan and China is needed. But even then, it will require vigilant upkeep for a much longer period. It would be unwise to abandon all forms of state intervention in favour of a completely free flow of ideas and feelings about past conflicts. Indeed, management by both governments and non-government institutions is still needed to steer the often-volatile relationship away from rupture and to provide a necessary framework for more honest exchanges on issues of war and trauma. The obligations of both countries will not be the same. As Zhu Jianrong, a Chinese scholar based in Japan, has suggested, to break this vicious cycle between the two countries, it is necessary to create a mechanism

28 Daqing Yang

that 'identifies the source of fire and prevents it'. Gradually, he argues, mid- and long-term efforts will be needed to take the bilateral relations onto a track where 'Japan will not forget the history while China will not talk about history'.[68]

Since Jiang's visit in late 1998, the history issue has taken a back seat, as the Chinese government seems to have undergone a policy shift in its Japan policy. In the last year or two, there has been some open discussion in China of the need for a new approach to relations with Japan. This is itself an unprecedented phenomenon. Many of these voices emphasise the importance of maintaining good neighbourly relations with Japan, and call for a better understanding of the postwar Japan as well as a better appreciation of the public sentiment in Japan.[69] One Chinese scholar has even argued that the Chinese government should be prepared for the 'irreconcilability of the history problem' and take measure to contain the history problem within a realistic framework.[70] There are already indications that the Chinese leadership has taken particular care on a number of occasions to emphasise the positive side of the relationship between the two countries and assigned much less prominence to the history problem. The visit by Premier Zhu Rongji to Japan in October 2000, during which he took great care not to offend Japanese public sentiment, is perhaps the most recent demonstration of such a policy shift in China. The long-term prospect remains to be seen, however. While such development may help stabilise China–Japan relations at a time when other issues – such as the Taiwan question – may prove to be more disruptive, a radical swing like this may still leave the impression that the history problem may once again end up like a card in the diplomatic game.

Notes

1 Jiang Zemin, 'Yi shi wei jian, kaichaun weilai', *Renmin Ribao*, 29 November 1998.
2 Major works include Allen S. Whiting, *China Eyes Japan*, Berkeley, CA, University of California Press, 1989; Caroline Rose, *Interpreting History in Sino-Japanese Relations: A Case Study in Political Decision-Making*, London, Routledge, 1998 and Ian Buruma, *Wages of Guilt: Memories of War in Germany and Japan*, New York, Farrar, Straus Giroux, 1994.
3 Given the fact that Japan's occupation of Manchuria was in 1931, it is perhaps more accurate to refer to it as the Fifteen-Year War (13 years 8 months to be precise), as many Japanese writers now do. The commonly used Chinese term is the 'Eight-Year War of Resistance' (*ba-nian kang-zhan*), which sees the Marco Polo Bridge incident in July 1937 as the beginning of the full-scale conflict.
4 PRC Ministry of Foreign Affairs website.
5 Ibid.
6 For Japanese and Chinese-language texts of Ambassador Tanino's speech, see Japanese Ministry of Foreign Affairs website.
7 Ibid.
8 Yamada Tatsuo, 'Cong jingdaishi kan Zhong-Ri guangxi', in *Ri-Zhong guanxi mianmian guan*, ed. Li Tingjiang, Zhongguo guoji guangbo chubanshe, Beijing, 1991, pp. 79–93; Hatano Sumio, 'Nitchūsensō no isan to fusai', in *Ajia no naka no Nihon to Chūgoku: Yūkō to masatsu no gendaishi*, ed. Matsuda Hiroshi and Hatano Sumio, Tokyo, Yamakawa Shuppan, 1995, pp. 57–76; Osaki Yuji, 'Aratana Nitchū kankei no kōchiku,' in *Nihon, Amerika, Chūgoku: Kyōchō e no shinario*, ed. Kokubun Ryosei, Tokyo, TBS-Britannica, 1997, pp. 169–224.

Mirror for the future or the history card?   29

9 See Whiting, *China Eyes Japan*, pp. 157–61.
10 For a list of lawsuits related to war reparations in Japan, see www.linkclub.or.jp/ ~teppei-y/tawara%20HP/sengo%20hoshou.html
11 *Zhongguo Qingnian Bao*, 15 February 1997.
12 Tahara's on-camera interview of the Chinese ambassador to Japan on 20 March 2000 on TV Asahi.
13 Ijiri Hidenori in Nakajima Mineo, ed., *Kingendaishi naka no Nihon to Chūgoku*, Tokyo, Tokyo Shoseki, 1992, p. 251.
14 Komori Yoshihisa, 'Machigaidarake no Chūgoku enjo', *Chūō Kōron*, March 2000, pp. 94–109; Miyamoto Yūji, 'Tai-Chū keizai enjo dōsuru ka', *Gaikō Forum*, August 2000, p. 83. A much more bitter attack running along similar lines of argument is Tanabe Toshio, 'Nihon no ketsuzei de tsukutta Chūgoku kōsha rakusei kinenhi no hitosa', *Seiron*, July 2000. China is the second largest recipient of Japanese ODA, after Indonesia.
15 Nicholas D. Kristof, 'The Burden of Memory', *Foreign Affairs*, vol. 77, no. 6, November/December 1998, pp. 38, 47.
16 Chalmers Johnson, 'The Patterns of Japanese Relations with China, 1952–1982', *Pacific Affairs*, vol. 59, no. 3 (Fall 1986), p. 424. Johnson did, however, go on to discuss 'collective Japanese amnesia about Asia' after the war.
17 Buruma, *Wages of Guilt*, pp. 126–7.
18 Nakajima Mineo, 'Imakoso "rekishi no chōbo" no kessan o', *Shokun*, August 1987, p. 95.
19 'Japan in the Right', *Economist*, 5 December 1998.
20 Quoted in Yamaguchi Kikuichiro, *Hoshutō kara mita shin Chūgoku*, Yomiuri Shimbunsha, Tokyo, 1955, p. 130.
21 Tagawa Seichi, *Nitchū kōryū to Jimintō ryō so tachi*, Tokyo, Yomiuri Shimbunsha, 1983, p. 219.
22 For a mildly critical analysis of Chinese textbook portrayal, by a Chinese scholar in Japan, see Zhao Jun, 'Chūgoku rekishi kyōkasho ni okeru kingendai Nitchū kankeishi' (http://www.est.hi-ho.ne.jp/zhaojun/jiaoke.htm).
23 While reiterating the policy of asking for no war reparation, the Chinese government was somewhat vague about these citizens' efforts, claiming 'to safeguard the legitimate interest and protect the interests of its people', by asking Japan to 'deal with them seriously and properly'. See Chinese Foreign Ministry website.
24 Mo Bangfu, 'Nihon no sensō sekinin Chūgoku de susumu kenkyū no "shinchōryū"', *Ronza*, May 2000, pp. 146–51.
25 Ambassador Tanino's speech, MOFA website.
26 Ijiri, p. 65. Here Professor Ijiri, like many Japanese commentators, fails to mention that such revision did occur in the previous year, and leaves the impression that the whole affair was created out of thin air by the media.
27 (Japan) Rekishi Kenkyū Iinkai compiled, *Dadongya zhanzhen de zongjie*, Beijing, Xinhua chubanshe, 1997. This is the Chinese translation of *Daitōa sensō no sōkatsu*, published for internal use by government and party officials in China.
28 Kotake Kazuaki, in *Genten Chūgoku gendaishi 8: Nitchū kankei*, compiled by Ando Masashi and Kotake Kazuaki, Tokyo, Iwanami shoten, 1994, p. 242.
29 Buruma, *Wages of Guilt*, p. 122.
30 For studies exploring such continuities, see John Dower, *Empire and Aftermath*, Cambridge MA, Harvard University Council on East Asian Studies, 1979; Chalmers Johnson, *MITI and the Japanese Miracle*, Stanford, Stanford University Press, 1982.
31 See Carol Gluck, 'The Past in the Present', in *Postwar Japan as History*, ed. Andrew Gordon, Berkeley, University of California Press, 1993, pp. 64–95.
32 For an update of their activities, see Tarawa Yoshifumi's homepage (www.linkclub. or.jp/~teppei-y/tawara%20HP/doukou.html).

30   *Daqing Yang*

33 International relations experts tend to downplay such internal factors. Notable exceptions include William Lee Howell, 'Inheritance of War: Japan's Domestic Politics and International Ambitions', in *Remembering and Forgetting: The Legacy of War and Peace in East Asia*, ed. Gerrit Gong, Washington, CSIS, 1996; Mike Mochizuki, *Japan Re-Orients*, Washington, Brookings Institution, 2000.

34 Amago Satoshi, 'Nitchū kankei – sengo sedai kara no teigen', *Sekai*, July 1988, pp. 258–70.

35 Japanese Foreign Ministry website.

36 Ijiri Hidenori, 'Sino-Japanese Controversy since the 1972 Diplomatic Normalization', in *China and Japan: History, Trends, and Prospects*, ed. Christopher Howe, Oxford, Clarendon Press, 1996, p. 63.

37 Kotake, *Genten Chūgoku Gendaishi 8*, p. 243.

38 *Sōrifu yoron chō sa*, Internet version.

39 Asano Akira, 'Nitchū Kankei no Shinten o Motome, Chokusetsu Kōryū no Kakudai', in *Nihon no Gaikō Anzenhōsho Option*, Tokyo, Nihon Kokusai Kōryū Senta, 1998. Internet version.

40 Chae-jin Lee, *China and Japan: New Economic Diplomacy*, Stanford, Hoover Institution, 1984, p. 146. On one such figure on the Chinese side, Kurt Radtke, *China's Relations with Japan: The Role of Liao Chengzhi*, Manchester, UK, Manchester University Press, 1990.

41 Toynbee made this comment in a 1968 article for *Mainichi Shimbun*, quoted in Albert Axelbank, *Black Star Over Japan*, New York, Hill & Wang, 1972, p. 151.

42 Ian Nish, 'China–Japan Relations, 1895–1945', in *China and Japan: History, Trends, and Prospects*, pp. 43–4.

43 De Beauvoir was puzzled by her Chinese hostess who preferred to forget. The episode is described in Simone de Beauvoir, *The Long March*, translated by Austryn Wainhouse, Cleveland, The World Publishing Company, 1958, p. 438.

44 Masahide Shibusawa, 'Japan's Historical Legacies: Implications for its Relations with Asia', in *The Process of Japanese Foreign Policy: Focus on Asia*, ed. Richard L. Grant, London, The Royal Institute of International Affairs, 1997, pp. 25–36.

45 Mo, 'Nihon no sensō sekinin', pp. 146–51.

46 *Nihon Keizai Shimbun*, 2 May 1997.

47 Kabashima Ikuo, 'Zenkokkai giin ideorogi chōsa', *Chūō Kōron*, May 1999, pp. 46–61.

48 See Elazar Barkan, *The Guilt of Nations: Restitution and Negotiating Historical Injustices*, New York, Norton, 2000. A critical view of the use of the 'victim consciousness', in the Jewish state of Israel, is Tom Seger, *The Seventh Million: The Israelis and the Holocaust*, translated by Haim Watzman, New York, Hill & Wang, 1993.

49 Quoted in *The Psychodynamics of International Relationships II: Unofficial Diplomacy at Work*, edited by Vamil D. Volkan *et al.*, Lexington MA, Lexington Books, 1991, p. x.

50 See, for example, Andrei S. Markovits and Simon Reich, *The German Predicament: Memory and Power in the New Europe*, Ithaca, Cornell University Press, 1997; Ann Phillips, 'The Politics of Reconciliation: Germany in Central-East Europe', *German Politics*, vol. 7, no. 2, August 1998, pp. 64–85. Also useful is Jeffrey Herf, *Divided Memory: The Nazi Past in the Two Germanys*, Cambridge MA, Harvard University Press, 1997.

51 Edward Hunter, 'The France and Germany of Asia', *Esquire*, April 1938, pp. 16–20. The author noted that 'there are more differences, although they belong to the same yellow race, than between any two variations of the white race'. The article is subtitled 'Contrasting the Imitative Japs [sic] with the inventive Chinese, you find they have nothing in common but slant eyes.'

52 Ogawa Akira, 'Nitchū Kyōdo no Bunkateki Sozō no Hōkōsei to Sono Junbi Toshiteno Nitchū Wakai', posted at the Okazaki Institute website.

53 See, for instance, 'Seoul, Tokyo Have Long Way to Go to Reach Shared View on Korea–Japan History', *The Korea Times*, 31 May 2000.

Mirror for the future or the history card? 31

54 Nagashima Akihisa's comment can be found at the Okazaki Institute website.
55 For criticisms, see Kuroda Katsuhiro, 'Shazai boom wa owaranai', *Seiron*, January 1999, pp. 74–83; Tanaka Akira, '"Kyōtsū no rekishi ninshiki" to iu bōgen', ibid.
56 'Japan in the Right', *Economist*, 5 December 1998.
57 Noting that Japan has been rightfully criticised for lack of repentance for its aggression in China, Li pointed out that although the Chinese have all the more reason to repent for their own crimes against their own people, they have not done so. Li Shenzhi, 'Fengyu canghuang Wushinian', Internet version.
58 Ogawa, 'Nitchū Kyōdo'.
59 Phillips, 'The Politics of Reconciliation', pp. 64–85.
60 Okazaki Hisahiko, 'Let Historians Handle Japanese History', *Daily Yomiuri*, 17 April 2000.
61 Joseph V. Montville, 'The Arrow and the Olive Branch: A Case for Track Two Diplomacy', *The Psychodynamics of International Relationships II*, p. 7.
62 Barry Buzan, 'Japan's Future: Old History versus New Roles', *International Affairs*, vol. 64, no. 4, Autumn 1988, p. 570.
63 See, for example, 'Seoul, Tokyo Have Long Way to Go'.
64 I have discussed some of the specific issues related to the Nanjing Massacre in 'Historians and the Nanjing Massacre', *SAIS Review*, XIX, summer–fall 1999, pp. 133–48.
65 Kojima Tomoyuki, 'Nitchū kankei "Atarashii hatten dankai"', in *Ajia Jidai no Nitchū Kankei*, Tokyo, Simul, 1995, p. 32. He considered the fiftieth anniversary to be 'perhaps the last chance'.
66 Ozawa Ichiro, *Blueprint for a New Japan: The Rethinking of a Nation*, Tokyo, Kodansha International, 1994, pp. 128–9.
67 *Sankei Shimbun*, 9 May 1998.
68 Zhu Jianrong, 'Rekishi o wasurezu, "doku o motte rin o nasu" kankei e', *Sekai*, February 1992, p. 77.
69 For example, He Fang, 'Women neng tong Riben youhao xiaqu ma', *Huanqiu Ribao*, 11 May 1997; Feng Zhaokui, 'Zengyang zuo lingju – dui shiji zhijiao Zhong-Ri kuanxi de sikao', *Shijie Zhishi*, January 2000, pp. 28–30. It may be pointed out that the latter piece, published in a popular international affairs magazine, has received a largely negative response from the public.
70 Yang Bojiang, 'Yi lixin siwei mouqiu Zhong-Ri guanxi de kuashiji fazhan', *Xiandai Guoji Guanxi*, September 1999, pp. 1–6.

2 Sino-Japanese relations in the context of the Beijing–Tokyo–Washington triangle

Quansheng Zhao

When one examines international relations with regard to any region or specific countries, the method of levels of analysis is one of the most efficient ways to conduct research.[1] When we look at Sino-Japanese relations, there are obviously many ways to conduct research at various levels, such as political leadership at the individual level, domestic politics and institutions at the state level, and the world structural system at the international level. This chapter will concentrate primarily on the external factors at the international level to conduct research on Sino-Japanese relations.

There are a number of key external factors or countries that would significantly affect relations between Beijing and Tokyo. In this regard, one can cite such actors as the United States, Russia and Korea, and factors such as the issue of Taiwan and financial and security problems in the Asian–Pacific area. Of course, it is clear that the United States is the most significant external actor/factor, and has had a tremendous influence on the direction of Sino-Japanese relations ever since the establishment of the People's Republic of China (PRC) in 1949.

This paper will examine Sino-Japanese relations in the context of the Beijing–Tokyo–Washington triangle. It will not, however, make much reference to the 1940s and 1950s. Rather, it will concentrate on developments since the end of the Cold War – primarily the 1990s. Other external factors, such as Russia, Korea and the issue of Taiwan, will also be discussed. In order first to get a comprehensive picture, let us look at the dynamics of the predominant triangular relationship in the Asia–Pacific region.

East Asia's new configuration of major power relations

Sino-Japanese relations have been tremendously influenced by the new configuration of power relations in East Asia. Although not everybody agrees with Francis Fukuyama that the end of the Cold War in the late 1980s constituted 'the end of history',[2] the events – especially the collapse of the Soviet empire, were indeed a landmark in contemporary history in the twentieth century. Similarly, the end of the Cold War has greatly affected the configuration of international relations in the Asia–Pacific region. The new global structure can be described, as some Chinese observers do, as *yi chao duo qiang* – meaning one single super-power faced with many strong powers, and referring to the phenomenon that the United States has become the only, or as Samuel Huntington has claimed, 'the lonely superpower',[3] *vis-à-vis* multiple powers including the European Union (EU), Russia, the People's Republic of China (PRC) and Japan. This new structure has replaced the so-called Beijing–Moscow–Washington 'strategic triangle' which prevailed in the 1970s and most of the 1980s.

Tremendous changes in great-power relations have taken place in East Asia in the post-Cold-War era. I would like to refer to this reconfiguration as the 'two ups' and 'two downs', which have become apparent since the early 1990s. The 'two ups' concern the rise of the United States and China. The United States' rise to sole superpower status has given Washington a dominant role in all four dimensions of world affairs: political, strategic, economic and technological/cultural. Meanwhile, China has achieved a spectacular economic performance for the past two decades, sustaining high growth rates (even with the slowdown from 11–12 per cent to 7–8 per cent growth rates in 1998–2000), and escaping, so far, the Asian economic crisis. This expansion has greatly increased China's influence in regional and global affairs.

The 'two downs' refer to the cases of Russia and Japan. With the collapse and dismemberment of the former Soviet Union in the early 1990s, Russia experienced major setbacks in all respects, and it will have a long way to go to return to its previous status and influence in the region. The nature of Japan's downturn is quite different, as it is reflected in economic terms only, and is a result of consecutive economic recessions rather than the major financial crises that befell Korea and Southeast Asia.

The following four tables demonstrate the dynamics of these 'ups' and 'downs'. Since the Russian economic downturn is so obvious and Russia is not a primary consideration of this article, the tables all focus on China, Japan and the United States. When we look at the most recent decade of available data on gross domestic product (GDP) in the three countries (see Table 2.1), we will see that, whereas the US maintained steady growth, China's lag behind both the US and Japan was significantly reduced while Japan's gap with the US grew. To be more specific, in a comparison of GDP in 1989, China's GDP is little more than 8 per cent of the United States', while Japan's is roughly equivalent to 55 per cent of the United States'. However, ten years later in 1999, China's GDP has increased from 8 to 11 per cent of the United States' and 23 per cent of Japan's. At the same time, Japan's GDP level relative to the US decreased from roughly 55 per cent in 1989 to approximately 44 per cent in 1998, with a rebound to 50 per cent in 1999.

Similar trends may be observed by comparing total trade during the same decade (Table 2.2). China's gap with the US and Japan's levels of total trade reduced from seven times and four times respectively in 1988 to five times and twice in 1998. At the same time, Japan's total trade level relative to the US decreased from roughly 60 per cent in 1988 to about 40 per cent in 1998.

Similarly, the United States maintained its position as the top recipient of foreign direct investment (FDI) from the late 1980s to the late 1990s (see Table

34   *Quansheng Zhao*

Table 2.1 Comparisons between US, China and Japan, gross domestic product (1989–99) (US$ billion)

Year	USA	China	Japan
1989	5438.7	449.1	2897.3
1990	5743.8	387.8	2996.2
1991	5916.7	406.1	3413.9
1992	6244.4	483.0	3725.5
1993	6558.1	601.1	4292.8
1994	6947.0	540.9	4700.3
1995	7269.6	697.7	5144.1
1996	7661.6	815.4	4591.2
1997	8110.9	901.5	4187.6
1998	8511.0	961.0	3782.7
1999	8708.9	996.3	4395.1

Sources: Economic Planning Agency, Japan, 1998, pp. 374–7; Economist Intelligence Unit, London, 4Q 1998, 1999; The World Bank Annual Report 1999.

Table 2.2 Comparisons between US, China and Japan, total trade (1988–98) (US$ billion)

Year	USA	China	Japan
1988	781.9	102.3	452.3
1989	856.7	111.7	483.7
1990	910.6	115.4	523.6
1991	930.1	135.7	552.4
1992	1002.1	165.5	573.2
1993	1068.2	194.1	603.9
1994	1201.8	236.7	672.3
1995	1355.6	277.9	779.2
1996	1447.1	290.1	760.1
1997	1555.3	325.0	759.5
1998	1592.1	317.7	625.7

Source: *Yearbook of International Trade Statistics*, vol. II, United Nations, 1997; Economist Intelligence Unit, London, 4Q 1998, 1999.

2.3), helping fuel its current economic boom. The US experienced steady growth from US$58.6 billion of FDI in 1988 to US$70.8 billion in 1997. China and Japan, however, followed very different paths during the decade. The two countries began at roughly the same level in 1988 at US$3.2 billion. By ten years later, China was receiving US$45.3 billion in FDI, an increase of fifteen times the original amount. In contrast, FDI in Japan only moved up to US$5.4 billion in 1997 – far behind the United States and China. Although it can be argued that Japan and China followed different paths of economic growth in terms of need for FDI, one can see, nevertheless, that China and the United States are clearly experiencing an upward trend in this regard.

When we analyse this 'two ups and two downs' structure in the post-Cold-War era, we have to bear in mind the following three points. First, China's rising

The Beijing–Tokyo–Washington triangle 35

Table 2.3 Comparisons between US, China and Japan, foreign direct investment (1988–97) (US$ billion)

Year	USA	China	Japan
1988	58.6	3.2	3.2
1989	69.0	3.4	2.9
1990	48.4	3.5	2.8
1991	22.8	4.4	4.3
1992	18.9	11.0	4.1
1993	43.5	27.5	3.1
1994	49.9	33.8	4.2
1995	60.8	37.5	3.3
1996	79.9	42.4	3.2
1997	70.8	45.3	5.4

Source: Economic Planning Agency, Japan, 1998, pp. 314, 359; OECD, *International Direct Investment Statistics Yearbook 1997*, pp. 177, 330; Economist Intelligence Unit, London, Q4 1998.

position is primarily reflective of positive general trends. However, when inspected more closely, the PRC's situation is far more fragile. There are widespread domestic difficulties such as state-owned enterprise (SOE) reform and disparities between coastal and internal regions, along with the problem of severe corruption, and many other problems that may not only slow down China's development but also plunge it into internal chaos if Beijing loses control of the pace of change.

Second, everything is in relative terms. Despite Japan's economic downturn, it remains the second largest economy in the world. Furthermore, when we look at GDP per capita, China is far behind both Japan and the United States (see Table 2.4). Although China more than doubled its GDP per capita from 1988 to 1998, China's US$773 yearly GDP per person in 1998 compared with US$29,900 in Japan and US$31,488 in the United States is a clear indicator that China is still a developing country in this sense.

Third, Japan's slowdown is primarily reflected in economic terms, whereas Russia's total economic, political, strategic and technological/cultural downturn is due to the collapse of the former Soviet empire. Despite its consecutive economic recessions, Japan has managed thus far to escape the major financial crises that befell Korea and Southeast Asia in 1997–8. Furthermore, since the end of the 1990s, some indicators suggest that the Japanese economy has begun to recover, as demonstrated by Japan's GDP growth from 1998 (US$3782.7 billion) to 1999 (US$4395.1 billion), despite some experts' more cautious assessments as to whether this is a true recovery.

Therefore, the picture of 'ups' and 'downs' is relative and is only a reflection of the past decade – the 1990s and early 2000. It is difficult to say at this point how long the current trends will continue, and each country will definitely experience a variety of upward and downward trends in terms of its own development over the decade to come; that is to say, countries currently on the rise may face a downward trend, whereas debilitated countries may move

36 *Quansheng Zhao*

Table 2.4 Comparisons between US, China and Japan, GDP per capita (1988–98)*
(US$)

Year	USA	China	Japan
1988	20,606	364	23,843
1989	21,989	401	23,550
1990	22,983	342	24,273
1991	23,421	354	27,557
1992	24,450	415	29,979
1993	25,406	508	34,449
1994	26,658	427	37,632
1995	27,636	584	41,975
1996	28,863	670	36,521
1997	30,263	733	33,231
1998	31,488	773	29,900

* Not adjusted for purchasing power parity (PPP).
Source: Economic Planning Agency, Japan, 1998, pp. 378–81; Economist Intelligence Unit, London, 4Q 1998, 1999.

upwards. Nevertheless, the 'two ups and two downs' structure has affected regional strategic configurations enormously, and has become a crucial factor in the foreign policy calculations of the major capitals in the world. The impact of this change can be analysed with reference to economic, political and strategic factors.

The economic dimension

An important element that characterises post-Cold-War international relations is the trend towards globalisation, or economic interdependency, which has increased enormously. The China–Japan–US triangular relationship is no exception. From Table 2.5, we can see that, in terms of top trading partners, each one of the three countries places the other two high on its list. Excluding Hong Kong, Japan and the US were the numbers 1 and 2 top trading partners of China, together accounting for 33.8 per cent of China's total trade. Similarly, the US and China are Japan's top trading partners, in combination counting for 36.3 per cent of its total trade in 1998. Meanwhile, the US conducts most of its trading activities with its NAFTA partners (number 1, Canada, number 3, Mexico, collectively totalling 31 per cent of American trade), but Japan and China occupy the number 2 and number 4 positions, together totalling 16.7 per cent of the United States trade. Also notable is the fact that, in the case of China, Hong Kong's trade with the US is not included in these statistics, which would increase the figures.

This extensive economic interdependency means that each bilateral relationship in the China–Japan–US triangle is considered to be of vital national interest to these countries. For example, the United States has long regarded the maintenance of the region's stability and prosperity as a top priority in its world

The Beijing–Tokyo–Washington triangle 37

Table 2.5 Top trading partners of China, Japan and the US (in 1997) (%)

Rank	China	Japan (1998)	US
1	Japan (18.7)	US (27.7)	Canada (20.9)
2	Hong Kong (15.6)	China (8.6)	Japan (11.9)
3	US (15.1)	Taiwan (5.4)	Mexico (10.1)
4	Korea (ROK) (7.4)	Germany (4.5)	China (4.8)
5	Taiwan (6.1)	Korea (ROK) (4.1)	UK (4.4)
6	Germany (3.9)	Hong Kong (3.4)	Germany (4.3)
7	Singapore (2.7)	Australia (3.1)	Taiwan (3.3)
8	Russia (1.9)	UK (3.1)	Korea (ROK) (3.1)

Sources: *Directions of Trade Statistics Yearbook*, IMF, 1998; 'Japan 2000: An International Comparison', Keizai Koho Center (Japan Institute for Social and Economic Affairs), (15 December 1999), p. 60.

strategy. As the two most powerful countries in the Asia–Pacific region, relations with China and Japan are critical to American regional and global interests.

In foreign policy, China and Japan regard their relationship with each other as second in importance only to the United States. Understandably, Japan will not change the foundation of its foreign policy, which is based on its alliance with the United States (discussed below).

On the other hand, Japan has played a continuous bridging role between China and the West. In 1990, for example, Japan was the first industrialised country to lift its economic sanctions imposed on China in the wake of the Tiananmen Square incident.[4] Similarly, Japan was the first industrialised country to offer its approval, in July 1999, for China's entry into the World Trade Organisation.[5] Obviously, Japan will continue to play a significant role in integrating China into the world economic system.

Additionally, Japan has a vital interest in China's development and stability because of its historical, cultural and geopolitical proximity. It is a common belief that Japan's biggest nightmare would be a China devolving into internal chaos, as such a situation would disrupt regional stability and prosperity enormously. If this scenario were to take place, Japan would be one of the first countries affected. Therefore, it is in Japan's interest to continue its cooperative and stabilising relationship with China, and in particular to continue its official development assistance (ODA) programme to promote China's modernisation effort and help with the PRC's incremental development toward a more open and democratic society.

As for China, much has changed over the decades in terms of its immediate foreign policy concerns. In order to understand the importance China currently attaches to economic modernisation, we need to look at how the priorities of Chinese foreign policy have altered as its leadership has changed over time. Under the leadership of Mao Zedong and Zhou Enlai, Beijing's major concern was China's strategic position within the Washington–Moscow–Beijing triangle. China's primary concerns with Japan and the United States at that time were how to counterbalance the threat from the former Soviet Union and address the

38 *Quansheng Zhao*

issue of Taiwan – a point perceived as crucial to the legitimacy of the Beijing regime.

Meanwhile, the priorities of the Deng Xiao-ping era were such that modernisation became the major focus of Chinese foreign policy. Therefore, China came to view the United States and Japan, along with the European Union, as primary suppliers of capital, markets and advanced technology. Therefore, economic cooperation with the United States and Japan became crucial to China. As a result of China's change in perception towards Japan and the United States, trade and investment between China and the other two countries increased rapidly and Japan became the largest donor of aid to China, in the form of ODA.[6]

Thus, economic interdependence between the three countries has developed rapidly during the last quarter of the twentieth century and will continue into the twenty-first century. Furthermore, the dynamics of technological transfers and personnel visits has raised the number and extent of mutual exchanges among the three countries to new levels.

Meanwhile, the United States' interest in China has its roots in the two countries' ambivalent historical relationship. Over time, the character of the US–China relationship has shifted starkly from missionary activities in the nineteenth century to the search for business opportunities in contemporary times. It has also involved a transition from being wartime allies in World War II to Cold War rivals in the 1950s to 1980s, and then to a 'strategic partnership', as confirmed by President Bill Clinton's 1998 visit to China. That is to say, China's attractions are its enormous population and rapidly modernised economy, and it has become virtually the last untapped market for American and Japanese business circles. Regardless of whether the dreams of profit are fulfilled or not, the fact that China has moved up quickly to become a significant trading partner and a leading destination for foreign investment is a major factor in US foreign policy toward Beijing.

The powerful voices of the business community in providing Beijing with a permanent normal trading relations (PNTR) status and entrance to the WTO offer one more example of American economic interests in China. Furthermore, many people believe that China's economic modernisation will help to create and enlarge an incipient middle class in China which will promote an enhanced civil society and democratisation process. This mixed political–economic consideration has become a foundation for the engagement policy advocated by the Clinton administration. Yet the concerns in strategic dimensions – namely the fear of the 'China threat' – as will be examined below, has created significant opposition to this engagement policy, notably from the US Congress.

The strategic dimension

When examining the strategic dimension in the China–Japan–US triangle, we may clearly see divergent interests yet with overlapping concerns over a variety of issues. As pointed out earlier, both the US and Japan view their alliance as the central point of their Asian policies. This position has been a clear landmark since

The Beijing–Tokyo–Washington triangle 39

1945, the beginning of the American occupation of Japan, which was further confirmed in 1951 when the US–Japan Security Treaty was signed.

According to a recently published book entitled *Alliance Adrift*, written by well-known Japanese journalist Yoichi Funabashi, although US–Japan relations have broadened and deepened, 'the intellectual and political underpinnings of the bilateral relationship are, in fact, frail'.[7] While the two countries maintain close ties, each side worries frequently about the other country getting too close to Beijing. When President Clinton visited Beijing in 1998, he did not even make a stop in Japan, leading some Japanese observers to worry that the United States had shifted from negative 'Japan bashing' to indifferent 'Japan passing' – considering it not worth the same attention as its troubled relationship with China. By the same token, the American leadership frequently expresses concerns that China's growing power may force Japan to become 'neutralised' – thereby moving away from the US–Japan alliance, a cornerstone of American foreign policy in Asia.

Meanwhile, the momentum of China's rise has made Chinese foreign policy more assertive as well as more sensitive to the increasing nationalistic sentiment among the Chinese people. This new development has made the strategic calculations of Washington and Tokyo more complicated. On the one hand, this change may be viewed as a natural move for any rising power. In this view, China could legitimately claim greater influence over international affairs as long as it does not jeopardise regional stability and prosperity. On the other hand, however, the rising nationalism in China's populace places more pressure on the current Beijing leadership to address sovereignty issues such as Taiwan and attempt to redress negative historical legacies such as the Japanese wartime invasion.

In regard to its relationships with Washington and Tokyo, a central locus of concern for Beijing is the issue of Taiwan. Indeed, Beijing regards the United States as a major obstacle to its goal of reunification with Taiwan. This issue can be traced back historically to the Chinese Civil War period (1946–9), when the US supported the Chiang Kai-shek regime, and when, at the cessation of the Korean War in the early 1950s, the US signed an official Mutual Defence Treaty with Taiwan which effectively prevented the PRC from taking over the island. In the late 1960s and early 1970s, both Beijing and Washington were willing to normalise their relations primarily out of concern about the threat from the Soviet Union. Richard Nixon's visit to China in 1972 – preceded by Henry Kissinger's visit to Beijing in 1971 – was the historical moment which spotlighted the two countries' *rapprochement*. It took seven years before the PRC and the United States completed their normalisation process in 1979.

However, while Washington has recognised Beijing officially and ceased its official relations with Taipei, there are two issues which Beijing still views as unwarranted 'intervention in internal affairs'. The first issue is that the United States continues to sell arms to Taiwan despite the 17 August Shanghai Communiqué of 1982 which stipulates that the United States should reduce its arms sales to Taiwan both quantitatively and qualitatively. The other issue relates to the Taiwan Relations Act – passed by the US Congress in 1979 – which, in addition to restricting the United States to non-official economic and cultural relations with Taiwan, required American commitment to peaceful settlement of the Taiwan Strait conflict. Both actions, from Beijing's perspective, represent continued intervention in China's internal affairs, and will continue to affect Sino-American relations well into the twenty-first century.

Beijing's perception of US interference may have been enhanced by the February 2000 vote in the US House of Representatives that passed the Taiwan Security Enhancement Act by the vote of 341 to 70.[8] At the time of this article's submission, the Act is in the midst of Senate preparation for the floor, but the Clinton administration clearly indicated that it would veto such a document.

China's deep concern is that America's arming of Taiwan may in fact prolong Taiwan's separate status, thereby promoting its eventual independence. Given that fear, in February 2000 the State Council of the PRC issued a Taiwan White Paper which states:

> If a grave turn of events occurs leading to the separation of Taiwan from China in any name, or if Taiwan is invaded and occupied by foreign countries, or if the Taiwan authorities refuse, *sine die*, the peaceful settlement of cross-Straits reunification through negotiations, then the Chinese Government will only be forced to adopt all drastic measures possible, including the use of force, to safeguard China's sovereignty and territorial integrity and fulfil the great cause of reunification.[9]

This passage indicates clearly that one more situation has been added which would prompt the PRC to use military force against Taiwan – that is, if Taiwan indefinitely delays negotiations with the mainland. Also, it is important to note that this statement was designed to influence the impending presidential election in Taiwan a month later.

The issue of Taiwan has also remained a problem between China and Japan, who is a 'loyal follower' of the United States in international affairs. Beijing's main concern is the new security guidelines for the US–Japan Security Treaty announced in 1997.[10] Specifically, China's concern is over Part V of the 'Guidelines for US–Japan Defence Cooperation' as to whether 'surrounding areas' are meant to include Taiwan itself. Although the document specifically indicates that this term is not a geographical but a situational term, one can hear conflicting statements from a variety of Japanese government officials on different occasions about whether the guidelines should indeed be considered to include Taiwan.

A tendency in Japanese foreign policy is to follow closely behind the United States. The Taiwan issue is no exception. Whenever they are asked about the inclusion of Taiwan, the typical informal answer from the Ministry of Foreign Affairs is that since this topic refers to joint guidelines, Washington will have to be asked for clarification – a move allegedly initiated by Washington. This kind of statement understandably alarms the PRC, and Beijing has insisted upon clarification from the Japanese government.

The Beijing–Tokyo–Washington triangle   41

One other example of Japan following America's lead is related to the controversial visit of Taiwanese President Lee Teng-hui to the United States in 1995 for the stated purpose of attending an alumni reunion at Cornell University. Similarly, there were extensive deliberations or preparations for Lee Teng-hui to visit Japan, also under the guise of attending an alumni event, since Lee also attended Kyoto University as an undergraduate. This plan did not get very far, since Beijing immediately gave a stern warning against such an action, but speculation has continued that Lee Teng-hui may still have the opportunity to visit Japan now that he has stepped down from the Taiwanese presidency.

There are other problems between China and Japan, especially a territorial dispute over a chain of islands between Taiwan and Okinawa, called Diaoyu in Chinese and Senkaku in Japanese,[11] as well as the potential resurgence of Japanese militarism, memories of which stem from past Japanese aggression.[12] The US factor has always been a top consideration for any new direction in Japan's China policy, and this was vividly demonstrated in the process of Sino-Japanese *rapprochement* in 1972. The US also played a significant role in the Diaoyu/Senkaku territorial disputes between China and Japan, at least in the initial stages. Even the current US position regarding this dispute remains ambiguously neutral. The historical fact is that when the US returned Okinawa to Japan in 1971, the Diaoyu/Senkaku islands were included in the package.[13] There has long been speculation about the possibility of US involvement in the event of a military clash between China and Japan over these disputed islands. Furthermore, Tokyo's emphasis on the human-rights issue in its China policy in recent years can also be seen as influenced by Washington.

Despite many discussions about the rising power of China and the potential threat to regional international affairs, the majority of China observers abroad hold the sober view that, in terms of military and strategic capacity, China is far from presenting a formidable force. Andrew Nathan and Robert Ross even call China's defence capacity merely 'an empty fortress', citing one of the master strategists of the Three Kingdoms period almost two thousand years ago, Zhuge Liang, in describing a strategy designed to promote the enemy's misperception of your strength and avoidance of military entanglement when you are actually weak.[14]

This line of thinking may well reflect reality. In terms of comparative levels of defence spending, China is far behind other major powers. The United States spends more than twenty-seven times the amount of China and six times the investment of Japan in military spending.[15] One must, however, be aware that Chinese figures are not necessarily as reliable as Western ones for a variety of reasons. Nevertheless, even with the inflated figures projected by various China observers, Chinese military numbers are still significantly lower than American and Japanese levels of spending. For the past few decades, China's defence expenditure as a percentage of its GDP has actually been in decline, from 4.63 per cent in 1978 to about 2 per cent in 1986, and was reduced further to 1.09 per cent in 1997. Furthermore, comparatively, in terms of defence expenditure as a percentage of national GDP, China's 1.09 per cent in 1997 was far lower than the

42 Quansheng Zhao

United States' 3.4 per cent, Russia's 3.8 per cent, Britain's 2.8 per cent, and only slightly higher than Japan's 0.99 per cent.[16]

While Chinese and Japanese strategists focus primarily upon the United States, the only superpower in the post-Cold-War era, Beijing and Tokyo also pay close attention to the other key players in the region, such as Russia and the two Koreas. For example, on the one hand, Beijing has been trying its best to be cooperative with the United States. On the other hand, Beijing has also prepared itself to face the strategic challenge presented by the new guidelines of the US–Japan Security Treaty, and subsequent preparations for a TMD system in East Asia. To counterbalance this perceived hostile environment, China has developed the following four strategies in its foreign policy:

First, China has further enhanced its cooperation with Russia and other former Soviet states, not only in economic and political areas, but more importantly in security matters. Second, Beijing has rekindled its interest in maintaining substantial influence over Pyongyang, so that China will have greater leverage in terms of political and strategic manoeuvring in the Korean peninsula. Third, China has moved further to improve its relationship with its neighbours in Southeast Asia, that is, to strengthen ties with ASEAN countries. Finally, China has increased its community-building efforts in East Asia, as demonstrated by the establishment of the China–Japan–Korea Forum in economic and technological areas. This three-way forum was decided upon at the recent summit meeting between the three countries during the 'ASEAN plus Three' conference held in Singapore in November 2000.[17]

In terms of the manoeuvres of China and Japan with regard to their relations with Russia, Beijing has worked very hard to bring Moscow to its side. At the same time, Russia is eager to secure China's support, as it has its own grudges – namely, the eastern expansion of NATO, the bombing of Kosovo, and the situation in Chechnya. Under these circumstances, with the two powers moving towards closer ties in political, economic and strategic dimensions, the most alarming development is Russia's willingness to help China modernise its military forces. In October 1999, for example, the two countries' Defence Ministries signed an agreement to conduct joint training and to share information on the formation of military doctrine. In early 2000, China purchased two Russian-built destroyers worth US$800 million each.[18] This development has certainly raised concerns in Washington and elsewhere.

Tokyo, however, has its own agenda to improve relations with Moscow. Japan has taken a positive position towards the major obstacle to bilateral relations: that is, the dispute over the four northern islands between the two countries.[19] Although the process for achieving a workable resolution has been slow, Japan's security concerns with Russia have almost entirely disappeared (except with regards to the northern islands).

Instead, Japan's attention has shifted toward China's potential military power and the Korean peninsula. With the generational change in Japan, younger politicians and foreign policy bureaucrats alike may feel less pressured by a sense of guilt surrounding its aggression towards China and the rest of Asia. At the same time Japanese nationalism has also been on the rise.[20] Although there is still a lack of proper recognition of its wartime behaviour, Japan's nationalistic sentiment today is very different from that of World War II. This change primarily reflects Japan's pride in its achievements in the postwar period and its desire to play a greater role in the international community.

The Korean peninsula may well be considered a good example of overlapping interests between China, Japan and the United States. In many respects, China holds the key to the security interests of the US and Japan in the Korean peninsula, which is a core issue of northeast Asian security configurations. Indeed, China's positive contributions to peace and stability in the region can be demonstrated by its role in the four-party talks on the Korean peninsula.[21] Japan and Russia were not included in the Korean four-party talks. Nevertheless, both countries would like to play an active role in any deliberations.[22] Although the four-party talks have not produced concrete results thus far, as proved by the most recent round of meetings in Geneva in the summer of 1999,[23] China's constructive role has been widely recognised.

As discussed earlier, strategic concerns in the region are also different between Beijing, Washington and Tokyo. Due to widespread concerns over past and future North Korean missile tests, there has been a significant change of mood among the Japanese people, which has led to the parliamentary approval in 1999 of revisions to the US–Japanese Security Treaty. Among several steps that Tokyo has adopted, the most noticeable development is Tokyo's announcement that it will participate in the development of a ballistic missile defence system with the United States, known as theatre missile defence (TMD). Although the tension in the Korean peninsula has appeared to be significantly reduced due to the Kim Dae Jung–Kim Jong Il summit in June 2000, the TMD plan is still ongoing. This development has alarmed Beijing, which fears not only a new US–Japan alliance to contain China but also the alliance's potential involvement in any future Taiwan Straits military crisis, should Taiwan 'officially' announce its independence.[24] Let us now look at these issues from a political perspective.

The political dimension

It should be noted that the China–Japan–US triangle is not an equidistant one. Obviously, Tokyo and Washington have a much closer relationship than either of them has with China. In light of the US–Japan military alliance and the new TMD initiative, as discussed above, it has been speculated that this triangle actually represents a 'two against one' framework: that is, on most occasions, if not all, the United States allies itself with Japan – most notably in the political and strategic dimensions.

The relationship between China and Japan has had its ups and downs since 1972, when the two countries normalised relations. But for most of the 1990s, their relationship has been deteriorating and this trend has cast a shadow over regional and global affairs in the post-Cold-War era. In light of this, the two sides have worked hard to reverse the downward slide, as exemplified by the recent

44 *Quansheng Zhao*

visits of the heads of state, namely Chinese President Jiang Zemin's trip to Japan in November 1998, and Japanese Prime Minister Obuchi Keizo's visit to China in July 1999.[25] Despite some positive results achieved from these visits, they have also highlighted the difficulties each side faces in handling this relationship.

The decline in Sino-Japanese relations began in the late 1980s. It was accelerated by the downfall of Chinese Communist Party Secretary General Hu Yaobang in 1987. Hu's removal was due largely to Beijing's domestic politics, but additional factors in his removal were criticisms that he was too 'soft' towards Japan and too personal in dealing with Japanese leaders.[26] This decline was compounded by the Tiananmen Square incident in 1989, when Japan followed the Western lead and imposed economic sanctions on China.

Unfortunately, there is a lack of true mutual understanding between the two countries. Although state visits occur virtually every year, there is a lack of in-depth discussion and multilayered exchange. Neither country has a clear understanding of the nature of the other's domestic politics and foreign policy direction. Beijing may ask such questions as, has Japan moved irreversibly down the path of a peaceful and democratic nation or might it still revert to militarism? By the same token, Tokyo's image of China also varies between that of a friendly and economically promising country, and that of a military threat.

China's policy toward Japan in the post-Deng era has primarily followed the previous lines of Mao and Deng, but some changes in policy priorities have become evident. While Taiwan and economic cooperation remain central aspects of Sino-Japanese relations, Chinese pressure on Japan to address the historical legacy of its wartime behaviour and its potential for a return to militarism has also been strengthened. Sometimes it appears that wartime history has become a leading factor in China's Japan policy.

What both countries need to do to improve their ties with each other is to conduct thorough studies of the contemporary history of the other country to gain greater insight into the nature of its politics and society. Tokyo must continue to learn lessons from its past wartime behaviour since there will always be a small circle in Japan that ignores or denies its historical experience. At the same time, China should recognise that the overwhelming majority of the Japanese people do not want to repeat the mistakes of the past and that Japan has become a democratic society striving to cultivate a peaceful environment in the Asia–Pacific region. To ensure long-lasting and peaceful cooperation between the two countries, Beijing needs to educate and utilise more Japan specialists in formulating its policy toward Tokyo. Promoting mutual understanding should be a central position in bilateral exchanges, and educational exchanges should be further expanded and institutionalised.[27]

In the political dimension, a prominent problem between China and the US is a difference of opinion and policy regarding human-rights-related issues, and Japan, in general, sides with Washington in this regard. The issue of human rights has increasingly become a top priority of American foreign policy toward China. The priority of Chinese foreign policy, however, has moved from 'revolution' under Mao to 'modernisation' under Deng. In other words, since

The Beijing–Tokyo–Washington triangle 45

1978, the central theme of Chinese foreign policy has been modernisation, namely economic development. In many ways, political considerations such as revolution or socialism have become much less prominent.[28] With these two opposite foreign policy priorities, it is inevitable that there have been and will continue to be confrontations between China and the United States around the issues of democratisation and human rights.

Another important background development regarding the human-rights issue is the changing international environment. With the end of the Cold War in the late 1980s, US foreign policy has shifted away from containing communism and there has been increasing attention to the differences between civilisations and cultures. A primary advocate of this consideration is Samuel Huntington's *Clash of Civilizations*. Huntington argues that future conflicts in the international community will be largely derived from the confrontation of Western and non-Western civilisations. He has further singled out Confucianism and Islam as two key components of non-Western civilisation.[29] Being controversial in itself, this notion of the 'clash of civilisations' has become a prominent factor among some academics and practitioners in their study of contemporary international relations. This emphasis on Western/non-Western differences has become a source of conflict regarding the process of China's democratisation and its human-rights record.

When we look at the human-rights issue in this triangular relationship, it is clear that America's China policy combines a variety of factors: strategic considerations and economic interests, as well as ideological elements such as human-rights issues. In a pluralistic society such as the United States, there are a range of priorities regarding foreign policy within different sections of society. Influential figures within the US Congress and human-rights, religious and other non-governmental organisations (NGOs) tend to put human rights as a top priority, whereas the White House and the State Department have to calculate United States foreign policy primarily from the perspective of national interest, such as security concerns and economic interest.

Two important developments in the 1990s may push Washington's China policy further toward strategic and economic considerations as a top priority rather than human-rights considerations. First, summit meetings between China and the United States have begun to be held regularly, as may be seen by Jiang Zemin's visit to Washington in October 1997, and President Clinton's China visit in June–July of 1998, and Premier Zhu Rongji's trip to the United States in the spring of 1999. The issue of nuclear development in North Korea, the economic crisis in Southeast Asia, the increasing tensions between India and Pakistan caused by the recent nuclear tests, and the explosive and uncertain issue of Taiwan require close cooperation and effective coordination between the two major powers, China and the US. The United States, therefore, does not have the luxury of making human rights the top priority most of the time.

Second, as mentioned earlier, China has undertaken fundamental economic reforms that have significantly shifted its social and political system toward a more pluralistic one. Recent reports indicate that while still maintaining its

46 *Quansheng Zhao*

authoritarian rule, the Chinese Communist Party has started to allow more extensive debate on political issues and to tolerate the activities of certain dissident groups.[30] Furthermore, China has gradually learned how to deal with external pressure on human-rights issues, and Beijing appears to be more accommodating toward outside demands. A sign of China's willingness to engage in dialogue over such delicate matters is that Beijing allowed, in September 1998, the visit of Mary Robinson, the chief of the UN Commission on Human Rights. This was the first such visit from a leading human-rights official. Beijing's continued accommodation may reduce pressures from the outside world.[31]

All of these developments, however, do not necessarily mean that the US will take a significantly lighter approach to human-rights issues in its future relations with China. Domestic pressures from interest groups and lawmakers will remain a powerful force within the United States. One can expect Washington to continue to raise the human-rights issue with Beijing.[32] It is important to note that China's human-rights policy has always followed an up-and-down mode, namely, an alternation between the periodic tightening and loosening of social controls. Needless to say, if there are major backward developments in Beijing, such as what happened in Tiananmen Square in 1989, there will be another major campaign from the United States to put pressure on China regarding human-rights issues. One may, nevertheless, also speculate that this is an unlikely development in the near future for US–China relations.

There are various characteristics in China's response to US promotion of human rights and democracy. China has insisted upon its own sovereign power regarding human rights, and it has resisted external interference, including US demands for democracy. China defends its position on human rights and has criticised US pressure by invoking sovereignty rights protected by the UN Charter, particularly 'The Declaration on the Inadmissibility of Intervention and Interference in the Internal Affairs of States'.[33] China argues that the UN Charter extends sovereignty to include human-rights issues by citing provisions such as 'Every state has an inalienable right to choose its political, economic, social and cultural systems, without interference in any form by another state'.[34] The protection of human rights only becomes an international issue when a state violates treaties it has signed, commits 'large-scale, gross' violations or endangers the peace and security of neighbouring countries.[35] In the absence of these conditions, according to China, human rights are internal matters.

On the other hand, China has been willing to make concessions under certain circumstances. It should be noted, however, that these concessions have been made despite continued human-rights violations. Partial concessions have been timed to coincide with the levels of external pressure, the priority of human rights in US China policy and debate on China's human-rights conditions in the US and internationally. These concessions, nevertheless, do not represent uniform changes in China's political system and have been made alongside the continued arrest of dissidents.[36] Ultimately, the issues of democracy and human rights are still regarded as internal matters. Concessions and regressions coincide with each other and are employed strategically to influence debate between China's supporters and critics, to undermine the overall efficacy of external pressure and to maintain Beijing's ability to set its own human-rights agenda. However, as China further integrates into the world economy and international affairs, its internal behaviour, including the human-rights issue, will inevitably be affected by external influences.

In sum, China may, in fact, be alarmed by the possible 'two against one' dynamic within this triangular relationship, particularly when facing a perceived 'encirclement' led by the US and Japan. This sense of encirclement may also involve the actions of such regional players as India and Vietnam.[37] Thus, both the United States and Japan should recognise that China's fear of being 'ganged up on' by the other two is not without cause, and they should be more sensitive regarding this concern.

Prospects for Sino-Japanese relations

Any discussion of the future directions of the Sino-Japanese relationship in the context of the Beijing–Tokyo–Washington triangle must first analyse each side's perspective. For example, China's Japan policy needs to be re-examined and Beijing needs to clarify its true national interests. Obviously, the emphases on strategic considerations and the Taiwan issue under Mao and the stress on economic modernisation under Deng should continue to be priorities in China's policy towards Japan. Other issues such as territorial disputes and historical legacies should be addressed, but not at the expense of major strategic and economic goals. It is in Beijing's interests to recognise the extremely important role Japan could play in creating a healthy and conducive international environment for China.

One may expect that Beijing will view its relationship with Tokyo from an overall global–strategic perspective. China will continue to promote friendly and cooperative relations with Japan, not only to facilitate its modernisation but also to limit its economic and strategic dependence on the United States. While focusing on economic exchanges between the two countries, Beijing is likely to begin regular consultations with Tokyo on regional strategic and security issues, including the recognition of Japan's legitimate concern about strategically important areas such as the South China Sea, and about sensitive issues such as human rights. As long as its legitimacy and sovereignty concerns over such issues as Taiwan are not threatened, Beijing will work closely with Tokyo on a wide range of regional issues, such as stability on the Korean peninsula and the Asian economic crisis. In doing so, Beijing will not only enhance its relationship with Tokyo but may also improve its position *vis-à-vis* the US in dealing with global affairs.

As for Japan, it may slowly develop a national consensus over time acknowledging its wartime role in Asia, especially in relation to China and Korea. Japanese politicians are likely to be cautious about any move toward revising the Japanese constitution, particularly article 9, known as the 'peace clause', since this is still a sensitive issue among Japan's Asian neighbours. Based

48 *Quansheng Zhao*

on this consensus, Tokyo may work out an official document with Beijing, specifically and precisely expressing its sincere remorse for its past behaviour.[38] In return, Beijing may agree that this document will serve as a foundation to conclude – as much as is possible – the unfortunate history between the two countries and to move ahead toward a new relationship.

In addition, Tokyo will probably continue to stick to its 'one-China policy' regarding Taiwan. Beijing has been particularly sensitive to any Japanese involvement in the Taiwan issue, considering that Taiwan was ceded from China to Japan in 1895 and remained Japan's colony for the next half century. Many older generations of Taiwanese politicians, such as Lee Teng-hui, Taiwanese President from 1988 to 2000, have a special emotional tie to Japan. It is understandable that any move by Tokyo to perpetuate the separation of Taiwan from the mainland would be interpreted as a continuation of Japan's long-term regional ambitions and would not be tolerated by any leadership in Beijing. Therefore, Tokyo will probably continue to make clear that it will not support Taiwanese independence, and that its proposed TMD systems would not include coverage of Taiwan.

From the perspective of Washington, when dealing with this crucial yet sensitive relationship between Beijing and Tokyo, the United States will continue to play a balanced role in order to maintain stability in the Asia–Pacific region. Washington will continue to maintain its alliance and further enhance its ties with Tokyo, which serves as the foundation for US policy in the region. There is no reason to believe that an anti-American 'Tokyo–Beijing axis' will develop in the foreseeable future. The US–Japan relationship is well developed, deeply rooted, mature and solid. The US–Japan alliance will continue for the decades to come, and will not be overtaken by encouraging the further development of Sino-Japanese relations, given the complicated historical, political and emotional elements between Beijing and Tokyo as outlined above.

While the US itself continues fully to engage Beijing politically, strategically and economically, Washington is also likely to encourage Japan to enhance its relationship with China, particularly in the political and security realms. There are understandably different lines of argument regarding how to deal with the 'rise of China', such as implementing a Cold-War-style containment policy similar to that used against the Soviet Union. Yet, while being fully prepared for potential conflict, it is in the best interests of all parties that a more cooperative rather than a confrontational approach should be given first consideration in dealing with these complicated yet delicate relationships. Clearly, stability and prosperity in the Asia–Pacific region will not be maintained without properly handling the unfolding drama of Sino-Japanese relations.

Notes

The author would like to thank Elizabeth Dahl and Ben Ludlow for research assistance.

1 The best-known example in this regard is Kenneth Waltz, *Man, the State and War*, New York, Columbia University Press, 1959.

The Beijing–Tokyo–Washington triangle 49

2 Francis Fukuyama, *The End of History and the Last Man*, New York, Free Press, 1992.
3 Samuel P. Huntington, 'The Lonely Superpower', *Foreign Affairs*, vol. 78, no. 2, March/April 1999, pp. 35–49.
4 See Chapter 5 of Quansheng Zhao, *Japanese Policymaking: The Politics Behind Politics: Informal Mechanisms and the Making of China Policy*, Hong Kong and New York, Oxford University Press, 1993.
5 Susan V. Lawrence, 'Prickly Pair: China and Japan Remain Civil – and Deeply Divided', *Far Eastern Economic Review*, 22 July 1999, p. 20.
6 Zhao, *Japanese Policymaking*, p. 163.
7 Yoichi Funabashi, *Alliance Adrift*, New York, Council for Foreign Relations Press, 1999; quoted in Richard Halloran, 'Awakening the Giant', *Far Eastern Economic Review*, 24 February 2000, p. 35.
8 Robert G. Kaiser and Steven Mufson, '"Blue Team" Draws a Hard Line on Beijing: Action on Hill Reflects Informal Group's Clout', *Washington Post*, 22 February 2000, p. A1; Thomas Legislative Information webpage, http://thomas.loc.gov/cgi-bin/bdquery/z?d106:h.r.01838
9 'The One-China Principle and the Taiwan Issue', *Renmin Ribao* (People's Daily), 22 February 2000, p. 1. Previously, the conditions for China's intervention were the declaration of Taiwan's independence or foreign power occupation.
10 See Part V of 'Guidelines for US–Japan Defence Cooperation' (US–Japan Security Consultative Committee release) as follows:

> V. Cooperation in Situations in Areas Surrounding Japan that Will Have an Important Influence on Japan's Peace and Security
>
> Situations in areas surrounding Japan will have an important influence on Japan's peace and security. The concept, situations in areas surrounding Japan, is not geographic but situational. The two Governments will make every effort, including diplomatic efforts, to prevent such situations from occurring. When the two Governments reach a common assessment of the state of each situation, they will effectively coordinate their activities. In responding to such situations, measures taken may differ depending on circumstances . . .
>
> When a situation in areas surrounding Japan is anticipated, the two Governments will intensify information and intelligence sharing and policy consultations, including efforts to reach a common assessment of the situation.

11 Suisheng Zhao, 'China's Periphery Policy and Its Asian Neighbors', *Security Dialogue*, vol. 30, no. 3 (September 1999), p. 340.
12 Thomas J. Christensen, 'Chinese Realpolitik', *Foreign Affairs*, vol. 75, no. 5, September/October 1996, p. 40.
13 For an excellent and detailed discussion on the US role in the Diaoyu/Senkaku dispute, see Jean-Marc Blanchard, 'The U.S. Role in the Sino-Japanese Dispute Over the Diaoyu (Senkaku) Islands, 1945–1971', *China Quarterly*, no. 161, March 2000, pp. 95–123.
14 Andrew J. Nathan and Robert S. Ross, *The Great Wall and the Empty Fortress: China's Search for Security*, New York, W. W. Norton, 1997, p. 25.
15 From Text of State Council, Information Office, 'White Paper on China's National Defense' (taken from SWB, FE/3291), originally printed by Xinhua News Agency, Beijing, in English 03.39 GMT 27 July 1998, quoted in 'Quarterly Chronicle and Documentation, July–September 1998', *China Quarterly*, no. 156, December 1998, pp. 1115–17.
16 Ibid.
17 *Renmin Ribao* (People's Daily Overseas Edition), 25 November 2000, p. 1.
18 John Pomfret, 'Russians Help China Modernise Its Arsenal: New Military Ties Raise U.S. Concerns', *Washington Post*, 10 February 2000, pp. A17–A18.

50 *Quansheng Zhao*

19 *Washington Post*, 11 February 2000, p. A32.
20 Chester Dawson, 'Flying the Flag', *Far Eastern Economic Review*, 12 August 1999, pp. 18–19.
21 In 1995, South Korea suggested a four-power peace conference that included the United States, China and the two Koreas for the purpose of working out a new peace agreement to replace the armistice and thereby bring a formal end to the decades-long Korean War. Initially, Pyongyang did not want Chinese participation, Selig Harrison, 'Promoting a Soft Landing in Korea', *Foreign Policy*, no. 106, spring 1997. After prolonged negotiations with the United States and South Korea in New York in July 1997, North Korea finally agreed to hold the four-power conference. The first preparatory talks were held in New York on 5 August 1997 ('Pyongyang Accepts Framework for Peace Talks', *Straits Times*, 2 July 1997, p. 21). After several on-again, off-again negotiations among the four parties, the talks broke down once again on 19 September 1997, without even an agreed agenda for further conferences to be held in Geneva, Steven Myers, 'N. Korea's Talks with U.S. Fail Over Demand for G.I. Pullout', *New York Times*, 20 September 1997. A major previous obstacle was that the North Koreans insisted that conference participants agree in advance to discuss the removal of the 37,000 American troops stationed in South Korea: Robert Reid, 'Korean Peace Talks Break Down', Associated Press, 20 September 1997.
22 In July 1997, Russian Foreign Minister Yevgeny Primakov visited Seoul and made a joint statement with South Korea on peninsula issues. The Russian side proposed that it host an international conference on the Korea issue parallel to the four-way talks: 'South Korea, Russia Issue Joint Statement on Peninsula Issues', *Korea Herald*, 25 July 1997. A month later, Japan also resumed its negotiations with North Korea over the normalisation of diplomatic relations.
23 Shin Yong-bae, 'Sixth Round of Four-Way Peace Talks Ends with Little Progress', *Korea Herald*, 10 August 1999 from http://www.koreaherald.co.kr/cgi-bin/searched_word.asp?qstr=four|party|talks&path=/news/1999/08/__02/19990810_0208.htm.
24 Frank Ching, 'A Tale of Two State Visits', *Far Eastern Economic Review*, 20 May 1999, p. 36.
25 Lawrence, 'Prickly Pair: China and Japan Remain Civil – and Deeply Divided', p. 20.
26 For further discussion, see Quansheng Zhao, *Interpreting Chinese Foreign Policy: The Macro–Micro Linkage Approach*, Hong Kong and New York, Oxford University Press, 1996, p. 192.
27 One such suggestion is to establish a new comprehensive and internationally oriented university in China, jointly developed by China and Japan with substantial financial and academic support from Japan. This university should be first-rate – comparable to Beijing and Qinghua universities, the two leading higher-education institutions in China. An important function of this university would be to enhance China's understanding of international affairs with a special emphasis on Japan. In addition, each side could also send a certain number of university professors annually to conduct lectures on aspects of the social, political, economic and legal environments of their own country.
28 For a detailed analysis of the changing priority of Chinese foreign policy, see Chapter 3 of Zhao, *Interpreting Chinese Foreign Policy: The Micro–Macro Linkage Approach*.
29 Samuel P. Huntington, *The Clash of Civilizations and the Remaking of World Order*, New York, Simon and Schuster, 1996, p. 20.
30 Rena Miller, 'Taking Liberties: Beijing Turns a Blind Eye to Small-scale Protests', *Far Eastern Economic Review*, 10 September 1998, pp. 32–3.
31 John Pomfret, 'Reform Hot Topic of Group in Beijing', *Washington Post*, 13 September 1998, pp. A37–8.
32 Murray Hiebert and Susan V. Lawrence, 'Trade Tightrope', *Far Eastern Economic Review*, 24 February 2000, p. 22.

The Beijing–Tokyo–Washington triangle 51

33 'A Report Which Distorts Facts and Confuses Right and Wrong – On the Part about China in the 1994 'Human Rights Report' Issued by the U.S. State Department', *Beijing Review*, 13 March 1995, p. 21.
34 Ibid.
35 Andrew J. Nathan, 'Human Rights in Chinese Foreign Policy', *China Quarterly*, no. 151, September 1997, p. 629.
36 Ibid., pp. 641–2.
37 Nayan Chanda, 'After the Bomb', *Far Eastern Economic Review*, 13 April 2000, p. 20.
38 See, for example, Frank Ching, 'A Tale of Former Allies', *Far Eastern Economic Review*, 2 March 2000, p. 35.

3   Engagement Japanese style

Reinhard Drifte

The Japanese–Chinese relationship is one of the most important variables in the formation of a new strategic environment in the Asia–Pacific region and one which has global implications. The management of China's rise to great-power status by Japan will be of crucial importance for regional and global stability and for access to the most populous market of the future.

To deal with China's challenge to the established power constellation, Japan has been pursuing a policy of engagement. This chapter critically examines the assumptions and feasibility of this policy whose dualistic character is usually ignored. This engagement intends to steer China towards a peaceful and sustainable path by assisting it with economic policy tools (trade, investment, technology transfer, ODA) while hedging against any Chinese strategic breakout or policy failure through the bilateral military deterrent with the US as well as political front-building with other Asian countries. I will look first at Japan's changing security perception of China since 1989 and then describe how Japan has been reacting to this perception at various policy levels (unilateral, bilateral, multilateral).

Background of Japanese–Chinese security relations in the 1990s

In the immediate post-Cold-War era, Japanese–Chinese relations enjoyed a brief honeymoon, not only because of Japan's accommodating attitude towards China in the wake of the Tiananmen Square incident, but also because China hoped that Japan's growing strength and assertiveness, as well as its rising friction with the US, would speed up the advent of Beijing's aspiration of a multipolar world in order to better resist the emergence of an increasingly unilaterally acting US after the end of the East–West conflict and its victory in the Gulf War. This favourable climate in Japanese–Chinese relations was soon changed, as the Japanese watched with increasing concern how economic growth enabled China to enhance its military capabilities behind a veil of secrecy, while issues like bilateral territorial conflicts in the East China Sea and around the Senkaku Islands, or China's resumption of nuclear testing, gave an indication of China's greater assertiveness. Japanese sensitivity towards China's greater political and military assertiveness occurred against a background of greater uncertainties in a much more fluid regional and international security environment in the post-Cold-War era, as well as harsh Western criticism for Japan's cheque-book diplomacy during the allied war against Iraq in 1991. The uncertainties of the new era also extended to the viability and duration of the future US security commitment to the region. Moreover, the ups and downs of Sino-American relations began to affect Japanese–Chinese relations as well.

Domestic changes in the wake of the temporary end of the LDP's rule in 1993 hastened a weakening of pro-China forces in Japan and facilitated a more hard-nosed view on Chinese security policies. The beginning of the post-Cold-War era saw a shift to a new generation of politicians with fewer sympathies towards China, a greater willingness to consider Japan's security interests, and a weakening of the LDP which had single-handedly ruled Japan since 1954. Even those in Japan who did not worry too much about China's potential military capabilities realised that there were many non-military challenges emanating from China, ranging from China's political and economic uncertainties and unfulfilled economic expectations (e.g. the problem of access to the Chinese market) to illegal immigration into Japan and Chinese piracy.

China's military growth

In order to regain what it considers its rightful place in the world and to cope with the unwelcome rise of a unipolar world in the post-Cold-War era, China has been reviewing its strategy, defence doctrine and force structure in the 1990s. The 15th National Party Congress in 1997 set the basic directions for China's defence policies for the coming five years, and basically reaffirmed the strategy of 'qualitative army against limited and high-tech warfare' which was adopted by Deng and other party and military leaders in the late 1980s.[1] In line with Deng's policy, China has been devoting considerable funds to the modernisation of its military forces, but has also reduced their size to achieve a more professional armed force.[2]

What has particularly raised concern in Japan since 1991 has been the consistent and relatively high level of budgetary increases for military expenditures, the opaqueness of the military build-up, and China's growing arms exports. In 1988–9 China's military budget started to increase by above 10 per cent annually. Official defence spending increased from yuan 91 billion ($11 billion) in 1998 to yuan 120.5 billion ($14.5 billion) in 2000, the latter being an increase of 12.7 per cent over the previous year. Official defence budget figures, however, do not include many other allocations and benefits accruing to China's armed forces and are not transparent.[3]

China's strategic nuclear forces are still small, but although Beijing has vowed not to attack a non-nuclear country with nuclear weapons, it is doubtful that such a guarantee extends to Japan which is under the US nuclear umbrella and hosts around 40,000 US troops. Closely related are reports about Chinese exports of nuclear weapons and missile technology to countries that are also of strategic importance to Japan.

54 Reinhard Drifte

These Chinese developments, on their own, might not have led to a change in Japanese perceptions of China beyond the small circle of security specialists, as was illustrated by Japan's limited public concern about the emergence of a Chinese nuclear deterrent in the 1960s or the upheaval of the Chinese Cultural Revolution. However, in the 1990s, China's political, economic and military importance had come to loom much larger on a regional and even global level because these developments interacted with changes in the international strategic environment, in the Japanese–American alliance and in Japan's domestic politics as mentioned before. Against this background the following bilateral security issues became more contentious.

Territorial disputes

The protection of territorial integrity is at the heart of every national security policy. In the case of Japanese–Chinese relations, territorial issues around the Diaoyu/Senkaku Islands and the delimitation of the exclusive economic zone (EEZ) in the whole of the East China Sea also involve substantial economic interests (fisheries, seabed resources). As Japan's protection of maritime interests depends on the US, in collaboration with its own maritime self-defence force (MSDF), alliance considerations are also involved.

Due to the improvement of relations between China and both Japan and the US since 1971, the territorial dispute over the Senkaku Islands was put to rest during the 1970s and 1980s. It flared up again with the promulgation of China's territorial law in 1992 and with the increase of Chinese survey and naval ships around the Senkaku Islands in the 1990s. Both governments started to take a more assertive stance and incidents were triggered by nationalists on the Japanese as well as the Chinese side (mainly Chinese from Hong Kong and Taiwan). While China still maintains that both sides agreed in 1978 and 1983 to shelve the Senkaku issue for the time being (statements made by Deng Xiaoping), the Japanese government is now publicly negating any such tacit agreement and denies even the existence of a territorial issue (over the Senkaku) which is rather ingenious since it did not contradict Deng's statements at the time.[4]

The Senkaku issue is closely linked to the delimitation of the continental shelf (on which depends the delimitation of Japan's EEZ) in the wider area of the East China Sea and both disputes block a solution of the other. The continental shelf in the East China Sea covers 300,000 square kilometres. China claims the whole shelf as far as Okinawa, including an unspecified portion of the Japan/South Korea Joint Development Zone. As a result, China does not recognise Japan's 1996 proclaimed EEZ since it lies between China's coast and the rim of Okinawa that faces China.

A solution of these territorial problems is made difficult by China's reluctance to get involved in serious negotiations, by the tactical need of both sides to fundamentally refute the stance of the other side, and China's growing encroachment on Japan's EEZ, accompanied by the rise of incursions by Chinese

Engagement Japanese style 55

oil-exploration-related vessels and naval vessels into Japan's EEZ and even territorial waters. The number of intrusions by Chinese research vessels into Japan's EEZ increased from 7 in 1995 to 33 in 1999, including the territorial waters around the Senkaku Islands.[5] Since May 1999, Chinese warships have been operating for the first time in the vicinity of Japanese territorial waters. The number of sightings of Chinese warships in waters around Japan (including passage through Japanese straits like the Tsuruga Strait) by the MSDF increased from 2 ships in 1998 to 27 in 1999.[6] Finally, Chinese oil and gas exploration and production is taking place very close to Japan's maritime border with China, which is bound to lead to more incursions of Chinese research and naval vessels.

In addition, Japan's trust in US support has diminished. Until the reversion of Okinawa which included the Senkaku Islands, the US de facto supported Japan's territorial claim. However, since 1971 the US claims that the reversion of the administrative rights to Japan did not signify a bias towards any of the territorial claims of the parties involved while at the same time confirming the applicability of the Japan–US security treaty to the Senkaku Islands.[7] The background to the US statements in 1971 as well as their reconfirmation in October 1996 was an American desire to improve relations with China.

Looking at the triangular dynamics involved, this indicates that the bilateral security treaty will for the foreseeable future most likely prevent any military confrontation over the Senkaku Islands, but in the meantime US political support for a solution in Japan's favour will remain very limited. Rather, any flare-up of tensions will highlight the rivalry between US–Chinese relations and Japanese–US relations. Finally, Japan cannot expect much US support in its conflict with China about the EEZ or territorial waters in the East China Sea. As in the case of the South China Sea, the US does not pronounce itself on any territorial claims and China is therefore free to continue its gradual encroachment on Japan's EEZ and underwater resources. The US merely reminds China occasionally of its demands for a peaceful resolution of territorial conflicts and the security of international maritime traffic while patrolling the area with the 7th Fleet.

What has been said about the Senkaku Islands and the East China Sea applies to a certain extent also to the South China Sea which is related to Japan's security because the safety of the country's major sea lanes and air corridors are involved. The South China Sea has been linked to piracy and more recently illegal immigration from China. The area's natural resources and fishing are very promising. Any conflict between China on the one hand, and other claimants and beneficiaries of the South China Sea on the other hand would have a negative impact on Japan's security environment and make compromise in the East China Sea even more difficult. It would be an indicator of China's willingness to use military force. Again, China seems to be playing for time while reinforcing its physical presence and its military potential to protect this presence. The US limits itself to cautionary statements about the need to protect the freedom of sea lanes.

56 Reinhard Drifte

China's nuclear testing

The beginning of a new Chinese nuclear test series in May 1995 at a sensitive moment of global efforts to enhance the nuclear non-proliferation regime further added to the negative impact created by China's rising military budget and territorial claims. Rather than any immediate perception of threat it was the delicate moment in global nuclear arms control and China's insensitivity towards Japan's anti-nuclear feelings which led to an unprecedented clash with China over the latter's resumption of nuclear testing.

First of all, the tests were in contravention of the new Japanese ODA Guidelines of 1992 which call for a reconsideration of ODA in the case of production of weapons of mass destruction. But since then Japan had only expressed its regret when China has tested its nuclear arsenal. This time, however, it was more difficult to ignore because the new series of tests occurred just when in April/May 1995 the NPT Extension Conference took place to decide on the indefinite extension of the treaty. It was particularly shocking for Japan that Socialist Prime Minister Murayama Tomoichi had just visited China and had urged Beijing to refrain from testing.[8] This prompted the Japanese government on 22 May to reduce its grant aid to China rather than only sending a formal protest to the Chinese government, as they had done in the past. At the same time, however, the government declared that it continued to support China's economic modernisation efforts.[9] Despite public calls for more severe sanctions, the government felt that the suspension of all yen loans, with its impact on China's five-year plan, would have been too strong a political signal and China would still go ahead with the testing.[10]

Taiwan Strait confrontation, 1996

Arguably the greatest impact on Japan's shifting security perception of China derived from the latter's military exercises and missile tests around Taiwan in 1995–6. These events were very close to Japan's own territory, they raised concern about China's willingness to use military force (and US willingness to reciprocate), they drew attention to China's missile force and proliferation of weapons of mass destruction, and they highlighted the role of the unresolved Taiwan issue in Japanese–Chinese relations.

The culmination of the crisis with the missile tests in March 1996 (around the time of the Taiwan elections) attracted the widest media attention in Japan, while officially the government tried to stay aloof and merely expressed the hope of a peaceful resolution of the confrontation. The missile tests drove home to the Japanese public how close the dispute is to Japan and how any widening of it could affect the country's own security and economic interests. One of the four missiles in March 1996 landed in the sea off the Taiwanese city of Hualian, about 60 kilometres from Japan's southernmost island, Yonaguni (Prefecture of Okinawa), affecting its fishing industry. However, when the residents of Yonaguni asked for naval protection, Prime Minister Hashimoto ruled out sending the MSDF in order not to provoke China.[11]

One high official in the Prime Minister's Office (PMO) involved in the crisis management admitted to Funabashi Yoichi that the government could not admit the seriousness of the situation because it might have triggered a Chinese attack on Taiwan or some similar dangerous situation.[12] The Japanese government maintained its cautious approach throughout March 1996. No threats about cutting ODA were made. The Japanese government explained that its position was more vulnerable than that of the US and Prime Minister Hashimoto even expressed the hope that 'the US will exercise self-control'.[13] The USS *Independence* which the US deployed to the area of the Taiwan Strait, is based in Yokosuka. According to Funabashi Yoichi, the US bases in Okinawa were not used except for radar support.[14] Fukuyoshi Shoji of Osaka Keizai Hōka University mentions that the US stationed its missile-tracking ship *Observation Island* in Yokohama harbour during spring 1996.[15] However, the Japanese MSDF supplied oil to US carrier group vessels.[16]

There was also concern that the Taiwan crisis, having highlighted the strategic importance of Okinawa for the US forward deployment in Asia, might wreck the compromise reached over the return of one US base in Okinawa, Futemna, and thus endanger again the public acceptance of the US military presence in Japan.[17] Zhang and Montaperto conclude from the absence of any Chinese diplomatic action against Japan and the limited amount of Chinese criticism of Japan that Japan's restraint was well appreciated.[18] However, Funabashi Yoichi quotes Foreign Minister Qian Qichen telling his Japanese counterpart, Ikeda Yukihiko: 'Leaving aside the fuss made by the Americans, you're the only other country kicking up a fuss. China is shocked by that'.[19]

Statements even by pro-China politicians were very critical of the tests. LDP Secretary General Kato Koichi was quoted as saying that 'China's missile testing in international waters in the Taiwan Strait was behaviour that cannot be tolerated'.[20] Some parliamentarians asked for a stronger reaction than simply a protest by the Director General of the Asian Bureau of the MOFA to the Chinese embassy in Tokyo.[21]

Finally, the Taiwan crisis in 1995–6 highlighted the role which the unresolved issue of Taiwan plays in Japanese–Chinese security relations and which assumed even greater importance after the 1996 Hashimoto–Clinton Declaration strengthening Japanese–US security cooperation and the beginning of Japan's involvement in TMD.

Japan's legal position on the Taiwan issue raises in the eyes of the PRC suspicions about Japan's ultimate intentions towards Taiwan and also has some bearing on Taiwan's designs of independence. Whereas the PRC insists that the postwar settlement leaves no doubt that Taiwan is part of its territory, the Japanese government has always insisted on keeping alive an ambiguity surrounding this settlement. Tokyo basically maintains that it renounced its territorial rights over Taiwan in the 1951 San Francisco Peace Treaty and has therefore no right to determine the new owner.[22]

Taiwan is for Japan a 'minimally strategic concern'.[23] It makes fundamentally no difference to Japan's sea lane security if the relatively short stretch along

58 *Reinhard Drifte*

Taiwan is added to the much longer stretch along the Chinese coast and notably through the contested South China Sea. The security interests of Japan in Taiwan lie not so much in the island being part or not part of the PRC, but in the process which would lead to a change of the status quo. If this process is violent – and the Taiwan crisis in 1995–6 invoked such fears – it would destabilise Asia and raise concern about China's future behaviour to a new height, possibly leading to an arms race and new military alignments. The possible involvement of the US would severely test Japan's security policy because it would have to decide between the long-term security relationship with its most powerful neighbour and the stability of its security alliance with the US which is thousands of miles away. Since the integration of Hong Kong into the PRC and the new dynamics in the PRC–Taiwan relationship, Chinese determination and willingness to use force if needed seem to have become a greater possibility to many Japanese. Japan would prefer the status quo, but the issue is whether it is sustainable in the light of the changes in Taiwan to assert the island's independence started under President Lee Teng-hui.

Non-military challenges

As a 'civilian power' with the world's second largest economy, Japan is wearily watching China's economic problems, including China's long-term economic challenge to Japan. There is a much greater awareness in Japan than, for example, in the US, let alone Europe, that China may internally disintegrate or become unable to handle its environmental degradation as a result of failed social and economic policies.[24] Japan's concern is that this may lead to a considerable stream of refugees into China's neighbouring countries.[25] There are already signs of this in the form of increasing Chinese illegal immigration to foreign countries, including Japan, piracy in the South China Sea, and Chinese involvement in regional and domestic crime. Japan and the Korean peninsula already suffer from Chinese transboundary air and sea pollution.

According to the Japanese police, about 90 per cent of people entering Japan illegally come from the PRC. Until 1991, the number of Chinese nationals arrested for entering the country illegally remained in double figures, but it rose sharply to 1209 in 1997 and 824 in 1998. There is considerable Chinese involvement in the smuggling of firearms and drugs into Japan. Hundreds of Chinese mobsters from more than 10 of Shanghai's 300 gangs are now active in Japan. The real figures may be several times higher. Therefore, in May 1998, the governments of both countries started talks on how to deal with this situation.[26]

Although these developments are still minor, particularly if one compares, for example, illegal immigration into Western Europe, they have a very high impact on the perception of a relatively crime-free society like Japan and further enhance the perception of a 'Chinese threat'. Moreover, Japanese trust in the communist regime successfully handling the economic and environmental problems of China are not high, and there is concern that the central government will continue to lose control.

The problems of engagement

In order to deal with the above security challenges and safeguard its national interests, Japan pursues a policy of engagement towards China. To evaluate this policy, we have to gain a better understanding of its dualistic character, appreciate the implications of the Japanese–American security alliance, and investigate how engagement can adequately cope with China's size, demography, ideology, national identity or serious structural economic problems.

The policy of engagement is most often associated with the liberal school of international relations which gives rise to considerable confusion because it obfuscates the role of force in the way it is pursued by the major powers, including Japan. In fact, engagement relies as much on realist foundations, with its deterrence and balance of power elements, as on liberal foundations, which stress the positive forces of increasing international economic interdependence and integration, the spreading of international norms, and the establishment of rules and institutions to regulate and enable peaceful cooperation between nations.

The following definition of engagement by Alastair Iain Johnstone and Robert S. Ross probably best describes the dualistic character of this policy: 'The use of non-coercive methods to ameliorate the non-status-quo elements of a rising power's behaviour. The goal is to ensure that this growing power is used in ways that are consistent with peaceful change in regional and global order'. The authors explicitly state that amelioration of the rising power's behaviour does not seek to limit, constrain, or delay the newcomer's power nor prevent the development of influence commensurate with its greater power.[27] They attach four conditions to making a policy of engagement effective:

1 The new rising power has only limited revisionist aims and there are no irreconcilable conflicts of interests with the established powers.
2 The established powers are strong enough to mix concessions with credible threats, i.e. a sticks and carrots policy.
3 Engagement is a complement and not an alternative to balancing.
4 The established powers must live by the same principles they demand of the new rising power.[28]

Looking carefully at this statement it becomes clear that, for the rising power, 'coercive means' still have to be an item in their calculation about the established powers despite their goal of the non-use of 'coercive methods'. This is not only related to the established powers' realist objectives *vis-à-vis* the intentions of a rising power (i.e. balancing and hedging), but is in the first instance due to the simple fact that all the established powers, including Japan, maintain considerable military forces and are involved in military alliances. Incorporating realist as well as liberal elements, engagement is a dualistic strategy. The real problems of engagement are therefore the emphasis and the robustness as well as the mix of policy tools with which some rather than other goals associated with engagement are pursued.

60 *Reinhard Drifte*

The liberal element of engagement dialogues and economic interaction

As part of the liberal agenda of engagement, Japan is engaging China bilaterally and multilaterally through political dialogue as well as economic interaction. For reasons of space other policies such as cultural diplomacy (at official as well as private levels) have to be omitted.

The bilateral political dialogue encompasses almost all levels of governmental activities and is operating at various governmental levels, depending on the issue. Recent summit meetings, notably President Jiang Zemin's Japan visit in November 1998, have led to a cooperation agenda of 33 different items on bilateral as well as multilateral levels.[29] Just to mention security-related issues, it includes arms control, exchange of military officials, the law of the sea, piracy, etc.

However, although the security area would particularly necessitate more dialogue because of often widely differing opinions (e.g. territorial disputes), a closer look reveals that often very basic contacts more relevant to confidence-building than anything else, let alone direct talks on difficult issues, face considerable obstacles. In the case of military exchanges, China insists on starting with the top level and gradually expanding downwards to the operational (individual unit) level. Yet China has been reluctant to facilitate such high-level contacts, often claiming scheduling problems and/or mentioning 'inimical' Japanese defence policies like the 1996 Hashimoto–Clinton reaffirmation of Japan–US cooperation or the revised Japan–US Guidelines of 1997. Although there have now been exchanges of Defence Ministers, the first senior uniformed self-defence force official's visit occurred only in 1995 when Admiral Nishi visited the PRC. In 1998 the first summit meeting for eleven years took place when Defence Agency Director General Fumio Kyuma met his PRC counterpart Chi Haotian in Tokyo. But although senior-level exchanges have increased, there have still not been fleet visits although China's navy sent ships to over 20 countries during the 1990s, including Africa.

A regular security dialogue only started in 1993, but initially China did not send any military representatives. Only in 1997, at the fourth meeting, did representatives of the Chinese general staff at colonel level take part for the first time. Earlier, only people from the Ministry of Defence joined in, which a Japanese Defence Agency official qualified as merely 'ceremonial' in terms of power.[30] In 1999 the Chinese side proposed to upgrade the level of the security dialogue to Deputy Minister, but the Japanese side has not responded to this proposal and the recent seventh dialogue was still at the level of Director General. A telephone 'hot line' was only established in autumn 2000.

There are several reasons for these difficulties. To the Chinese, the exchange of visits is seen as a favour granted to the other side, and their withholding can serve reasons of admonition against the other side's policies which China does not appreciate. There is also a certain disdain for Japan because of its past but also its lower rank in comparison to the US or other more independently acting Western countries. Moreover, the military in China is certainly the sector which

Engagement Japanese style 61

is the most negative towards Japan and most reluctant to discard its suspicions. PLA officers admit in private that their leadership has intentionally slowed the development of relations or even tried quietly to bring them to a halt.[31] China displays the same tactical approach to confidence building measures (using confidence building measures in talks as a lever to achieve certain objectives) as well as fundamentally misunderstanding the concept (requiring confidence, i.e. agreement with Chinese policies, as a prerequisite for confidence building measures rather than as their intrinsic goal) as Japan did during the Cold War towards the Soviet Union in relation to their territorial dispute. The contrast with the positive developments of confidence building measures with South Korea and particularly with Russia is striking.

Japan is strongly promoting China's integration into multilateral forums, with the ASEAN Regional Forum (ARF) being particularly relevant. For Japan multilateral forums can be an opportunity to bring up critical issues shared by other countries but which it would not like to raise bilaterally. An important part of Japanese diplomacy now is conflict prevention which is supported for various reasons (e.g. non-military international burden-sharing) but which also has Chinese involvement very much in mind (e.g. in the ARF) in order to dissuade China from using force for dispute settlement (e.g. Taiwan).

China often uses these forums to attack Japanese security policies like theatre missile defence (TMD) and the new Guidelines. Its representatives often act as obstacles rather than promoters, let alone initiators. Moreover, China is using its membership of the ARF to prevent the discussion of the most troubling subject to all members, i.e. China's territorial claim, making use of the ARF's procedural rule of consensus. The multilateral involvement of China is also a double-edged vehicle for Japan's engagement policy as there is the distinct impression that China is opposing Tokyo's greater regional and international role, knowing that such a role needs some kind of Chinese agreement to be legitimised. China does not want to recognise Japan as an Asian representative, as was illustrated when China kept Japan out of US-proposed discussions on the India–Pakistan nuclear tests in 1997, or when former Prime Minister Obuchi tried to involve China in the G8. On a global level, China has also demonstrated on several occasions its opposition to Japan becoming a more global player. China is, for example, opposed to Japan's permanent UN Security Council bid.[32]

In the context of the liberal agenda of engagement one may also point out Japan's cautious treatment of China. The most famous recent case is Japan's strong campaign for the ending of sanctions by the West against China in the wake of the Tiananmen Square massacre in order not to isolate Beijing and hurt its integration into global society. The Japanese government has also been careful in other areas, where the US or other countries have been much more outspoken and critical of China, for example over human rights. Another example is Japan's prudence about suspending loan aid to China in 1995 after China's resumption of nuclear tests, compared with a total suspension of aid to India and Pakistan after their nuclear tests in May 1998, although Japan is the biggest ODA donor to both countries, far ahead of the second biggest donor.

62 Reinhard Drifte

The involvement of private business in the PRC is actively supported by the Japanese government, not only for economic reasons, but also in the interest of engagement, because of its positive contribution to the creation of a more interdependent relationship and China's integration into the global system. Trade in 1999 amounted to $65.8 billion and the cumulative total of Japanese investments in China was $33.5 billion up until fiscal year 1999. China received a total of $13.18 billion in ODA from Japan up to 1998, being Japan's second largest aid recipient after Indonesia, while Japan is China's biggest aid donor.[33] The Japanese government enunciated under Prime Minister Ohira Masayoshi in 1979 ODA principles specifically for China, stipulating among other things that no military assistance would be provided. In the general ODA Guidelines of 1992 Japanese ODA was made even more contingent on the security policy of the recipient. Japan's ODA has recently come under fire because there are increasingly critical comments that it is often wasted, that China does not stick to its conditions, that it should go to areas where there is real need, including the environment, that China is not grateful, that China is itself an ODA donor, that domestically China does not acknowledge the aid, and that China spends too much on the military. Moreover, there is a feeling that Japan is losing its ODA leverage on China because of its successful economic modernisation[34] (see also Söderberg in Chapter 7).

In conclusion, one can say that Japan's liberal agenda of engagement has been very considerable, notably in the area of economic development, and that it has had a positive influence on the security relationship, building towards greater mutual understanding. The security dialogue is less advanced, and military exchanges are particularly weak. The important aspect here is that China's attitude hinders the development of more normal relations which would help to overcome the many bilateral differences. Apart from serious security policy differences, to be discussed next, the Japanese side has not helped the situation by not coming to terms with its past. Japan's economic interaction with China has certainly been the most positive feature of Japanese–Chinese relations which has had a soothing influence on bilateral disputes. There have been several incidents in the past, including over the Senkaku Islands, where China's wish for continued Japanese help played a decisive role in cooling, if not stopping, a conflict from escalating.[35] Japan's recent ODA policy change also helps directly to address sources of Chinese instability by shifting more aid to western and central China, away from the overcrowded east coast rim, and by increasing ODA for environmentally related projects. China's likely admission to the WTO in 2001 certainly owes a great deal to Japan's economic support. However, the liberal part of the engagement agenda has not achieved its full potential because of enduring Chinese suspicion of Japan and increasing strategic competition with Japan. The current transition to a less generous and domestically more scrutinised ODA programme by Japan may raise frictions of its own while the absolute amount of ODA decreases and Japan loses a certain amount of its influence because of China's economic progress. One may also ask whether the solutions offered so far as part of the liberal agenda of the engagement strategy

Engagement Japanese style 63

are not several orders of magnitude below the scale of China's political, economic and environmental problems. Finally, the revisionist goals of the liberal agenda are offensive to many Chinese because they are regarded 'as a means for the West to bring about a peaceful transformation of China's international and domestic behaviour in accordance with rules and norms set by the West', endangering Chinese regime stability.[36]

The realist elements of engagement – power balancing and hedging

Against the background of serious differences between Japan and China, the effect of the liberal element of engagement is partly curtailed by the realist policies of balancing and hedging, which are also closely connected to Japan's comprehensive alliance with the US. Balancing has a political as well as a military side, although the latter is much more important. However, it is important to point out that Japan's growing links with Mongolia, Central Asia, India, Myanmar, Vietnam and ASEAN in general are supported by a range of policy constituencies whose motivations range from providing China with incentives to construct its Asian policy on peaceful foundations to the goal of ultimately building up 'soft containment' against China.

The military side of balancing relies on Japan's own defence efforts, as well as close integration into the Japan–US alliance. Japan's self-defence forces rank now, after US forces, as the second most modern military force in Asia. The Chinese armed forces are vastly more numerous and have nominally greater amounts of hardware, but in spite of China's nuclear weapons and missiles, Japan's armed forces are superior in terms of technological sophistication. Japan has the potential to expand its military, at least economically, but its pacifist orientation, the anticipation of offsetting military efforts by other countries (including the US), and Japan's lack of strategic depth put severe limits on any such development. The reconfirmation (critical voices speak of redefinition of the Japan–US security pact) by Prime Minister Hashimoto and President Clinton in April 1996 and the passing of laws to implement the new Guidelines for Japan–US military cooperation in case of conflict in spring 1999 would not have been achieved had there only been the more immediate concern about North Korea's security policies. Rather, it was the uncertainty about China's future course which was at the back of the minds of Japanese policy-makers and which facilitated domestic acquiescence, if not support.

China has made very clear its opposition to recent Japanese security policies through:

1 criticism of the reconfirmed security treaty expanding from a bilateral security treaty to the protection of the whole region;
2 criticism that the new Guidelines are aimed at containing China;
3 criticism of the ambiguity of the new Guidelines and suspicion that they include Taiwan to prevent national reunification.

64 *Reinhard Drifte*

In addition, a new issue is the US-initiated TMD system in whose research phase Japan has joined. China's greatest concern is again the impact on Taiwan, since it asserts that TMD is to include Taiwan (see also Hughes in Chapter 4).

The Japan–US alliance does not only underpin Japan's balancing and deterring of China. Some of its complexities actually render the operationalisation of engagement difficult.[37] These complexities result from the following factors:

1   Japan and the US do not agree that all the four conditions for engagement as mentioned by Johnstone and Ross are met. At least the Taiwan issue comes very close to or may even be considered an 'irreconcilable conflict' between the US and China, but not between Japan and China. Arguably the US attachment to human rights or the Tibet issue may come into the same category.
2   There are differences between Japan and the US on how important Taiwan is, but possibly also on other regional issues like the continued presence of US troops on the Korean peninsula after reunification.
3   In the American debate the emphasis and the robustness with which the principles of engagement are to be pursued is not only unclear and constantly shifting, but is also subject to domestic politics which often have more to do with scoring points against the executive than with protecting American national interests on a long-term basis, let alone the interests of close allies like Japan. Necessary coordination between Japan and the US is therefore not easy. In contrast to the US, engagement as a policy is hardly contested in Japan.
4   These Japan–US divergences are related to Japan's pacifist inclinations, asymmetries in power and geography and the dynamics resulting from triangular relations and the 'alliance game' (abandonment and entrapment).

Analysing the triangular dynamics between Japan, China and the US (see also Zhao in Chapter 2), one has to consider that in theory there is always the possibility that two may gang up against the third and that the third may play the two others against each other. Another possibility is for one power to engage in offshore balancing or to act as a balancer of last resort. Two of the countries (Japan and the US) have a relationship with each other which cannot be rivalled by China's relationship with either the US or Japan. There is therefore an inherent and an a priori two-against-one triangular relationship. China is therefore naturally trying to drive a wedge between the two, to amplify any Japan–US differences and to play one against the other. Under these circumstances, it is not in China's interests to give the appearance that it could be convinced that a strengthened Japanese–American security alliance is not directed against it.

Military policies like the new Guidelines or TMD on the one hand aim at reducing the risk of abandonment by the US ally, and on the other they reinforce the dilemma of entrapment. Japanese accommodation of the US has recently been motivated by the apparent ambiguity of the second Clinton administration

Engagement Japanese style   65

concerning the relative importance of Japan to the US in relation to China, triggered by various official actions and statements.

Conclusions

The challenge for the global community as well as for Japan's engagement policy is how to help China achieve its goals as a peaceful power despite the latter's territorial and ideological revisionism, and how to help China reconcile its rapid economic growth with domestic political stability and environmental sustainability. Japan wants to prevent a situation where China's current policies are merely a temporary accommodation which aims at extracting maximum benefit from economic powers like Japan, until China feels strong enough to secure its objectives in a way which is less compatible with a peaceful and stable world, and which notably disregards the legitimate interests of other East Asian countries. Even apart from the possibility of China's tactical reaction to engagement, we have seen that this dualistic policy contains conflicting dynamics which diminish its efficiency, including that of the liberal agenda.

There are, however, considerable centrifugal dynamics in the policy of engagement. One fundamental problem is China's suspicion of Japan and of the reaffirmed Japan–US relationship. Japan presents China's realists with a dilemma. Opposing alliances, US preponderance in Asia and dependence on other countries, China would logically have to encourage Japan to become more independent from the US and to have a security policy commensurate with its economic power. Moreover, since Japan is, after the US, China's most important economic partner to achieve the goal of regaining its former status as a great power, good relations with a prosperous Japan should be important. However, as realists the Chinese are also convinced that big economic powers inevitably become big military powers although this historical determinism is put into question by Japan's rise as a global civilian power and the resulting difference between Japan's economic might and performance and its military might and willingness to use it. A majority of Chinese strategists believe it to be impossible, against the background of their historical determinism, that a greater Japanese military role can be contained within the Japanese–American security alliance (e.g. TMD is considered a shield behind which Japan may develop an offensive capability).

Obviously, China does not want to follow realist prescriptions in Japan's case and encourage Tokyo's independent military growth (the period of anti-hegemonic struggle in the 1980s was an exception), nor does it want to hasten the realisation of its historical determinism about Japan's future path because of its own national ambitions, its concern about strong Japanese–American links inhibiting the advent of a multipolar world, and its deep distrust of Japan resulting from the past.

But by either working towards the end of the Japanese–American security alliance and/or threatening Japan with a rapid and non-transparent build-up of its conventional and nuclear military forces, as well as with destabilising acts to

66   *Reinhard Drifte*

assert its territorial claims, the unwanted scenario of either a stronger Japanese–American military alliance or a stronger independent Japanese military power may become reality. Even if China's political and strategic leaders abandoned their historical determinism as some have done, ending the Japan–US alliance would force Japan to overcome its hesitance towards military force and nuclear armament, at least from a realist point of view.

Against this background of suspicion, competition and tactical elements in China's Japan policy, and combined with its economic weakness and historical memory of colonialism and exploitation, accentuated by its own brand of communism, Chinese leaders are still more inclined towards a realist and zero-sum game approach to international relations. One has therefore to ask whether China's policy-makers and strategists are able to respond to Japan's engagement policy in the way Japan desires, or whether their realist inclinations will prompt them to react more to the realist than to the liberal elements of this policy.

Since engagement is basically a policy to buy time for a peaceful change in China while it copes with its serious political, social, economic and environmental problems, Japan has to reconsider the mix of policies under the liberal and realist agenda in order to make engagement more effective in good time. Bilaterally Japan has to make ODA more relevant for the current major economic and ecological problems of China. But even Japan's economic interaction with China and ODA bear the risk of enhancing the environmental and political damage caused by economic growth. A more sincere attitude towards the past would not only force China to abandon its suspicions towards Japan, but would deprive it of a strong lever against Japan. Tokyo might also consider using greater clarity on the legal position of Taiwan as a lever for constructive talks about territorial issues. The more Japan becomes an important and indispensable security dialogue partner for other Asian countries, the more China would feel the necessity to give up its reserve towards Japan. Multilaterally, Japan would be well advised to be more active and imaginative in integrating China into regional and global organisations and frameworks.

The most difficult adjustments would have to be made concerning the policies associated with the realist agenda of engagement because they are so dependent on the Japanese–American alliance and therefore hostage to US consent. For the hedging element of engagement should not only be the deepening of the bilateral alliance, but also the prevention of an economic or ecological collapse in China. The precondition for this is a US China policy which broadens rather than limits its array of policy tools, notably in the multilateral arena. Japan and the US would have to work much more seriously on coping with the negative dynamics of the triangular Japan–US–China relationship. The inclusion of Japan into TMD, let alone Taiwan, would wreak havoc with security in East Asia. Japan and the US will ultimately have to include China in a regional security system which takes over some functions of the two Northeast Asian security alliances which the US has with Japan and Korea (for example the 'cap in the bottle' function). Just 'explaining' to China the inoffensive intentions of the new Guidelines and their non-geographic meaning is not convincing and contradicts

Japan's insistence on Chinese military transparency. Some consideration might therefore be given to an East Asian equivalent of 'Partnership for Peace' which would reduce China's concerns.[38]

Notes

1 Charles Morrison, ed., *Asia Pacific Security Outlook 1998*, Japan Center for International Exchange, JCIE, p. 46.
2 For a good presentation of China's strategy see June Teufel Dreyer, 'State of the Field Report: Research on the Chinese Military', *Accessasia Review*, Summer 1997 (http: 'www.accessasia.org/products/aareview/Vol1No1/Article1.html').
3 Richard A. Bitzinger and Bates Gill, *Gearing up for High-Tech Warfare? Chinese and Taiwanese Defense Modernization and Implications for Military Confrontation across the Taiwan Strait, 1995–2005*, Washington, DC, Center for Strategic and Budgetary Assessment, February 1996, p. 15.
4 For a negation of having ever shelved the issue see, for example, the report on talks between Prime Minister Hashimoto and Deputy Foreign Minister Tang Jiaxuan in October 1996, *Yomiuri Shimbun*, 30 October 1996. For a negation of the very existence of a territorial issue, see, for example, the statement by the press secretary of MOFA at the press conference on 19 July 1996, MOFA website.
5 Kaijō Hoanchō, *Kaijō Hoan no Genkyō*, September 2000, p. 49.
6 Japanese White Paper on Defence 2000, p. 56.
7 Funabashi Yoichi, *Alliance Adrift*, Washington, DC, Council on Foreign Relations, 1999, pp. 404–5.
8 This account is largely based on Kokubun Ryosei, Reisengo no anzenhoshō to Nicchū kankei, in Okabe Tatsumi, Takagi Seiichiro and Kokubun Ryosei, eds, *Nichi-Bei-Chū. Anzen hoshō kyōryoku o mezashite*, Tokyo, Keisō Shobō, 1999, p. 24 ff.
9 Wakisaka Noriyuki, Nichi Bei no tai Chū keizai kyōryuoku, in Kokubun Ryosei, ed., *Nihon, Amerika, Chūgoku: Kyōchō e no shinario*, Tokyo, TBS Britannica, 1997, p. 227. For further information on the reduction of grant aid see Japan's Official Development Assistance Annual Report 1997, Tokyo, Ministry of Foreign Affairs, 1998, p. 72.
10 Kokubun Ryosei et al., op. cit., p. 25, *Asahi Shimbun*, 3 and 10 June 1996.
11 Funabashi, op. cit., p. 394.
12 Funabashi, op. cit., p. 401.
13 Zhang Ming and Ronald N. Montaperto, *A Triad of Another Kind. The United States, China, and Japan*, New York, St Martin's Press, 1999, p. 88.
14 Funabashi, op. cit., pp. 386–91.
15 Fukuyoshi Shoji, *Chūgoku no gunjiryoku to Nichi Bei ampo saiteigi*, Higashi Ajia Kenkyū, no. 15, 1997, pp. 56–7.
16 Thomas A. Drohan, *The US–Japan Defence Guidelines: Toward an Equivalent Alliance*, Tokyo, Institute for International Policy Studies, November 1999, p. 9.
17 Nakai Yoshifumi, Turbulence threatens, *The World Today*, vol. 55, no. 11, November 1999, p. 18.
18 Zhang/Montaperto, op. cit., p. 99.
19 Funabashi, op. cit., p. 423.
20 *Far Eastern Economic Review*, 15 August 1996, p. 28.
21 Funabashi, op. cit., p. 394.
22 *Asahi Shimbun*, 2 October 1997. See also MOFA spokesman Numata Sadaaki in his press conference on 16 October 1998, MOFA website.
23 Nakai Yoshifumi, US–Japan Relations in Asia: The Common Agenda on the Taiwan Issue, p. 5, at http://www.stanford.edu/group/APARC/publications/papers/nakai.pdf

68 *Reinhard Drifte*

24 Sato Hideo, Japan's China perceptions and its policies in the alliance with the United States, *Journal of International Political Economy*, vol. 2, no. 1, March 1998, pp. 11–13.
25 Amako Satoshi, ed., *Chūgoku wa kyōi ka*, Tokyo, Keisō Shobō, 1997, p. 9.
26 *The Daily Yomiuri*, 20 June 1999. *Asahi Shimbun*, 24 June 1999.
27 Alastair Iain Johnstone and Robert S. Ross, *Engaging China. The Management of an Emerging Power*, London, Routledge, 1999, pp. xiv–xv.
28 Johnstone/Ross, op. cit., pp. 14–15.
29 Joint press announcement on strengthening cooperation between Japan and China toward the twenty-first century, 26 November 1998. http://www.mofa.go.jp/region/asia-paci/china/visit98/press.html
30 Interview with a senior official of the Defence Agency, 25 June 1997.
31 Benjamin L. Self, Confidence-building measures and Japanese security policy, in Ranjeet K. Singh, ed., *Investigating Confidence-Building Measures in the Asia-Pacific Region*, Report no. 28, Washington, DC, The Henry L. Stimson Center, May 1999, p. 64.
32 Reinhard Drifte, *Japan's Quest for a Permanent Security Council Seat. A Matter of Pride or Justice?*, London/Oxford, Macmillan/St Antony's College, 2000, pp.150–1.
33 *Japan Times*, 13 May 2000. For an overall official evaluation see Miyamoto Yuji, Tai Chū keizai enjo o dō suru ka, *Gaikō Forum*, no. 144, August 2000.
34 Murai Tomohide, Ajia no anzenhoshō to Nicchū kankei, *Gaikō Jippō*, January 1998, p. 18.
35 For such a role in the Senkaku conflict in 1996, see Funabashi, op. cit., p. 407.
36 Takahashi Takuma, Economic interdependence and security, in Mike M. Mochizuki, ed., *Toward a True Alliance. Restructuring US–Japan Security Relations*, Washington, DC, Brookings Institution Press, 1997, p. 119.
37 See Reinhard Drifte, US impact on Japanese–Chinese security relations, *Security Dialogue*, vol. 31, no. 4, 2000, pp. 449–62.
38 A similar suggestion has been made by Thomas Berger, Set for stability? Prospects for conflict and cooperation in East Asia, *Review of International Studies*, vol. 26, no. 3, July 2000, pp. 427–8.

4 Sino-Japanese relations and ballistic missile defence (BMD)

Christopher W. Hughes

Introduction: Japan and the strategic implications of BMD

Japan and BMD

On 25 December 1998, the National Security Council of Japan approved the initiation of cooperative technological research with the United States (US) into ballistic missile defence (BMD) systems.[1] This Japanese cabinet decision was then followed on 16 August 1999 by an 'Exchange of Notes Concerning a Programme for Cooperative Research on Ballistic Missile Technologies' between the governments of Japan and the US.[2] In accordance with these agreements, the Japanese government committed itself to cooperative technological research into providing a shield for Japan against ballistic missile attack, to provide initial funding in the 1999 budget of yen 16 million for general research into BMD and the modality of Japan's defence, and another yen 962 million into four key technologies associated with Japan's possible participation in the Navy Theatre Wide Defence (NTWD) component of BMD (explained in more detail below).[3] In the 2000 budget, a further yen 2.05 billion was earmarked for research into these four technologies.[4] The Japan Defence Agency (JDA), the Ministry of Foreign Affairs (MOFA) and other government policy-makers stress that the BMD project remains purely at the research stage, and that separate government decisions will be necessary before any progression is made towards the stages of development, production and deployment. Nevertheless, even at the research phase it is clear that both Japanese policy-makers involved with BMD and outsider commentators alike envisage a host of problems associated with the project at each potential stage of its development, which have implications for Japan's entire security policy.[5]

BMD, or theatre missile defence (TMD) as it is still most commonly referred to in Japan and the US – much to the exasperation of Japanese government officials who wish to draw a distinction between US TMD projects, designed to protect US forces despatched to overseas theatres and allied states, and Japan's own BMD, designed with the stated intention of protecting only Japanese national territory, but which necessarily would have the near simultaneous function of protecting US forces stationed in Japan – generates a number of concerns for Japanese policy-makers. These include questions over the technological

70   *Christopher W. Hughes*

feasibility of BMD; the final cost versus effectiveness (*hiyō tai kōka*) of research, development, production, and deployment; and legal and constitutional issues connected to missile defences.[6] Nevertheless, whilst all of these issues may become crucial 'make or break' considerations for the future course of BMD, the principal focus of this chapter, and indeed for Japanese policy-makers themselves, is the political, diplomatic and strategic consequences of Japan's potential participation in BMD for its overall security policy and for international relations in East Asia.

Japan, China and BMD

Since the launch of a Taepodong-1 'missile' over Japanese airspace on 31 August 1998, the ballistic missile threat from North Korea and a Korean peninsula contingency have been the most immediate concerns and the public legitimis-ation for Japan to undertake BMD research.[7] But it is also clear – and of greatest relevance to the theme of this volume – that BMD carries major implications for Japan's security policy towards international relations with the People's Republic of China (PRC) (hereafter referred to as China), and, due to the triangular nature of the 'great power' security nexus in East Asia explained in other chapters, inevitably engenders problems for Japan's relationship with its own US alliance partner. The argument of this chapter is that for Japanese policy-makers the pursuit of BMD will make the security relationship with China, which has already become highly complex due to the introduction since 1997 of the revised Guidelines for US–Japan Defence Cooperation, even more fraught and hazardous. The revised Guidelines have without doubt been responsible for ratcheting up tensions between Japan, China and the US over the last three years, but their cautious framing with a vague definition of their scope has provided Japan, the US, and to some extent China also, with sufficient room for strategic manoeuvre to allow them to assuage tensions and avoid final conflict scenarios if deemed necessary. However, in contrast to the uncomfortable but near tolerable *modus vivendi* offered to all sides by the revised Guidelines, BMD presents Japan with a qualitatively more dangerous challenge for the management of its bilateral security relations with China and the US–Japan alliance. This is because the inherent technological and military logic of BMD dictates that Japan becomes more fully integrated than ever before into US military strategy in East Asia and towards China. Taken to its extreme, and without sufficiently careful manage-ment by Japanese policy-makers, the subsequent logic of BMD could be to undermine Japan's political, diplomatic and strategic freedom and to set it on a collision course with China's inviolable security interests.

Nevertheless, as indicated above, this chapter also argues that the BMD issue, although it possesses the potential to eliminate Japanese 'escape clauses' in managing its strategic relations with China and the US, could, if managed with extreme care, also be turned to the perceived advantage of Japan's security. Thus, this chapter seeks not only to evaluate the potential risks and advantages of BMD for Japanese security, but also how these are perceived by Japan's security policy-makers themselves and what strategies, if any, they have devised to navigate their way through them.

Japanese participation in BMD

BMD systems

BMD, or TMD in the case of identical US anti-missile defences intended for eventual deployment in the Asia–Pacific and other theatres, comprises four types of upper-tier and lower-tier weapon systems based on land and sea (see Table 4.1). These BMD/TMD weapon systems are designed to use hit-to-kill missile technology (in essence, using a bullet to hit another bullet) in order to intercept and destroy incoming ballistic missiles at varying heights in their descent and re-entry phase. In the process of developing TMD systems, the US government has attempted to reach agreement with Russia that these technologies are compliant with the bilateral Anti-Ballistic Missile (ABM) treaty of 1972. The ABM treaty does not prohibit the development of TMD systems, but it does prohibit the development of anti-ballistic missile systems intended to defend against either side's strategic missiles. In 1997, the US and Russia adopted a joint government statement to differentiate between TMD and ABM systems, agreeing that TMD systems with interceptor velocities of more than 3 kilometres per second, and tested against ballistic missiles flying faster than 5 kilometres per second and with a range of over 3500 kilometres, were non-compliant with the ABM treaty.[8] The imposition of an upper threshold upon TMD capabilities is designed to ensure that these systems do not jeopardise the effectiveness of US and Russian strategic nuclear deterrent – the intercontinental ballistic missiles (ICBM) of either side typically travelling at velocities of at least 7 kilometres per hour and equipped with ranges of between 9000 and 16,000 kilometres. However, as will be seen in

Table 4.1 BMD/TMD systems

Lower-tier	Ground-based	PAC-3	Existing PAC-2 system upgraded by the adoption of new GEM missiles and improvement of radar and firing control
	Sea-based	NAD	Existing Aegis system upgraded by improvement of radar, firing controls and Standard Missile-2 Block IV A, and provision of ballistic missile intercept capability
Upper-tier	Ground-based	THAAD	Development of new large-scale mobile radar and high-speed high altitude missile interceptor and firing control
	Sea-based	NTWD	Existing Aegis system upgraded as in NAD, and addition of LEAP ballistic missile intercept capability

Source: Yamashita Masamitsu, Takai Susumu and Iwata Shuichiro, *TMD: Seniki Dandō Missairu Bōei*, Tokyo, TBS Buritanika, 1994, pp. 151–200.

Acronyms: PAC-3: Patriot Advanced Capability-3; NAD: Navy Area Defence; THAAD: Theatre High Altitude Area Defence; NTWD: Navy Theatre Wide Defence; GEM: Guidance-Enhanced Missile; LEAP: Lightweight Exo-Atmospheric Projectile.

72 *Christopher W. Hughes*

more detail below, strong suspicions exist about the limits in practice of TMD capabilities, and their compliance with the joint statement. The lower-tier and less capable systems of PAC-3 and Navy Area Defence (NAD) are undoubtedly compatible with the ABM Treaty, but research has suggested that the Theatre High Altitude Area Defence (THAAD) system, and very likely the NTWD system, possess interceptor speeds of between more than 3 and 5 kilometres per second.[9] These capabilities for a US TMD system, represent possible non-compliance with the ABM Treaty and could enable the NTW system to counter the strategic ballistic missiles of Russia and other nuclear powers.

The US envisages the use of lower- and upper-tier and ground- and sea-based TMD systems in combination in order to protect its military forces overseas. The combination of upper- and lower-tier systems is designed to provide mutually reinforcing layers of protection to guard against 'leakage' in the event of major ballistic missile attack, whilst the combination of land- and sea-based systems offers differing advantages in terms of mobility – the PAC-3 and THAAD systems are able to be loaded on C-141 transport aircraft for rapid airlift to combat theatres, and the NAD and NTW systems take advantage of the sea mobility of Aegis-equipped destroyers.[10]

In addition, and integral to its TMD programme, the US has also developed sensor systems for the detection of ballistic missile launches and battlefield management (BM) and command, control, communications and intelligence (C3I) systems to operate the response of the TMD weapons systems. THAAD systems possess ground-based radar which have some capability to detect incoming ballistic missiles.[11] However, the effectiveness of TMD systems is really dependent upon the early warning provided by space-based infrared sensors. US Defence Support Programme (DSP) satellites detect the heat plumes from ballistic missile launches, and then transmit this information to North American Aerospace Command (NORAD) and US Space Command (USSPACECOM). In turn, information concerning missile launches has to be transmitted on and processed through a C3I system, so that decisions and instructions concerning the response of the TMD weapons systems can be carried out in a framework of real time. As will be seen below, Japan's need also to develop these identical detection and command systems in its own BMD system may greatly influence the degree of its independence in security planning.

Japan and the development of BMD

Japanese interest in BMD stretches back to the inception under the Reagan administration in 1983 of the Strategic Defence Initiative (SDI) (better known as 'Star Wars'), and the subsequent agreement of the Nakasone Yasuhiro administration in September 1986 to participate in SDI research. Although Japan's participation in SDI at the time was replete with problems, and the US eventually abandoned SDI after the failure of the Bush administration to transform the programme in January 1991 into the less ambitious Global Protection Against Limited Strikes (GPALS), both sides maintained an interest in anti-ballistic missile technology following the end of the Cold War. Based on the 1986 US–Japan governmental agreement, the US government Strategic Defence Initiative Office (SDIO) and US and Japanese private defence contractors carried out a joint study on Western Pacific Missile Architecture (WESTPAC) from December 1989 until May 1993.[12] Meanwhile, US and Japanese government interest in BMD technology in the post-Cold-War period continued to be driven by the proliferation of ballistic missile capabilities globally and in the East Asia region – the growing missile threat illustrated by Iraq's use of Scud missiles during the Gulf War of 1990–1. Japan, partly in reaction to the experience of the Gulf War when the US used the Patriot system even to intercept Iraqi missiles, and partly in reaction to North Korea's test launch of Nodong-1 missiles in the Sea of Japan in May 1990 and May 1993, initiated the purchase from the US of an upgrade to its existing Patriot SAM missiles to the PAC-2 missile system with some anti-ballistic capabilities.[13]

In September 1993, the US Secretary of Defence, Les Aspin, and Director General of JDA, Nakanishi Keisuke, agreed to establish under the bilateral Security Subcommittee (SSC) a TMD working group, which then met twelve times from December 1993 onwards. This was followed in June 1994 by direct US government proposals for bilateral collaboration with Japan on BMD. US BMDO was reported to have presented four options to Japan. First, an upper-tier NTWD and lower-tier Patriot system at a cost of US$4.5 billion, based on upgrades of existing Japanese plans to deploy four Aegis destroyers, and four Airborne Warning and Control System (AWACS) aircraft. Second, a NTWD and Patriot system costing US$16.3 billion, based on upgrades of the existing Japanese deployment plans already mentioned, and an additional two Aegis destroyers and new surveillance radar. Third, a THAAD and Patriot system at a cost of US$8.8 billion; and, fourthly, a combined NTWD, THAAD and Patriot system at a cost of US$8.9 billion.[14] US proposals for Japanese participation in BMD were matched by the report of the Prime Minister's Advisory Group on Defence released in September 1994, which recommended US–Japan collaboration in the development of Japan's own BMD.[15] The Japanese government established in the same month a specialist bilateral study (BS) under the SSC to investigate the technological feasibility of BMD systems, and this group instituted regular meetings from January 1995 onwards. In total between 1995 and 1998 the government devoted yen 560 million for study costs into TMD weapon systems, and sensor and C3^I systems, as well as commissioning private Japanese defence contractors to investigate key technologies to improve native BMD capabilities. However, for various reasons, some of which are explained below, the Japanese government remained reticent about committing itself to actual participation in cooperative research with the US into BMD.[16] Momentum for cooperative research was eventually provided by the US–Japan Joint Declaration on Security of April 1996 which stressed the importance of BMD as a means to enhance the credibility of the alliance, and then Japan's commitment to joint BMD research was assured by the North Korea missile test of August 1998. In accordance with the US–Japan exchange of

74   Christopher W. Hughes

notes mentioned at the start of this chapter, Japan has agreed to undertake joint research into the four key technologies: infrared seekers mounted in the nose cones of interceptor missiles to detect and pursue targets; the protection of the infrared seekers from heat generated in-flight from the atmosphere; kinetic interceptor warheads for the direct destruction of ballistic missiles; and the second-stage rocket motor of the interceptor missile.[17] As Japan already possesses many of the platforms for a BMD weapons system, including AWACS and Aegis-class destroyers, the NTWD system has been chosen for research as the most cost-effective option.[18]

Japan's involvement in BMD and the impact on Sino-Japanese security relations

Japan's original demonstration of interest in BMD research, and then its actual commitment to a cooperative programme with the US, has indicated the potential for renewed security tensions *vis-à-vis* China. Chinese policy-makers, from the outset, and intensifying their efforts since 1995, have communicated their concerns about BMD to their Japanese counterparts using a mixture of informal and official dialogue channels. Chinese concerns essentially revolve around the dual impact of BMD upon China's strategic nuclear deterrent and the course of the Taiwan issue.

Chinese officials and neutral observers have argued that a Japanese BMD or TMD system developed in conjunction with the US would lead to the effective negation of China's nuclear deterrent by providing Japan with both a 'spear' and 'shield'.[19] The spear of the US extended nuclear deterrent would be complemented by the shield of BMD, allowing Japan to enjoy *vis-à-vis* China capabilities of both deterrence by punishment and deterrence by denial.[20] The evidence presented above relating to the capabilities of advanced TMD systems suggests that Chinese concerns to a certain degree may be justified. Around 80 per cent of China's strategic arsenal consists of missiles with ranges of less than 3500 km (see Table 4.2). In accordance with US definitions used to develop TMD or BMD systems, these missiles would thus be classified as theatre weapons and within the threshold of US and Japanese NTWD system capabilities.[21] Moreover, as noted above, NTWD systems equipped with interceptor speeds of between 3 and 5 kilometres per second would also be capable of countering Chinese longer-range ICBMs which number only around twenty.

China may be able to overcome the possible negation by NTWD of its strategic nuclear deterrent through the employment of counter-measures and the ongoing upgrade of its missile force, and in particular through the development of Multiple Independently Targetable Re-entry Vehicles (MIRV) which could provide it with the capability to saturate and overwhelm BMD systems by force of numbers.[22] However, NTWD and other BMD systems would still possess the capability to negate or at the very least severely circumscribe China's other shorter-range ballistic missile capabilities, unless China were massively to increase the production of these missiles so as also to raise their numbers to saturation levels.

Sino-Japanese relations and BMD 75

Table 4.2 Chinese ballistic missile capabilities

DOD name/ designation	Chinese name/ designation	Static/ Mobile	Range (km)	CEP	Inventory (deployed/ stockpiled)
ICBM					
CSS-4	DF-5	Static	13,000	500	20
CSS-NX-5	JL-2	SLBM	8000	n.k.	12
CSS-X-9	DF-31	Mobile	8000	n.k.	n.k.
CSS-X-10	DF-41	Mobile	12,000	n.k.	n.k.
IRBM					
CSS-2	DF-3	Mobile	2800	1000	40
CSS-3	DF-4	Static	4750	1500	20–30
CSS-N-3	JL-1	SLBM	2150	700	12
CSS-5	DF-21	Mobile	2150	700	24
CSS-6	DF-15/M-9	Mobile	600	300	48
SRBM					
CSS-7	DF-11/M-11	Mobile	280	600	n.k.
CSS-8	M-7/Project 8610	Mobile	150	n.k.	n.k.

Source: International Institute for Strategic Studies, *The Military Balance 1999–2000*, Oxford, Oxford University Press, 1999, p. 312; Stockholm International Peace Research Institute, *SIPRI Yearbook 1999*, Oxford, Oxford University Press, 1999, p. 555; John Wilson Lewis and Hua Di, 'China's ballistic missile programs: technologies, strategies, goals', *International Security*, vol. 17, no. 2, pp. 9–11.

Acronyms: CEP: Circular Error Probable; CSS: Chinese Surface-to-Surface; CSS-N: Chinese Surface-to-Surface Naval; CSS-T: Chinese Surface-to-Surface Tactical; DF: Dong Feng (East Wind); DOD: Department of Defence; ICBM: Intercontinental Ballistic Missile; IRBM: Intermediate Range Ballistic Missile; JL: Julang (Great Wave); n.k.: not known; SLBM: Submarine Launched Ballistic Missile; SRBM: Short Range Ballistic Missile.

For Chinese policy-makers, Japan's possible acquisition of an NTWD system to counter its intermediate and short-range ballistic missiles would have significant ramifications for the second of its concerns, the Taiwan issue. China's weapon of choice in seeking to intimidate the Taiwanese government has been the IRBM, such as the D-15 test-fired across the Straits of Taiwan in March 1996. China's worst-case scenario would obviously be Japan's deployment, either individually or in conjunction with the US, of the Aegis-based and sea-mobile NTWD system to protect Taiwan in a future crisis situation.[23] The reluctance of Japan's policy-makers to become directly embroiled in a crisis in the Straits of Taiwan means that, in all but the most dire of conflagrations which would threaten Japan's own security and engender massive alliance pressure from the US, Japan would be highly unlikely to contemplate the actual deployment of a Japanese NTWD either to protect Taiwan directly or even to provide missile cover for US forces involved in a Taiwan conflict. Nevertheless, even if Japan is likely to distance itself from allowing its NTWD systems to become involved in a Taiwan crisis, and, indeed, it has made it very clear that it does not wish to see any third party such as Taiwan involved in Japan–US BMD research, Chinese

76 *Christopher W. Hughes*

fears remain that Japanese participation could bring BMD benefits to Taiwan and weaken China's security position.[24] Most particularly, the concern of China appears to be that BMD technologies developed jointly under a US–Japan programme, although they could not be transferred by Japan to Taiwan due to the former's ban on arms exports, could still be transferred by the US, regardless of Japan's intentions to prevent Taiwan from participating in BMD.

Hence, Japan's acquisition of a BMD system and especially NTWD is perceived by China to provide it with the capacity to intervene both directly and indirectly, and individually and jointly under the US–Japan alliance, in a conflict over Taiwan and in contravention of China's most basic national security interests concerned with the preservation of its sovereignty and territorial integrity. In this situation, it is hardly surprising that the protestations of Japan's policy-makers that BMD is a 'purely defensive' system confined to Japan and which poses no threat to its neighbours cut little ice with their Chinese counterparts.[25] For, as commentators both inside and outside Japan have noted, a purely 'defensive' weapon such as BMD can actually appear offensive if it threatens the status quo. China's principal security goal is to prevent Taiwan from moving from de facto to de jure independence, and has concluded increasingly that military coercion may be the only means left available to persuade Taiwan to desist. Consequently, Taiwan's access to any defensive weapon which could embolden a declaration of independence and overturn the status quo, such as a BMD system capable of countering China's ballistic missiles and a main tool of military coercion, and acquired by Taiwan either through the development of its own BMD system or the extension to it of a US or Japanese system in a crisis situation, can be perceived as an offensive move and detrimental to the balance of power in the region.[26] In particular, Chinese analysts seem to fear a scenario in which TMD could function to defend the forces of an external power, such as the US or Japan, attempting to intervene militarily in a Taiwan Straits crisis, and thus serve in effect to augment their offensive power.[27]

The end result of concerns about the combined potential defensive and offensive roles of BMD and TMD is that to date it has only succeeded in raising China's suspicions about Japan's security intentions – as shown by its recent tendency to switch increasingly the direction of its rhetoric away from the *fait accompli* of the revised Guidelines and towards BMD and TMD. BMD has even raised misplaced Chinese concerns that Japan could pursue its own nuclear option.[28] In turn, the BMD project, although it has certainly not initiated the process, will probably help to accelerate Chinese moves to upgrade its nuclear ballistic missile and other conventional military capabilities, so generating an arms race in the region.

Japan's potential security tensions with its US ally

Japan's participation in BMD has also generated potential new alliance security management problems versus the US, which could subsequently reinforce security tensions with China. Japan could face a difficult choice if it were called upon by its US alliance partner to extend its NTWD system to assist US forces involved in a conflict over Taiwan; either directly under intense US pressure, or, as noted in the preceding section, most likely in an indirect fashion by providing cover against missile attacks on the perimeter of the US combat zone and in Japanese territorial waters, so as to avoid charges of collective self-defence. Japan would experience intense domestic political difficulties in providing such support to its ally in a Sino–US conflict over Taiwan. If it were to fail to be seen to satisfy US requests for assistance in the case of extending BMD cover, then this could lead to a crisis of confidence in the alliance, as in the case of Japan's reluctance to support the US during the North Korean nuclear crisis of 1994.[29]

The technological nature of the BMD project also presents an intense and qualitatively new challenge to Japan's policy-makers in terms of the risks of being overly incorporated into US military strategy in East Asia. This is because Japan's attempts to develop an effective BMD system necessitate that its relies to a considerable degree upon technology and information provided by the US, which in turn necessitates tighter US–Japan military cooperation, and the erosion of Japan's strategic freedom. Matsumura Masahiro argues that Japan's lack of infrared satellite technology and related early-warning systems, so essential for the detection of ballistic missile launches, means it will be forced to rely upon the US for these capabilities and information, supplied via US DSP satellites and NORAD.[30] In addition, in order to access and utilise information on missile launches, Japan will be obliged to develop further C3^{I} systems identical to and procured from the US. As Cronin, Giarra and Green stress, the rebuilding of Japan's air defences will have to be based on Japanese acceptance of the necessity for 'effective bilateral integration, leading inexorably to the requirement for systematic bilateral co-ordination and rationalisation of design, development, procurement, fielding, doctrine and operations'.[31] The result of these developments would be that Japan would seek to replace its existing military command systems, which are largely distinct from and function in parallel to those of the US, and substitute instead command systems compatible with and reliant for their correct functioning upon technology and information supplied by the US. Japan's BMD and other military command systems would have to stop short of explicit integration with those of the US due to the ban on the exercise of collective self-defence, but implicitly would now assume a subsidiary position within the structure of the alliance due to their dependence upon information filtered top downwards from the US.

This technological and military set-up for BMD could then have considerable implications for Japan's exercise of strategic choice in a conflict situation. Japan's reliance upon US-supplied information in order to make a BMD system function would place it at a marked political and military disadvantage *vis-à-vis* both a potential adversary and its US ally. Japan might be unable to take an independent decision to deploy BMD in a crisis situation unless it had secured the consent of the US and had demonstrated that this action was compatible with its ally's interest. Moreover, taking Machiavellian calculations to their extremes, the US could seek to deprive Japanese policy-makers of vital information concerning

78 *Christopher W. Hughes*

missile launches which threaten Japan's security, and in this way ensure that Japan is left defenceless against an attack and thereby embroiled in a conflict on the side of the US. Finally, a scenario could be imagined in which US failure, deliberate or accidental, to provide Japan with the correct information, and the rapid communication possible between the US and Japanese forces enabled by compatible C3[1] systems, could lead to Japan deploying its BMD as a de facto TMD system in support of US forces. All of these scenarios, however, could occur in a conflict situation surrounding Taiwan and reinforce the adversary security dilemma for Japan against China.

Japan's 'escape routes'

Hence, Japan's participation in BMD research with the US in the long term and after deployment of an actual NTWD system could create an interlinked structure of technological and strategic dependence on Japan's part, and related tensions with both China and its US ally. The ability of Japan to escape limitations placed upon its strategic freedom in the case of BMD is doubtful. The technological logic of dependency, as dictated by BMD, can only be countered by the development of other technological options. Japan's decision since 1998, in response to the North Korea Taepodong-1 test, to develop its own imagery intelligence (IMINT) satellites based on optical and synthetic aperture radar (SAR) systems will provide a Japanese capability to detect preparations for a missile launch, but not the actual launch itself.[32] Indeed, even this programme sold to many LDP members as a means to lessen Japan's strategic dependency on the US may actually only end up increasing it, as Japanese indigenous production (*kokusanka*) still involves the purchase of key components from the US and reliance upon the US for the processing of satellite information.

Japan is thus faced with the uncomfortable situation of being squeezed between its security interests with regard to both China and the US, and from which there appears to be no ready escape exit. Chinese fears of even research into the feasibility of BMD threaten to provoke an arms race, whilst the US appears to have gained the potential to exert unavoidable technological and military leverage over Japan. BMD possesses, then, the real potential to place Japan on a disastrous and headlong path towards conflict in Northeast Asia. The only other option open to Japan would be to eschew cooperation with the US on BMD altogether, but domestic pressure building up in favour of BMD since 1998 and the political cost to the continuation of the alliance means that this could only be a drastic last resort.

In this situation, in which Japan is unable to refuse cooperation with the US on BMD, but is also aware of the risks involved in any eventual BMD deployment of integration into US strategy and the aggravation of relations with China, a number of observers have speculated that Japan's optimum strategy for pushing ahead with BMD might be one of cooperation in stages with the US, in conjunction with attempts to use BMD as a means to persuade China to moderate its security behaviour, thus obviating tensions with both sides. Hence, the argument runs that Japan can move through each of the stages of research, development and deployment of the different BMD systems so as to satisfy US demands for cooperation and provide for its own defence, but intimating as well at each stage that it still retains the option to cease BMD development and prevent itself being corralled into a situation of entrapment.[33] This staged approach would simultaneously present opportunities to ameliorate relations with China. For even though Japan would be communicating to China through its participation in BMD that it is willing to defend its security interests and that it will negotiate from a position of relative strength, the staged and characteristically Japanese incremental nature of the approach would also indicate to China that Japan's commitment to BMD is not irrevocable and that there is room for both sides to reach an accommodation on security issues. The eventual hope is that this type of Japanese approach could bring China to the negotiating table on arms control in East Asia.

In sum, then, this represents a form of hedging strategy, but one which is made all the more difficult by the compulsive logic of BMD technology which means that Japan could be locked into US strategy before it has had the opportunity to exercise the option to steer between the path of conflicting interests over the US and China. Having laid out the potential and complex problems that BMD presents to Japan over the medium to long terms with regard to the US and China, the task of the next and final section is to examine what is the exact perception of its policy-makers with regard to BMD, whether they are aware of all the strategic implications of the project, and whether they can conceive of such strategies to provide escape clauses and retain Japan's security options.

Japanese policy-makers and BMD strategic considerations

Japanese policy-makers have been criticised as lacking a true understanding of the strategic implications of BMD. Soeya Yoshihide comments that: 'In the minds of Japanese policy-makers, Japan's participation in the embryonic stages of TMD is an act of security co-operation with the US, and as such is an end in itself . . . There is no indication that the Japanese government has given any serious consideration to the strategic dimension of the TMD program'.[34] Evidence from various secondary and primary sources, and as yet limited interviews, would seem to support this conclusion to a certain extent, but also suggest that Japan's policy-makers are not entirely unaware of the strategic problems of the project.

MOFA officials certainly demonstrate concerns that BMD engenders for Japan potential security tensions with regard to Japan–US and Sino-Japanese relations. Soeya's criticism of Japanese involvement in BMD as simply forming part of a larger overall project, along with the revised Guidelines as described earlier, to rebuild the credibility of the US–Japan alliance, and thereby ameliorate concerns about abandonment, are hard to counter.[35] TMD's function as a vehicle to cement the political rather than military basis of the alliance appears to have been especially strong prior to the North Korean 'Taepodong shock' and the consequent emergence of an immediate ballistic missile threat which could be

80 *Christopher W. Hughes*

used to legitimise Japan's taking the plunge into joint BMD research. But Japan's subsequent participation in BMD research has meant that for its policy-makers the project now serves equally as a test of both the political and military resolve of the alliance. At the same time, MOFA policy-makers also seem to be cognisant of the enhanced probability of integration into US military strategy in the region and the generation of adversary security dilemma with China. As stated above, China's officials have used every opportunity in direct dialogue with their Japanese counterparts to express their concerns over BMD and Taiwan, and MOFA acknowledges, although strongly denies, the validity of these Chinese anxieties. Moreover, MOFA officials are aware that the BMD issue cannot strictly be separated from Russian and Chinese objections to possible US unilateral abrogation of the ABM Treaty, and the knock-on effect upon Japan's own role in working for international arms control – Japan in essence being seen as the US's accomplice in undermining arms control regimes. The result has been that Japan was relatively muted on the awkward issue of NMD and the ABM Treaty at the Okinawa G8 summit in July 2000. Furthermore, MOFA also realises that the conflicting international pressures on the Japanese government are complicated by domestic pressure from the LDP, the arms industry, and the general public to take steps to counter North Korea's ballistic missile programme.

MOFA's awareness of latent security dilemmas and risks with regard to participation in BMD is also accompanied by the sense of the need for a form of reserve exit strategy. MOFA officials stress that any Japanese decision to move ahead with BMD research and development will be taken based on considerations of the feasibility and cost effectiveness of the project, and, most crucially, whether it meets Japan's own strategic and defensive needs. Hence, they argue, Japanese participation in BMD research is not simply another case of Japan 'caving in' to US pressure for bilateral defence cooperation, and any future progress towards the stages of development and deployment will be judged in accordance with whether or not the project enhances Japan's defence capabilities. MOFA, then, views itself as negotiating with relative skill a pathway between satisfying US expectations for defence cooperation and limiting the risks of disruption to the alliance, but also making clear its determination not to participate in and become entrapped in a BMD programme dictated at the pace of the US unless it fits with the general interests of Japanese defence policy. Similarly, MOFA also appears to believe that it can assuage Chinese concerns about the programme to some degree by repeated dialogue and persuasion in bilateral and other forums. MOFA officials may believe privately that it is a futile task, given China's deep-rooted suspicion of Japan's security intentions, and that eventually China may simply be forced to accept the BMD programme as a hard fact of Japan's defensive needs, in much the same way as they have had to accept the revised Guidelines for Japan–US Defence Cooperation. But the hope still remains that with sufficient effort Japan can lessen Chinese nervousness over BMD and reach some form of *modus vivendi*.

MOFA's perception of and response to the security dilemmas involved with BMD thus do not quite amount to the type of highly sophisticated escape strategy outlined in the previous section. This is because there appears to be no attempt to use BMD as a bargaining tool to bring China into arms reduction talks, and Japanese concerns are much more focused on upgrading Japan's own defence capabilities than downgrading China's. Nevertheless, the impression is that Japanese policy-makers are at least attempting to provide themselves with some strategic leeway and to mitigate the risks of alliance and adversary games. In seeking to achieve this strategy they also appear to be employing the twin tactical devices of dogged persuasion and dialogue towards the US and Chinese sides, coupled with an incremental approach of stretching out decisions on whether to move between the stages of research, development and deployment so as to create a time-line for BMD participation which allows Japan, the US and China opportunities to reformulate their strategic and security relations and obviate potential conflict conditions between them. Indeed, there is some scepticism in MOFA that the US may abandon TMD in the same way as they have abandoned other large-scale cooperative technological projects in the past, such as SDI and the super-conductor, and that over the long term BMD may even disappear altogether as a major issue between Japan, the US and China. Therefore, for MOFA, in the final calculation, and based on the belief that Japan can still carefully manage its alliance relations with the US and bilateral relations with China and still maintain sufficient strategic freedom to hedge its bets, there is much to be gained from participation in BMD research. As one official remarked, 'we look at BMD, see that it fits the general profile of our defence policy', and say 'why not participate at least in research'.[36]

The position of the JDA on BMD matches that of MOFA to a large degree, generally subordinate as it is to MOFA on security planning issues, but also demonstrates some divergences. As is well known, the JDA is concerned that BMD may absorb too great a portion of the defence budget, and criticisms of Japan's policy on BMD similar to those of Soeya have been expressed in the national media.[37] For instance, JDA senior officials are quoted as stating that Japan's decision to participate in BMD research has been predicated more on the 'importance of the US–Japan alliance than the actual feasibility of the project', and that it resulted from a knee-jerk reaction to the Taepodong shock rather than from a careful analysis of the long-term international environment.[38] However, JDA officials also follow a similar line to MOFA, stressing that BMD will only proceed in accordance with Japan's defensive priorities; that Japan, regardless of the stance of the US, will retain the option of abandoning the project if it is shown not to be feasible in cost or strategic terms; and that Japan will continue to persuade China that BMD is a defensive system which it need not fear, and that the Chinese government should also look at the broader picture of Sino-Japanese security cooperation and not allow BMD to unduly hamper bilateral relations.[39]

The overall impression, therefore, is that Japan's policy-makers are not as strategically innocent as Soeya has argued, and that they do conceive of the necessity of an exit strategy from the potential risks of BMD. Nonetheless, there is also evidence to support Soeya's supposition that Japan's policy-makers may not be fully cognisant of *all* the implications and risks of BMD, and that their hedging strategy and related tactics could very easily come to nought. The principal difficulty of Japan attempting any hedging strategy over BMD through the use of dialogue is that once again it is a 'bottom-line' issue for China, from which its security interests cannot be unbundled or compromised. Hence, as long as Japanese BMD retains the technical capability of functioning as a TMD system for intervention in a Taiwan Straits crisis, it will remain a bone of contention between Japan, the US and China, threaten to bring their security interests into collision, and generate related alliance and adversary dilemmas. In this situation, the mantra-like statements of Japanese officials that BMD is a purely defensive system will fail to register with their Chinese counterparts. Even more importantly, Japan's incremental approach to BMD may fail to keep the window of opportunity open over the longer term for accommodation on divergent security interests. As argued in previous sections, the nature of the BMD system under research could eventually necessitate the near total integration of Japanese and US command and control functions of their respective militaries, but with the US very much enjoying a dominant position in the partnership. At the current stage of research, Japan is probably able to maintain a relatively equal status with the US and retain its strategic freedom. But, if as seems likely, Japan fails in efforts to persuade China or North Korea of the defensive nature of BMD and of the need to scale back their missile programmes, then a decision will come on whether to move towards the stage of development. It is probably at this stage, with the need for closer practical military cooperation, that Japan will reach a threshold of 'no return', the technological logic of BMD will begin to take over, and Japan will become increasingly integrated into the US military structure in the region. In this situation, any carefully constructed hedging strategy will collapse, as Japan is forced to make a choice between cooperation with the US and an explicit adversarial relationship with China, or to distance itself from cooperation with the US and embark on an uncertain strategic relationship with China. Japan's instinct to plump for the former could then become the cause of open and disastrous conflict with its East Asian neighbour.

Conclusion: Japan's BMD quandary

The above sections have argued that participation in BMD carries the potential to create serious and inescapable security tensions for Japan. The technological logic of BMD dictates that over the long term Japan may become wholly integrated into US military strategy and set on a collision course with China over its inviolable security interests in Taiwan. Japanese policy-makers certainly perceive many of the strategic risks involved with BMD, but perhaps do not yet fully grasp how the technological nature of the project can rapidly close off available avenues for it to temper its commitment to the US–Japan alliance and juggle its often contradictory security interests *vis-à-vis* the US and China.

The events of 2000 indicate that both the international and domestic momentum for Japanese participation in BMD research and eventually development is building, and is consequently reducing the timeframe available for Japan to follow a hedging strategy. Despite the recent failures of tests for related NMD technology in the US, and President Clinton's decision to defer a decision on deployment, the pressure from this quarter for joint Japan–US cooperation on TMD is unlikely to abate. The US presidential elections have brought in a George W. Bush administration committed publicly (currently at least) to both NMD and TMD programmes; and, even if NMD technologies are deemed to be unfeasible or too costly, this may only lead to increased US interest in the less costly TMD versions. These technologies might even include boost-phase intercept varieties of TMD, considered to be more accurate and harder to counter, but which would also possibly need to be mounted on naval platforms deployed closer to launch sites on the Chinese coast and thus appear even more provocative as a defensive–offensive weapons system with regard to Taiwan.[40] Moreover, even though 2000 has also witnessed important developments in the Korean peninsula security situation which may contribute to calls for TMD programmes to be scaled back, the fact that North Korea has yet to offer a compromise formula on its ballistic missile programme which will satisfy the US and Japan means that there will remain significant domestic lobbies in both states for TMD and BMD. China's awareness that BMD research in Japan serves the dual purpose of countering both North Korea and Chinese missiles means that the continuation of the programme will further ratchet up Sino-Japanese security relations. Indeed, the greatest concern could be that Japan's strategists in MOFA and the JDA begin to lose control of management of the BMD programme in the face of pressure from LDP factions, other political parties and the mass media. The almost hysterical nature of the reaction to the Taepodong launch in August 1998 indicates that these domestic forces could force Japanese policy on BMD in unpredictable directions, which would only serve to exacerbate Sino-Japanese security tensions.

In conclusion, BMD is an issue which is unlikely to go away and will only become more pressing; which could lead Japan into conflict with China and generate friction with the US; and for which Japan's policy-makers lack a strategy to finesse and deal with. Japan's policy-makers will need to exercise all their usual caution in moving from the stage of research to development if they are not to engineer at the same time a general destabilisation of the Japan–US–China security nexus and the entire security situation in Northeast Asia.

Notes

1 Bōeichōhen, *Bōeichō Hakusho 1999*, Tokyo, Ōkurashō Insatsukyoku, 1999, p. 137.
2 Ministry of Foreign Affairs, http://www.mofa.go.jp/announce/1999/8/816.html
3 Bōeichō, *Dandō Misairu Bōei (BMD) ni kansuru Kenkyū ni tsuite*, Tokyo, 1999, p. 11.
4 Asakumo Shimbunsha, *Bōei Handobukku 2000*, Tokyo, Asagumo Shimbunsha, 2000, p. 144.
5 Patrick M. Cronin, Paul S. Giarra and Michael J. Green, 'The alliance implications of theater missile defense', in M. J. Green and P. M. Cronin, *The US–Japan Alliance: Past, Present and Future*, New York, Council on Foreign Relations Press, 1999, p. 94.

84 *Christopher W. Hughes*

6 Japanese policy-makers and commentators have similar doubts to their US counterparts concerning the feasibility of BMD technology which involves hitting a 'bullet with a bullet', and their doubts have been reinforced by recent unsuccessful interceptor missile tests in the US, and by the fact that the deployment by adversaries of simple decoy measures may be sufficient to defeat more expensive BMD technology. The cost effectiveness of BMD is also viewed as questionable. The JDA has limited its estimates to research and not produced a costing for any eventual deployment of a BMD system. However, other estimates suggest that the entire project could cost up to US$16 billion for deployment. These costs would place considerable strain on the defence budget and severely limit the Japan Self Defence Forces' (JSDF) ability to acquire other new weapons systems. Hence, the suspicion is that the US may be using Japan as a source of funds for BMD in order to support the last remaining large-scale defence project available to maintain a Cold-War-style military–industrial complex. Handa Shigeru, '"Muda na heiki": jieitai kara hihan sareru TMD sanka', *Gunshuku Mondai*, no. 230, December 1999, p. 40.

  The legal and constitutional problems that Japan faces in seeking to develop BMD revolve mainly around the prohibition of the exercise of the right of collective self-defence, a Japanese ban on the possession of weapons with power projections capabilities, the ban on the export of weapons, compliance with the Missile Technology Control Regime (MTCR), and the May 1969 Diet resolution concerning the peaceful use of space. The prohibition on the right of the exercise of collective self-defence complicates any Japanese attempt to develop with the US an integrated BMD command system which could be seen to serve the defence of the US in a situation deemed not to be directly connected with Japan's own security. Japan's ban on weapons of power projection capacity and the export of weapons, together with compliance in the MTCR, means that it has never possessed its own ballistic missile technology which could be used as a basis for research into necessary anti-ballistic missile technologies (although it could be argued that Japan's H-2 rocket could fulfil this function). Japanese policy-makers have found it particularly difficult to dodge the 1969 resolution which states that Japan's activities in space should be limited to peaceful purposes (*heiwa no mokuteki ni kagiri*), interpreted in the Diet as meaning non-military activities (*higunji*). The use of upper-tier technologies would involve exo-atmospheric military activities in space and would appear to transgress the resolution. However, the Japanese government has justified its participation in BMD research by arguing that as it is charged with the responsibility of defending the life and property of Japanese citizens, and BMD is a purely defensive system and the only means available to it to defend itself against missile attack, then a BMD system would be in line with the purport of the resolution and the government would seek the indulgence of the Japanese people on this matter. In effect, the government is seeking to shift the interpretation of 'peaceful' in the resolution away from 'non-military' to 'defensive'. *Asahi Shimbun*, 24 December 1998, p. 2. Asakumo Shimbunsha, *Bōei Handobukku 2000*, p. 147.

7 For further details on the BMD issue and Japan–North Korea relations, see Christopher W. Hughes, 'Japan's strategy-less North Korean strategy', *Korean Journal of Defense Analysis*, vol. 12, no. 2, winter 2000, pp. 153–81; Patrick M. Cronin and Michael. J. Green, 'Theater missile defense and strategic relations with the People's Republic of China', in Ralph A. Cossa (ed.) *Restructuring the US–Japan Alliance: Toward a More Equal Partnership*, Washington DC, The CSIS Press, 1997, p. 112; Bōeichō Bōei Kenkyūjo, *Higashi Ajia Senryaku Gaikan 1998–99*, Tokyo, Ōkurashō Insatsukyoku, 1999, p. 58.

8 Stephen A. Cambone, 'The United States and theatre missile defence in North-east Asia'. *Survival: The IISS Quarterly*, vol. 39. no. 3, autumn 1997, p. 70; M. Saperstein, 'Demarcation between theater missile defense and strategic missile defense', *Security Dialogue*, vol. 27, no. 1, March 1996, pp. 110–12.

Sino-Japanese relations and BMD   85

9 Dean A. Wilkening, *Ballistic-Missile Defence and Strategic Stability. Adelphi Paper 334*, London, Oxford University Press, 2000, p. 47; Lisbeth Gronlund, George Lewis, Theodore Postol and David Wright, 'Highly capable theater missile defences and the ABM treaty', *Arms Control Today*, vol. 24, no. 83, April 1994, pp. 3–8; Michael O'Hanlon, 'Star Wars strikes back', *Foreign Affairs*, vol. 78, no. 6, November/December 1999, p. 77.

10 Ballistic Missile Defence Organisation, *Fact Sheet; Theater High Altitude Area Defense System*; *Fact Sheet, Navy Theater Wide Ballistic Missile Defense Program*.

11 Yamashita Masamitsu, Takai Susumu and Iwata Shuichiro, *TMD: Seniki Dandō Missairu Bōei*, Tokyo, TBS Buritanika, 1994, p. 205.

12 US defence contractors included Raytheon, McDonnell Douglas, Lockheed, GE Aerospace, and Boeing. Japanese contractors included Mitsubishi Heavy Industries, Mitsubishi Electric Corporation, Mitsubishi Corporation, NEC, JRC, Hitachi and Fujitsu. The report cost US$8 million and was released in May 1994. It calculated that in the event of a North Korean missile attack upon western Japan by six missiles, it could be expected that a Patriot system on its own would result in a 46.6 per cent leakage rate. Patriot and THAAD combined would reduce the leakage rate to 33 per cent. The report also stated that in a simulated saturation attack upon Sasebo naval base a Patriot system on its own would intercept 66 per cent of incoming missiles, and a combined Patriot and THAAD layering would make for almost a 100 per cent intercept. Hence, the report recommended the use of Patriot lower-tier and THAAD upper-tier systems in combination. It also examined the use of Aegis-class warships for BMD.

13 For a highly critical evaluation of the effectiveness of Patriot systems during the Gulf War, see Theodore A. Postol, 'Lessons of the Gulf War experience with Patriot', *International Security*, vol. 16, no. 3, winter 1991/92, pp. 119–71. The background to Japan's procurement of Patriot systems is explored in: Michael Chinworth, *Inside Japan's Defense: Technology, Economics and Strategy*, New York, Brassey's (US), 1992, p. 95; Reinhard Drifte, *Arms Production in Japan: The Military Applications of Civilian Technology*, London, Westview Press, 1986, pp. 69–70.

14 Michael J. Green, *Arming Japan: Defense Production, Alliance Politics, and the Search for Postwar Autonomy*, New York, Columbia University Press, 1995, p. 138; Steven A. Hildreth and Jason D. Ellis, 'Allied support for Theater Missile Defense', *Orbis: A Journal of World Affairs*, vol. 40, no. 1, winter 1996, pp. 109–10; James Clay Moltz, 'Viewpoint: missile proliferation in East Asia: arms control vs TMD responses', *The Non-Proliferation Review*, vol. 4, no. 3, spring/summer 1997, p. 66; Steven A. Hildreth and Gary J. Pagliano, *Theater Missile Defence and Technology Cooperation: Implications for the US–Japan Relationship*, Washington DC, Congressional Research Service, Library of Congress, 1995, p. 7.

15 Bōei Mondai Kondankai, *Bōei no Anzen Hōshō to Bōei no Arikata: Nijū Isseiki e Mukete no Tenbō*, Tokyo, Ōkurashō Insatsukyoku, 1994, p. 47.

16 For example, in mid-1995, the JDA contracted with Nissan Motors and Kawasaki Heavy Industries to develop a side thruster interceptor missile.

17 Bōeichōhen, *Bōeichō Hakusho 1999*, p. 138.

18 For a fuller explanation of the reasons for the choice of the NTWD system, including considerations of domestic industry and techno-nationalism, see Cronin, Giarra and Green, op. cit., p. 173. Techno-nationalism is further defined in Richard J. Samuels, *Rich Nation, Strong Army: National Security and the Technological Transformation of Japan*, Ithaca NY, Cornell University Press, 1994.

19 *International Herald Tribune*, 18 February 1999, p. 4; Alastair Iain Johnston, 'China's new "old thinking": the concept of limited deterrence', *International Security*, vol. 20, no. 3, winter 1996–7, p. 73.

20 Yamashita et al., op. cit., pp. 29–30.

21 Alastair Iain Johnston, 'Prospects for Chinese nuclear force modernization: limited

86 *Christopher W. Hughes*

deterrence versus multilateral arms control', *China Quarterly*, no. 146, June 1996, p. 573. Indeed, Gronlund et al. argue that the TMD threshold was set at the level of a 3500 kilometre range specifically to target missile such as China's CSS-2. Gronlund et al., op. cit., p. 4.

22 Ivo H. Daalder, James M. Goldgeier and James M. Lindsay, 'Deploying NMD: not whether, but how', *Survival: The IISS Quarterly*, vol. 42, no. 1, spring 2000, p. 15; Michael O'Hanlon, 'Theater missile defense and the US–Japan alliance', in Mike M. Mochizuki (ed.) *Toward a True Alliance: Restructuring US–Japan Security Relations*, Washington DC, Brookings Institution Press, 1997, pp. 186–7.

23 Banning Garrett and Bonnie Glaser, 'Chinese apprehensions about the revitalization of the US–Japan alliance', *Asian Survey*, vol. 37, no. 4, April 1997, p. 395.

24 For instance, Nonaka Hiromu, in his first stint as Chief Cabinet Secretary, offered the emphatic assurance that no third country, including Taiwan, would be included in Japanese participation in any BMD programme, and that the system was not designed to defend Taiwan. *Asahi Shimbun*, 9 March 1999, p. 3.

25 The ritualistic description of BMD for Japanese policy-makers connected with MOFA and the JDA as elaborated in the Diet and various publications has been that it is a purely defensive system (*junsui ni bōgyo teki na shisutemu*). The reliance of Japanese policy-makers upon persuasion by repetition of this phrase has become reminiscent of the use of the phrase that *shūhen* in the revised Guidelines was purely situational (*aku made mo jitai teki mono de aru*).

26 Thomas J. Christensen, 'China, the US–Japan alliance, and the security dilemma in East Asia', *International Security*, vol. 23, no. 4, spring 1999, pp. 65–6; Xinbo Wu, 'Integration on the basis of strength: China's impact on East Asian security', in Kyongsoo Lho and Kay Möller (eds.) *Northeast Asia Towards 2000: Interdependence and Conflict?*, Baden-Baden, Nomos Verlagsgesellschaft, 1999, p. 20; David Shambaugh, 'Sino-American strategic relations: from partners to competitors', *Survival: The IISS Quarterly*, vol. 42, no. 1, spring 2000, p. 103. The original thesis that defensive weapons promote stability is contained in Stephen Van Evera, 'Offense, defense and the causes of war', *International Security*, vol. 22, no. 4, spring 1998, pp. 5–43.

27 Yan Xuetong, 'TMD rocking regional stability', *Korean Journal of Defense Analysis*, vol. 11, no. 1, summer 1999, p. 70.

28 Chinese concerns revolve around Japan's ability, having acquired BMD technology, to convert this to the production of offensive missile technology and consolidate Japan's technological base for the production of nuclear-capable ballistic missiles. However, BMD is highly unlikely to promote Japan's interest in nuclear weapons if it already has an effective defence against such weapons. For an analysis which actually stressed the benefits for non-nuclear proliferation in Japan's case by eschewing its own need to develop nuclear weapons, see Bōeichō Bōei Kenkyūjo, *Higashi Ajia Senryaku Gaikan 1998–99*, p. 58.

29 Christopher W. Hughes, 'The North Korean nuclear crisis and Japanese security', *Survival: The IISS Quarterly*, vol. 38, no. 2, summer 1996, pp. 79–103.

30 Matsumura Masahiro, *Nichibei Dōmei to Gunji Gijutsu*, Tokyo, Keisō Shobō, 1999, pp. 141–2.

31 Cronin, Giarra and Green, op. cit., p. 182.

32 Jiyū Minshutō Seimu Chōsakai Jōhō Eisei ni kansuru Purojekuto Chiimu, *Jōhō Shūshū Eisei Dōnyū ni tsuite Teigen*, 29 October 1998.

33 Matsumura Masahiro, 'Deploying theater missile defense flexibly: a US–Japan response to China', in Nishihara Masahi (ed.) *Old Issues, New Responses: Japan's Foreign and Security Policy Options*, Tokyo, Japan Center for International Exchange, 1998, pp. 103–18. Variants of the argument that BMD could be used by Japan and the US to persuade China of the need to engage in arms control are contained in: Green, op. cit., p. 117; and Kori J. Urayama, 'Chinese perspectives on Theater Missile Defense: Policy Implications for Japan', *Asian Survey*, vol. 40, no. 4, July/August 2000, pp.

613–14. Also see Morimoto Satoshi's testimony in the House of Councillors, *142kai Sangiin Gaikō Bōei Iinkai 21gō*, 11 June 1998.

34 Soeya Yoshihide, 'In defense of no defense', *Look Japan*, vol. 45, no. 527, February 2000, p. 23.

35 Christopher W. Hughes, *Japan's Economic Power and Security: Japan and North Korea*, London, Routledge, 1999, pp. 202–3. For one Japanese view stressing the importance of TMD as a means to strengthen confidence in the US–Japan alliance and its function across the region, see Morimoto Satoshi, *Kyokutō Yūji de Nihon wa Nani ga Dekiru ka: Gaidorainu to Yūji Hōsei*, Tokyo, PHP Kenkyūjo, 1999, pp. 104–5.

36 This interpretation of Japanese BMD policy is based on an interview with a MOFA official of deputy vice ministerial rank, Tokyo, 8 December 1999.

37 Takagi Takashi, 'Dandō misairu bōei wa gukō de aru', *Sekai*, no. 672, March 2000, p. 136; A Henry L. Stimson Center Working Group Report, *Theater Missile Defenses in the Asia–Pacific Region*, June 2000, p. 69.

38 *Asahi Shimbun*, 15 August 1999, p. 2; 6 November 1999, p. 3 (Author's translation).

39 Interview with bureau director-level official, JDA, 9 December 1999, Tokyo.

40 Wilkening, op. cit., pp. 59–60.

5 The Taiwan question
Reconciling the irreconcilable

Phil Deans

Introduction

For twenty years the issue of Taiwan defined Sino-Japanese relations. All interaction between Japan and China – political, economic or social – had to be understood and mediated through the fact of Japan's formal diplomatic recognition of the Republic of China (on Taiwan) rather than the People's Republic. Surveying the twenty-eight years that have passed since the Japanese government switched recognition, perhaps the most remarkable thing is how little Taiwan has been a source of conflict. The three governments involved have proved adept at managing the relationship and all three have shown a willingness to accommodate and compromise for their mutual benefit. The key to enabling the relationship has been the ability of Japan and Taiwan to utilise informal channels and networks to handle contact and communication, and the willingness of the PRC to tolerate this. However, although Beijing and Tokyo have shown a significant willingness to compromise and accommodate one another over the Taiwan question, the CCP has a bottom line over which it cannot compromise: the leadership of the PRC is unwilling, and perhaps unable, to tolerate any change in the Japanese government's stance on the formal 'one-China policy'. This dictates that Japan must never assign any form of sovereignty to Taiwan, it must ensure that all contacts are informal/unofficial (or at least low-profile) and that issues related to reunification are a matter solely for Beijing and Taipei. Furthermore, changes in the international system related to globalisation mean that the space in which informal ties exist is becoming increasingly codified and formalised, which puts growing pressure on the informal channels.

Legacies of the colonial period and the period of full diplomatic relations

Taiwan was a colony of Japan from 1895 to 1945, and the colonial period has had a number of profound consequences for the significance of Taiwan in Sino-Japanese relations. Four issues rooted in the colonial period are of ongoing significance: the increased sensitivity of the PRC to Japanese involvement with Taiwan; the existence of significant pro-Japanese sentiment amongst influential sectors of Taiwanese society; the foundations of Japan's postwar 'Taiwan lobby';

and the foundations of Taiwan in Japan's postwar economic nexus. The period of full diplomatic relation between Japan and the ROC which existed from 1952 to 1972 are significant because of the way in which they deepened and strengthened these factors in the bilateral relationship and increased the suspicion on behalf of the leaders of the CCP with regard to Japan's true intentions toward Taiwan.

The project of the CCP since its foundation has been one of national development and of ending humiliation and subjugation by foreign powers. Taiwan is emblematic for the leadership of the CCP of China's humiliation at the hands of Japanese imperialism and American interventionism. The CCP's project of national reunification will only be completed when Taiwan is returned to the motherland and a historical wrong is righted. The CCP's acute sensitivity to Japanese actions and Japan's history in China is well documented,[1] and with specific regard to Taiwan, the Chinese leadership regards any Japanese involvement with Taiwan with far greater concern than that of any other Asian power.[2] While the rhetoric attacking Japan's 'neo-colonialism' in Taiwan in the context of the 'revival of Japanese militarism' that was common in the 1950s and 1960s has died down, the possibility of a visit by former President Lee Teng-hui to Japan is far more sensitive than visits by the former President to any other country. Before the March 2000 election in Taiwan a PRC Foreign Ministry spokesman stated, 'In whatever capacity and in whatever form, Lee Teng-hui's visit to Japan would constitute a serious political situation and the Chinese government is strongly opposed to that'.[3] This sensitivity is even stronger with regard to any possible Japanese military role with regard to Taiwan, as was shown by Beijing's reaction to the revisions of the US–Japan Security Guidelines.

Running in parallel to this, however, has been the emergence of a significant and influential body of pro-Japanese sentiment in Taiwan. Taiwan is perhaps unique in Asia as the only country where the Japanese are regarded in a positive light by large sectors of the population of all generations, in strong contrast to the open hostility that is common in the PRC or Korea. The reasons for this difference are complex, but are rooted in the relatively benign nature of Japanese colonialism in Taiwan (compared to Japanese actions in Korea and the Chinese mainland), interacting with the fact that a distinct Taiwanese identity only emerged as a consequence of Japanese colonialism and therefore Taiwan did not generate the vicious cycle of anti-Japanese nationalist reaction and imperialist counter-reaction that occurred in Korea or China. Secondly, the appalling brutality of the early period of Kuomintang (KMT) rule on Taiwan (1945–55) generated a distinct nostalgia for the Japanese amongst several generations of Taiwanese. This attitude of 'double colonialism', where the Japanese imperialists are regarded more highly than the mainland 'colonists', is encapsulated in the often heard Taiwanese remark – it was better to be ruled by dogs than pigs. Finally the emergence of pro-Japanese sentiment among younger Taiwanese should be understood as a form of subethnic differentiation amongst younger Taiwanese – espousing pro-Japanese attitudes is a means of demonstrated difference from the dominant construction of Chineseness that emerges from the

90 *Phil Deans*

PRC. Furthermore, as younger Taiwanese attempt to establish an identity that is distinct from the preferred meaning of 'Chineseness' promoted by Beijing, pro-Japanese sentiment is used as a means of demonstrating difference.[4]

Nowhere has this pro-Japanese sentiment been as clear as in the stance of former President Lee Teng-hui. President Lee repeatedly stated his desire to visit Japan and his feelings of sympathy for the Japanese. While Lee's attitude may be more pronounced than some he is not alone amongst his generation of Taiwanese. The new Democratic Progressive Party administration has also come in for severe criticism from the PRC over its sympathy for Japan, in particular the new ROC Vice-President, Annette Lu who has been called, 'a Japan-flattering traitor' who 'has beautified foreign aggressors and sung songs of praise for a traitorous treaty [the 1895 Treaty of Shimonoseki] of national betrayal and humiliation. By doing so she is simply dreaming about relying on the support of foreigners to confront the motherland, so as to realise her plot to "Taiwan independence".'[5] This marked pro-Japanese sentiment creates particular dilemmas for Japanese policy-makers who are constrained by the PRC from embracing a country that would otherwise be Japan's closest friend in Asia.

The colonial period, and to an extent Taiwan's pro-Japanese sentiment, were also significant in laying the foundation for the Taiwan 'lobby' in Japan's Liberal Democratic Party (LDP). Many of the Japanese involved in the colonial administration of Taiwan or in other ways linked with the island later took up significant positions in later Japan–ROC relations. Key figures are Prime Minister Kishi Nobusuke (1957–60) and his brother, Prime Minister Sato Eisaku (1960–72). The family were part of the Chōshū elite that dominated the Meiji Restoration and had a historical interest in Taiwan.[6] The two main formal organisations of pro-ROC/pro-Taiwan figures in the LDP were the Japan–ROC Cooperation Committee (Nikka Kyōryoku Iinkai, JRCC) which was founded in 1957 when Kishi Nobusuke was Prime Minister,[7] and its successor, the Japan–ROC Dietmembers Consultative Committee (Ni-Ka Kankei Giin Kondankai or Nikkakon). Nikkakon was founded in March 1973 by twenty-seven right-wing LDP members such as Ishii Mitsujiro and Funada Naka from the JRCC. Ishii Mitsujiro, one of Japan's key faction leaders of the 1950s and 1960s, was private secretary to General Ando Sadami, the Governor-General of Taiwan from 1915 to 1920. Another notable example is Shiina Etsusaburo. Shiina was MITI Minister, 1960–1 and was Foreign Minister under Sato in the late 1960s. Shiina played a very important and influential role in the JRCC and later in Nikkakon, including being charged with the task of conveying Prime Minister Tanaka's notice of derecognition to Taipei in 1972. He has remained active in the LDP's pro-ROC lobby.[8] Shiina was the nephew of Goto Shimpei, the first Japanese Chief of Civil Administration of Taiwan. Shiina also had considerable experience in colonial administration from the time he worked in Japanese-occupied Manchuria, where Goto was President of the South Manchurian Railway.[9]

The reasons given by Japanese politicians for supporting Taiwan are mixed. At the time of normalisation of relations with the PRC, Kaya Okinori, one of the key figures in the pro-ROC groups in the postwar era, stated at the time of

The Taiwan question   91

derecognition that there were four main reasons behind supporting the ROC: (1) Chiang Kai-shek had been 'strict but generous' toward Japanese soldiers and civilians in China after Japan's surrender, greatly assisting their repatriation; (2) Chiang had opposed the abolition of the imperial household after the war; (3) he had vigorously opposed the division of Japan into zones of occupation; and (4) Chiang had given up the right to reparations from Japan.[10] Iguchi Sadao, a Japanese ambassador to the ROC, cited Chiang's policy of 'returning malice with virtue' as contributing the most to the closeness felt between Japan and the ROC.[11] These factors continued to be relevant, and were frequently cited in interviews by Nikkakon members, but were of declining significance, as Kaya's generation died off. Other issues, such as an anti-communist ideology and the possible financial reward that could come from promoting Taiwanese interests are also significant. Since the mid-1970s Nikkakon has not campaigned for Japan's re-recognition of the ROC on Taiwan, but it has proved to be a vital channel of informal, high-level contact between Tokyo and Taipei, and has proved invaluable in resolving a range of sensitive issues between Japan and Taiwan.[12]

A final important legacy of the colonial period considered here is the foundation of Taiwan's postwar economic success and the manner in which Taiwan (along with South Korea) became part of Japan's postwar economic nexus. Much of Taiwan's infrastructure was created during the colonial period, and from the 1960s onwards Japanese business concerns resurrected colonial links to invest in Taiwan. As Cumings has shown, the island very quickly became integrated into a Northeast Asian product cycle, accepted declining Japanese industries and relied on the US market for exports.[13] This pattern has broken down to a certain extent in the 1990s as the relationship has shifted from being a triangular one involving the US, Japan and Taiwan to a quadrilateral one that includes the PRC. Nonetheless, Japanese products and technology still dominate the Taiwanese economy. Japanese investment into Taiwan is second only to that of the US, and, given its tendency to go towards smaller ventures (rather than large single plants), is more pervasive. Furthermore, Japan is Taiwan's third largest export market (after the US and the PRC). From the Japanese perspective, while trade with Taiwan was surpassed by trade with the PRC for the first time in the early 1990s, trade with Taiwan is weighted far more in Japan's favour, with Japan having run large surpluses since the late 1950s. The most important development in the 1990s has been the role that Taiwan has developed for channelling Japanese investment into the PRC. Identifying the 'origin' of goods is increasingly difficult given the increasingly globalised nature of production: a Japanese brand such as Panasonic may consist of components from Taiwan assembled in the PRC and therefore the product's 'nationality' is hard to define. Bearing this caveat in mind, Japanese investment in Taiwan has been central to much Taiwanese investment into the PRC.[14]

While the colonial period has begun to receive the attention it deserves in understanding contemporary Taiwan, less attention has been paid to the role of Japan in Taiwan in the 1950s and 1960s. Since 1945 the key determining factor

92 *Phil Deans*

in the Japan–PRC–Taiwan triangle has been US policy and US preferences, and the broad context of the relationship can only be understood through the framework of US policy in the region. However, within this broad framework, Japan, China and Taiwan have proved adept at pursuing their own preferences. Following Japan's defeat in 1945, authority over Taiwan was handed to the Republic of China, in line with the Cairo Declaration. Initially this was unproblematic, but the defeat of the KMT in the Chinese civil war, and the founding of the PRC in October 1949, put the legitimacy of KMT rule on Taiwan and the claim of the ROC to represent China in the international arena under severe challenge. However, the US perspective on East Asian politics saw these events through the lens of the Cold War that had developed in Europe. Although the US government was ambivalent toward Chiang Kai-shek, the attack on South Korea by North Korea in 1950 saw the US switch support fully behind Chiang Kai-shek and intervene in the Chinese civil war by ordering the US 7th Fleet to prevent any military action by either the PRC or the ROC in the Taiwan Strait.

In the international arena, the US government attempted to shore up the legitimacy of the KMT regime on Taiwan by continuing to recognise the ROC as the sole, legitimate government of China, blocking the PRC's entry into the UN and ensuring that America's allies also maintained the fiction that the ROC represented China. This was a particularly sensitive issue in Japan, and the US Secretary of State, John Foster Dulles, required the Japanese Prime Minster to issue a letter stating that, when Japan regained its full sovereignty, it would also recognise the ROC as the sole, legitimate government of China. As a result, when Japan regained full sovereignty in 1952, the Japanese government established formal diplomatic relations with the ROC. However, there was considerable pressure within Japan from opposition parties, certain groups within the ruling conservatives and from business interests to develop a relationship with the PRC, and as a consequence Japan quickly developed an informal relationship with Beijing which operated in parallel to its formal relationship with Taipei.

Throughout the 1950s and 1960s the Japanese government was able to maintain this uneasy relationship, although it was constantly subject to pressure because of changing domestic factors in the three countries. For example, the increased radicalisation of Chinese politics that accompanied the Great Leap Forward of 1958 saw a significant increase in military activity in the Taiwan Straits. At the same time, Japan had a markedly pro-ROC Prime Minister in Kishi Nobusuke, and Japan and the ROC developed closer links at the cost of Japan's informal ties with Beijing.[15] However, the early 1960s saw a far more pragmatic leadership in Japan under Ikeda Hayato, pursuing economic goals and therefore improving relations with Beijing at the cost of links with Taipei, which led to threats by Chiang Kai-shek to terminate relations.[16] What matters most about this period for current relations, however, is the way in which links dating from the colonial period were strengthened and deepened. This is clearest in the economic arena, where Japanese investment and expertise were to prove vital in

The way in which the Taiwanese economy developed. In the political arena also, right-wing ROC and Japanese figures developed close personal links that were to be of continuing relevance after derecognition.

Much as the Japanese government's move to recognise the ROC in 1952 had been determined in Washington, the timing and nature of Japan's derecogniton of the ROC and recognition of the PRC was a consequence of changes in US interests in East Asia. Although there was growing pressure in Japan in the 1960s to develop a stronger relationship with Beijing, it was only following Washington's surprise opening to China that the Japanese government was able to take a similar initiative. One of the most remarkable events of this period is the haste with which the Japanese government opened relations with Beijing, and the extent to which the Japanese were prepared to make concessions to the PRC – to the extent of allowing Mao Zedong and Zhou Enlai to effectively veto the prime ministership of the Taiwan-leaning Sato Eisaku. Disputes over the Taiwan question in the early 1970s saw very severe splits develop in the LDP, the most serious division in the ruling conservative group before the fracturing of the LDP in the 1990s.

The significance of the twenty-year period of full recognition for Taiwan in Sino-Japanese relations are threefold, and all relate to continuities across the supposed watershed of 1972. First of all 1952–72 saw the deepening of a number of the colonial ties that existed between Japan and Taiwan, whether in economic or political fields. As mentioned above, key political figures in Japan quickly resumed relationships with political figures in the ROC. On an economic level, Taiwan became one of the first destinations for Japanese overseas investment, brought about by geographical proximity and cultural and linguistic familiarity. This period also saw the emergence of the broad legitimating device – the principle of the separation of politics and economics – that was to manage Japan's relations with Taiwan after 1972. Finally, the period of full recognition highlights the ongoing dominance of US interests in determining the broad framework within which the Japan–China–Taiwan relationship exists.

Managing the Taiwan question: reconciliation through ambiguity

There are parallels between Japan–PRC relations from 1952 to 1972 and Japan–Taiwan relations from 1972 to the present, in part because of the Japanese government's insistence that both these relationships should be governed by the principle of the separation of politics and economics (*seikei bunri*, Chinese: *zhengjing fenli*). Operating this principle has been greatly facilitated by the fact that in capitalist developmental states such as Taiwan and Japan, the interpenetration of political and economic concerns has made distinguishing between political and economic and public and private realms particularly difficult.[17] Since official relations were severed in 1972, a range of formal and informal institutions have emerged to handle interaction between the two sides, and the 1990s have seen changes occur to both the formal (i.e. state-centred or 'official') institutions

94 *Phil Deans*

and the informal channels. The change of the name of Taiwan's 'virtual' embassy from the Association of East Asian Relations to the Taipei Economic and Cultural Representative Office (TECRO) in 1991 marked a notable change in the profile of Taiwan's presence in Japan. Not only does the new name reflect far more accurately the purpose and function of the office, but the name itself directly connects the institution to Taiwan, in contrast to the former ambiguous title. This is particularly significant in Japanese and Chinese where the abbreviated use of *Tai* can be understood to mean Taiwan, rather than Taipei.

In many respects the practice of Japan–Taiwan relations post-1972 mirrors that of Japan's relations with the PRC before 1972, but these parallels should not be taken too far. Japan's relations with Taiwan since 1972 are far more substantial than those between Japan and the PRC before 1972, in terms of the scale of personal and economic interaction, and the size and profile of their mutual 'virtual' diplomatic presence: Japan and the PRC never enjoyed institutions comparable to the Interchange Association or the Taipei Economic and Cultural Representative Office. The Taiwanese side has been able to achieve 'upgradings' in relations with Japan in part as a result of a number of changes in the circumstances surrounding the relationship. An important factor was the improvement in relations between Taiwan and the PRC that had taken place since the late 1980s. This improvement was viewed by the Japanese side as allowing a more flexible and pragmatic approach to the relationship.[18] Furthermore, Taiwan's worldwide efforts to increase its profile and recognition, and changes in third countries, have also made it easier for the Taiwanese side to encourage the Japanese to relax their restrictions. Particular pressure was brought to bear on the Japanese Foreign Ministry by the Diet's pro-Taiwan groups, centred around Nikkakon. When asked if the Interchange Association (Japan's representative office in Taiwan) would be likely to change its name in the light of these changes a senior official said that this was very unlikely given the possible reaction of the PRC.[19]

Relations between Japan and Taiwan have not been unaffected by political change on Taiwan, although the changes have resulted in new uncertainties rather than clear-cut improvements.[20] The relationship still depends on the informal groups of pro-Taiwan politicians within the Japanese government for the resolution of substantive issues. Political change on Taiwan has made this more complicated as the traditional basis for this support – ideology, ties to Chiang Kai-shek and historical links – become less relevant, and as money politics becomes more significant and Beijing's informal lobbying in Tokyo more effective. Personal ties are vital, but remain vulnerable to scandal and the passage of time: in the summer of 2000 supporters of Taiwan in the Japanese cabinet (defined in terms of current or previous membership of Nikkakon) were at their highest since the late 1960s, but there are no guarantees that this situation will last, or translate itself into concrete political action in Japan. ROC's ambition of getting Tokyo to establish a 'Taiwan Relations Act' based on the Washington model will not be achieved in the foreseeable future.

The response of the Japanese government to President Lee's 'Special State-to-State' announcement reinforces this. The Japanese government's reaction was to mirror the response of the US and to restate its main position on the Taiwan question. Japanese Foreign Ministry spokesman Numata Sadaaki stated that 'There is no change at all in the Japanese government's position on Taiwan'.[21] Prime Minister Obuchi Keizo quickly reaffirmed Japan's position that it 'understands and respects' Beijing's claim that Taiwan is an inalienable part of the PRC, and joined the United States and many other Asian countries in regarding Lee's statement as regrettable and ill advised. This formal response, though, masks a growing sympathy for Taiwan from across the political spectrum in Japan. When Jiang Zemin visited Tokyo in December 1998 he was unable to extract a Japanese equivalent to President Clinton's 'Three Noes' on Taiwan – no support for independence, no support for 'two Chinas' or 'one China, one Taiwan', and no support for Taiwanese membership of any international organisation for which statehood is a requirement.[22] There are those in Japan who call for a much closer relationship with Taiwan, however. For example, Kawamura Junihiko, a senior Japanese military commentator, has said that Japan is obliged to help the US if it acts military to defend Taiwan under the Taiwan Relations Act.[23] This was an important shift in Japan's usual stance of bowing a little lower than other countries when dealing with the PRC.

The current political sympathy for Taiwan in Japan is fragile, however. It is based on individuals rather than an institutionalised system, and as such is vulnerable to the vagaries of domestic politics – as the Taiwanese learnt following the disgrace of one of their former patrons, Kanemaru Shin. Many of Japan's Taiwan supporters are not simply motivated by an idealistic sympathy for Taiwan's achievements, but by a nationalist agenda for Japan's future. In addition, some of Taiwan's sympathisers in Japan can also be liabilities. Taiwan's highest-profile supporter is the outspoken mayor of Tokyo, the nationalist Ishihara Shintaro. Ishihara's venomous criticism of the PRC when he went to Taiwan to attend President Chen Sui-bian's inauguration and his well-known comments denying the Nanjing Massacre make him a difficult ally. What cannot be denied is that Taiwan's current pro-Japanese generation is a diminishing resource, and as they pass from the scene the ease of communication created by fluency in language and a degree of shared norms will decline. The implications of this are something which are already a concern for Taiwan's Foreign Ministry.

Tokyo's preferred option for cross-Straits relations remains the continuation of the status quo. This will enable the Japanese to avoid hard choices and difficult decisions – should military conflict occur in the Straits, Japan will be forced to choose between supporting the US in defence of a former Japanese colony and so offending its most important Asian neighbour, or charting a new course in the Chinese, rather than American, orbit. For the foreseeable future this second choice is highly unlikely, but despite Taiwan's numerous and influential friends in Tokyo, it is unlikely that the Japanese government will risk a direct confrontation with the PRC over this question either.

The (re-)emergence of security concerns

Several other chapters in this volume address security issues in Sino-Japanese relations as their main concern, so this section will briefly sketch the significance of Taiwan. For most of the post-1972 period security concerns were of minimal significance to the Taiwan issue in Japan–PRC relations. Military security re-emerged as a significant factor in 1995, but while the underlying factors behind the 'securitisation' of the Straits have shifted significantly, the external framework for managing the dispute – and Japan's putative role in this – has remained stable. The dangers of a PRC military invasion of Taiwan (or a ROC attempt to use military force) had receded by the late 1960s. While the US intervention in the Taiwan Straits in 1950 was primarily aimed at preventing a communist takeover of Taiwan, it also functioned to limit military adventurism by Chiang Kai-shek. Following Richard Nixon's visit to China in 1972 and US recognition of the PRC in 1979, the danger of military conflict receded further, although the basic parameters of US involvement remained the same, as they do to the present day: the US government adopts an agnostic position on Taiwan's status and future, but will only tolerate a peaceful resolution of the question. Different US administrations and advisers will have different preferences, but the American bottom line is that whatever happens (reunification, independence for Taiwan or the continuation of the status quo), has to happen peacefully. This was made clear in 1996 by Winston Lord, the Assistant Secretary of State for East Asia and the Pacific:

> we will continue to maintain self-sufficient defence for Taiwan and fulfil our obligations under the TRA . . . [the 1982 Communiqué] did suggest that the general level [of arms sales] would decline and we will not unduly upgrade [Taipei's] technological skills. But in that same Communiqué the Chinese stated that it was their fundamental policy to strive for a peaceful solution. Our whole policy toward China–Taiwan . . . is keyed to the premise that we will see an effort to resolve this issue peacefully.[24]

Japan's position in this relationship has also remained quite stable and broadly within the 'Yoshida Doctrine' of fundamental reliance on the US for security. This essential continuity of Japanese policy crosses the supposed fault line of the end of the Cold War – the high-profile debates of the revised Security Guidelines notwithstanding. These revisions are simply the latest configuration of a long-standing Japanese commitment to offer support to the US in the region. While the wording and the nuance may have changed, the debate about Japan's actions or otherwise in support of the US in the 'areas surrounding' Japan under the 'new' Guidelines should not be regarded as a significant departure, but a revised version of the 1978 agreements regarding defence of the 'areas surrounding'. These in turn should be regarded as the latest manifestation of the 1969 Nixon–Sato communiqué, in which Prime Minister Sato stated: 'the maintenance of peace and security in the Taiwan area is also an important factor for the security of Japan'.[25] US policy over Taiwan has been remarkably consistent throughout the Cold War and after, and the parallels between the US position in 1996 and US responses to the Taiwan Straits crises in 1954 and 1958 are uncanny. In the conclusion to his study of the 1954 and 1958 disputes Gerald Segal states: 'The Taiwan events remained overwhelmingly a bilateral US–China crisis as Beijing probed American intentions . . . But China lacked both the military power and the political will to overcome this US policy. So China settled for long-term goals where it could hope to encourage the decline of US power and/or will'.[26]

The missile 'crisis' of 1995, and to a lesser extent of 1996, clearly marked a new departure in post-1972 cross-Straits relations. It also marks the point where the 'Taiwan Question' re-emerges as an issue of major importance in Sino-Japanese relations rather than the irritant that it had been since 1972. However to understand the dynamics of this shift it is important to understand the changing nature of the cross-Straits conflict and shake off the misconception that it is a 'Cold War' conflict. Rather than a product of the Cold War, the origins of the Taiwan question lie in the unresolved Chinese civil war. The Chinese civil war should be understood not as a conflict between 'communism' and 'capitalism' but between the conservative and radical Chinese nationalisms that emerged in response to Western and Japanese imperialism.[27] While the Cold War is clearly central to the US involvement in the Chinese civil war and intervention in the Taiwan Straits in 1950, the Cold War is not the source or origin of the cross-Straits conflict. This is important in accounting for the fact that when the Cold War 'ended' the basic parameters of cross-Straits relations (like the situation in Korea) remained unchanged. American policy remains broadly similar as does the Japanese government's support for this policy.

The re-militarisation of the Taiwan question in 1995 is not the product of the end of the 'Cold War' *per se*. In many respects, as an organising idea for understanding intra-Asia conflict, the Cold War is of limited utility after the early 1970s – it remains of great significance for outlining the global context of East Asian politics but a 'Cold War' does not add much to an understanding of key issues in the international politics within Asia: the economic transformation of China that begins in 1978, the improvement in cross-Straits relations that begins in 1987, the ongoing hostility between Japan and Russia, to give three examples. The changes that occur in the military context of cross-Straits relations from 1995 onwards should not be seen in a 'post-Cold-War' context, but rather in the context of changing nationalisms in the PRC and Taiwan. The PRC's radical, isolationist nationalism of the Maoist period of 1949–78 has been transformed into an assertive nationalism that promotes integration into the world economy of national benefit but can offer no compromise over issues of territorial integrity, for which reunification with Taiwan is central. However, on Taiwan, Chiang's conservative Chinese nationalism has faded, to be replaced by an emergent liberal Taiwanese nationalism that appeals for Taiwan to be granted sovereign statehood on the basis of a normative claim rooted in Taiwan's development of successful and effective democratic institutions.[28]

During the missile crisis the Japanese government at first took an assertive line

98 *Phil Deans*

on China's actions. Foreign Ministry spokesman Hashimoto Hiroshi called China's missile tests 'undesirable'[29] and a few days later the Japanese Prime Minster Hashimoto Ryutaro expressed his regret over Chinese actions.[30] As tensions increased, the Japanese Foreign Ministry again called for calm, and, interestingly, stated that, because of Japan's alliance with the US, '[Japan] was not and could not be neutral'.[31] Hashimoto further called for self-restraint over what was a 'major cause of concern'.[32] This provoked an angry response from Beijing who warned Japan that the Taiwan question was 'an internal matter that brooks no interference'.[33] Following this admission the Japanese government remained very quiet about activities in the Straits, demonstrating their overriding concern not to damage relations with Beijing over the issue. By the end of the crisis, Gaimushō (MOFA) was increasing its ambivalence with statements such as '[Tokyo] understands that the US is determined to continue to play an important role in the region [but] China is a very important neighbour for us ... We have got to be on good terms with China and Taiwan for a long time'.[34] Japan's acute sensitivity over Taiwan was highlighted when Kato Koichi, Secretary-General of the Liberal Democratic Party (LDP) stated that he would not attend President Lee's inauguration. The reason for this was fear that showing a closeness to Taiwan might damage Kato's hope of becoming Prime Minster.

At the heart of this disagreement is the exact location or definition of the 'areas surrounding' Japan. Some members of Gaimushō have insisted that this definition is 'situational' rather than 'geographical' but this has been contradicted by other parts of the Ministry of Foreign Affairs (MOFA).[35] For example the Chief Cabinet Secretary Kajiyama Seiroku – a long-time Taiwan supporter – has said that the 'areas surrounding' Japan 'naturally include the Taiwan Strait'.[36] Interestingly, Lee Teng-hui has welcomed the greater security cooperation between Japan and the US.[37] The PRC has also been very critical of Japan's changing security relationship with the US and especially over what it perceives as Japan's stance over Taiwan. The Chinese claim that Japan is not adequately supporting Chinese reunification and that 'elements within Japan' support Taiwanese independence. At a summit in Japan in November 1997, Li Peng raised the issue and stated that Taiwan was sovereign Chinese territory and Hashimoto gave the stock response of commitment to the 1972 declaration and not supporting Taiwanese independence. The Chinese Defence Minister Chi Haotian visited Tokyo in February 1998 and he again pressed the Japanese on their stance over Taiwan, and Kyuma Fumio his opposite number gave a classic blank response of 'We hope the Taiwan question can be solved by the two parties concerned'.[38]

Conclusion

The role played by Taiwan in Sino-Japanese relations is complex and multi-faceted, involving as it does three actors with contending domestic forces, and operating in a context determined by US Asia–Pacific policy. One issue that should be mentioned though is the willingness of the leadership of the PRC to tolerate a range of significant and substantive relations between Taiwan and Japan. These contacts go beyond the simple 'economics' of trade and investment that would be tolerated under the remit of *seikei bunri* and comprise a major Japanese 'diplomatic' presence in Taiwan that is scarcely disguised. The PRC is the subject of constant criticism in the West and in Japan for its stance on Taiwan, but in the context of the domestic pressure that the leadership of the CCP is under it should perhaps be commended for its willingness to keep a low profile. The leadership of the CCP is suffering from a range of pressures, including the social unrest that results from the economic reform programme and the growing significance of nationalism as a means of legitimating its rule.[39] The 'success' Japan and the PRC have enjoyed over the Taiwan question is rooted in the use by both sides of ambiguous statements and positions to prevent open disagreement – it is a case where ambiguity decreases, rather than increases, tension. This skilful use of ambiguity can be seen in everything from the Japanese government's coded position that it 'understands and respects' the PRC's position, through the indeterminate status of Japan's quasi-diplomatic representation in Taiwan, to the 'situational' construction of the revised Security Guidelines which do – and do not – cover Taiwan. The space for this kind of relationship is narrowing, however. Globalisation brings with it a range of Western norms which are legalistic and intolerant of different practices. Accession to organisations such as the World Trade Organisation and participation in various regional organisations increases the formal, legalistic codification of Taiwan and hence narrows the space within which *seikei bunri* has operated.

With regard to Japan, it remains the case that Japan's approach to Taiwan and the role of Taiwan in Tokyo's relations with Beijing is determined by Japan's relations with the US. There are differences between Washington and Tokyo – in the 1950s and 1960s the Japanese were keener on links with the PRC, in the 1990s they have proved more cautious. The Japanese government is rarely pro-active in the realm of foreign relations, however, and Tokyo's stock response to problems in the Taiwan Straits is still to fall in line behind Washington's China policy. With this caveat borne in mind, the Japanese government is less susceptible to PRC pressure and more open to and supportive of Taiwan today than at any time since the normalisation of relations with the PRC in 1972. This openness and support is of vital significance to the future of Taiwan, but support is fragile, based on Japan's perception of its interests (rather than Taiwan's interests) and may be a diminishing resource.

Nevertheless, the 1990s have seen the emergence of significant discussion of Taiwan in the Japanese media after two decades of self-enforced silence. Until the early 1990s the only newspaper to maintain a permanent presence in Taiwan was the right-wing *Sankei Shimbun*. As Zhao has shown, the early 1990s saw the gradual return of other Japanese media organs to Taiwan and increasing coverage of Taiwan in Japan.[40] Japanese media groups had previously been unable to have representation in both Taiwan and the PRC. Taiwan's democratisation and the friendliness of the Taiwanese towards the Japanese certainly creates a groundswell of popular support for Taiwan in Japan – an

100 *Phil Deans*

opinion poll in the *Mainichi Shimbun* in 1993 indicated that 72 per cent of Japanese believed Japan should have diplomatic relations with both Beijing and Taipei.[41] The growth in media coverage reached its peak in March 2000 when all major Japanese news organisations gave extensive coverage of the presidential election, most of it portraying Taiwanese democracy in a very positive light and being critical of the PRC's stance.

Japanese concern over the Taiwan issue has grown considerably since security issues re-emerged in cross-Straits relations following President Lee's visit to the US in 1995. After over two decades of strategic and political neglect, Japanese policy-makers were rudely reminded of just how important Taiwan is to Japan on a number of levels, and of Taiwan's potential to be a source of serious difficulties in Japan's relations with the PRC. The impact of conflict in the Straits for Japan's economic security and on Japan's key trade routes was obvious. The debates concerning the revision of the Security Treaty Guidelines with the US were given special significance by the re-emergence of military tension, and the ongoing problems have been a significant catalyst in the creation of the current system. Furthermore, while the PRC surpassed Taiwan as an economic partner of Japan in the early 1990s, Japan–Taiwan trade remains far more profitable to the Japanese, and many Japanese companies are deeply and intimately bound up with Taiwanese companies – the Marubeni–Evergreen link being the most significant. There is much more to the relationship than business and commercial concerns, however. In particular, there is a considerable reservoir of goodwill, sympathy and support for Taiwan in Japan, a reflection of the open admiration of Japan by many Taiwanese.

Reconciliation between Beijing and Tokyo over the Taiwan question may not be possible, but there has been an admirable degree of compromise, from all three sides, over the maintenance of different levels of relationship. While Tokyo and Beijing have proved adept at compromising over Taiwan and allowing practical issues to override issues of substance most of the time, Beijing remains acutely sensitive to anything that challenges Beijing's claim over the island or Beijing's one-China policy. For most of the post-1972 period, form (i.e. adherence to the 'one-China principle') has mattered more than substance (trade and other contacts) for Beijing, and Beijing has been most vociferous in its complaints when form has been challenged. Serious problems may lie ahead, though, if the leadership in Beijing are less willing to accept the status quo as a neutral position between reunification and independence, and instead choose to see it as unacceptable de facto independence. To date, Japanese politicians have been unwilling and perhaps unable to change either the form or the substance of Japan's relations with Taiwan: for better or worse Japan's policy operates very much as a by-product of US China policy.

Notes

The author gratefully acknowledges the support of the Japan Foundation Endowment Committee (JFEC Grant no. 995) in preparing this chapter.

The Taiwan question 101

1 See Allen S. Whiting, *China Eyes Japan*, Berkeley, University of California Press, 1989.
2 See Ma Yuan, 'Riben jingqi tiaozheng dui Tai zhengce de yuanyin he yi tu', *Guoji Guanxi xueyuan xuebao*, no. 3, September 1997, pp. 18–28. For a discussion, see Rex Li, 'Partners or Rivals? Chinese Perceptions of Japan's Security Strategy in the Asia Pacific Region', *Journal of Strategic Studies*, vol. 22, no. 4, December 1999, pp. 1–25.
3 *China Times*, 4 February 2000.
4 See Phil Deans, 'What Have the Romans Ever Done for Us? Taiwanese Perceptions of Japan', Paper presented to the London China Seminar on Taiwan, 2 November 2000. See also Xu Zongmao, *Riben Qingjie: Jiang Jieshi dao Li Denghui*, Taipei, Tianxia Wenhua, 1997; Xu Zongmao, 'Riben Wenhua dui Taiwan zuqin de yingxiang', in *Tawianren Lun*, Taipei, Shibao Wenchu gongsi, 1993, pp. 181–8, and Hsieh Yamei, *Nihon ni koshita Taiwanjin*, Tokyo, Sogo Hōrei Shuppan, 2000.
5 *Ta Kung Pao*, Hong Kong, 5 May 2000 in *Summary of World Broadcasts (SWB)* FE/3833 F/6–F/7 (8), 6 May 2000.
6 John Welfield, *An Empire in Eclipse: Japan in the Postwar American Alliance System*, London and Atlantic Heights, Athlone Press, 1988, p. 116.
7 For background see Kurata Nobuyasu, 'Nikka Kyōryoku Iinkai no Rekishiteki Yakuwari', in Uno Seichi, *Kobun kara Ritokei e: Nikka 80-nen no Kiseki*, Tokyo, Waseda University Press, 1992, pp. 333–49 and Ikei Masaru, 'Nikka Kyōryoku Iinkai: Sengo Nichi-Tai Kankei no Kōsatsu', *Hōgaku Kenkyū (Law Studies)*, 1980, vol. 53, no. 2, pp. 1–28.
8 For background to this see Matsumoto Ayahiko, *Taiwan Kaikyō no Kakehashi ni: ima Akasu Nichi-Tai Dankō Hiwa*, Tokyo, Kenmun Bukusu, 1996.
9 Shiina Etsusaburo, 'Nihon Sangyō no Daijikenjo: Manshū', *Bungei Shunjū*, February 1976, pp. 106–14; Chalmers Johnson, *MITI and the Japanese Miracle: The Growth of Industrial Policy, 1925–1975*, Stanford, Stanford University Press, 1982, pp. 130–1.
10 Kaya Okinori, 'Taiwan kirisute no bōkyo o imashimeru', in *Senzen Sengo Hachijūnen*, Tokyo, Keizai Oruaisha, 1976, pp. 337–54.
11 Iguchi Sadao, 'The Taiwan Problem and US–China Relations', in Kajima Morinosuke (ed.) *Japan in Current World Affairs*, Tokyo, Japan Times, 1971, pp. 109–25.
12 For more details on Nikkakon and its predecessors, see Phil Deans, *Virtual Diplomacy: Japan–Taiwan Relations since 1972*, forthcoming.
13 Bruce Cumings, 'The Origins and Development of the Northeast Asian Political Economy: Industrial Sectors, Product Cycles and Political Consequences', in Frederic C. Deyo (ed.) *The Political Economy of New Asian Industrialism*, Ithaca and London, Cornell University Press, 1987, pp. 44–83.
14 Taiwanese officials spoken to by the author claim that as much as 60–70 per cent of all Taiwanese investment into the PRC is partly or wholly linked to Japanese investment in Taiwan or contains some kind of Japanese component. Unattributable interviews with TECRO officials in Tokyo, July 1999.
15 The late 1950s saw a range of issues in the relationship such as Kishi's state visit to Taiwan and the Nagasaki flag incident in 1957, the Offshore Islands crisis of 1958 and the negotiations over the security treaty between the US and Japan.
16 Central to the tensions were decisions in Japan to allow the use of Import-Export Bank credits by the PRC, and the controversy over the dissident Zhou Hongjing. See Lin Ch'in-ching, *Ume to Sakura: Sengo no Nikka Kankei*, Tokyo, Sankei Shuppan, 1984, pp. 178–80 and Douglas H. Mendel, 'Japan's Taiwan Tangle', *Asian Survey*, vol. 4, pp. 1073–84.
17 See Phil Deans, 'The Capitalist Developmental State in East Asia', in Ronen Palan and Jason Abbot with Phil Deans, *State Strategies in the Global Political Economy*, London, Pinter, 1996.
18 See the comment by President Lee Teng-hui that the end of the Cold War and the improvement of relations across the Taiwan Straits should lead to an improvement in ties with Japan, *Dacheng Bao*, 3 May 1993.

102 *Phil Deans*

19 Unattributable interview, September 1996.
20 See Phil Deans, 'A Democracy Craving Recognition: A Pessimistic View on the Impact of Democratisation on Taiwan's International Status', *China Perspectives*, no. 34, March–April 2001, pp. 35–47.
21 'Japan Affirms "One China" Stance after Taiwan Shift', Reuters, 13 July 1999, accessed on 11 October 1999 from http://taiwansecurity.org/Reu/Reu-990713-2htm.
22 'China, Japan Clash Over Three Nos' *Agence France Presse*, 2 November 1998, accessed on 6 December 1999 from http://taiwansecurity.org/AFP/AFP-981102.htm.
23 'Japanese Critic Urges Japan to Engage in Co-operation with Taiwan', accessed on 15 October 1999 from http://www.taipei.org/teco/cicc/news/english/e-10–13–99/e-10–13–31.htm/.
24 *Far Eastern Economic Review*, 4 April 1996, p. 17.
25 Cited in Wolf Mendl, *Issues in Japan's China Policy*, London, Macmillan, 1978, p. 25.
26 Gerald Segal, *Defending China*, Oxford, Oxford University Press, 1985, p. 136.
27 Chiang Kai-shek's conservative nationalism survived in Taiwan, and parallel conservative nationalism existed under Syngman Rhee and then Park Chung-Hee in South Korea and various US-supported regimes in South Vietnam. Mao's radical nationalism had its parallels in Kim Il-sung's North Korea and Ho Chi-minh's North Vietnam. This analysis is part of an ongoing project by the author on re-assessing the 'end' of the Cold War in Northeast Asia.
28 See Deans, 'A Democracy Craving Recognition'.
29 *SWB* FE/2553 E/1, 6 March 1996.
30 *SWB* FE/2556 E/1, 9 March 1996.
31 *SWB* FE/2560 F/10, 14 March 1996.
32 *SWB* FE/2563 E/2, 18 March 1996.
33 *SWB* FE/2565 E/1, 19 March 1998 and FE/2566 F/5, 21 March, 1996.
34 *Far Eastern Economic Review*, 21 March 1996, p. 15.
35 See the statement by Akiyama Masahiro, the Administrative Vice-Minister of the Japan Defence Agency, *SWB* FE 3274 E/1, 9 July 1998.
36 *SWB* FE/3002 F/1; *Japan Times Weekly International Edition*, 3–9 November 1997, p. 6.
37 *Japan Times Weekly International Edition*, 3–9 November 1997.
38 *Japan Times Weekly International Edition*, 9–16 February 1998.
39 For the significance of this for Sino-Japanese relations, see Phil Deans, 'Contending Nationalism and the Diaoyutai/Senkaku Dispute', *Security Dialogue*, vol. 31, no. 1, March 2000, pp. 119–31.
40 Suisheng Zhao, 'Changing Leadership Perceptions: The Adoption of Coercive Strategy', in Suisheng Zhao (ed.) *Across the Taiwan Strait: Mainland China, Taiwan and the 1995–1996 Crisis*, London, Routledge, 1999, pp. 111–12.
41 Poll cited by Ijiri Hidenori, *Taiwan Keiken no Reisengo no Ajia*, Tokyo, Keisō Press, 1993, p. 250.

6 The background and trend of the partnership

Jin Xide

Throughout the 1990s the Chinese–Japanese relationship has been undergoing a structural change. What has happened in the relationship? Why has it changed? How do we define the new stage of the Chinese–Japanese relationship? How do we foresee its future progress? We get the most reliable answers to these questions by shedding light on the background, the meaning and the future trend of the so-called China–Japan partnership.

In late November 1998, when Chinese President Jiang Zemin made an official visit to Japan, the governments of China and Japan published a joint declaration in which the two countries agreed on the future goal of building a Partnership of Friendship and Cooperation for Peace and Development. Subsequently many people, not only Chinese and Japanese, have expressed their doubts on the results of Jiang's visit to Japan, especially on the China–Japan partnership that is the key notion of the joint declaration. Not a few people regarded Jiang's visit as a total failure and even saw the so-called partnership as a meaningless word.

In my opinion, many people have failed to see the important breakthrough made during the visit for the following reasons: the too high and too idealistic expectations for the improvements of the Chinese–Japanese relationship and a failure to compare the positive trend of the relationship made by the visit of 1998 with that of the mid-1990s when China and Japan experienced the worst situation of political friction since they normalised their bilateral relations in 1972.

Moreover, many people focused their attention on the history issue and an emotionally charged atmosphere then existed between the two countries so that they could barely see the overall picture of the new bilateral partnership.

In addition, different approaches and standpoints between Chinese and Japanese people have also made great differences to how one evaluates the results of Jiang's visit and the declared goal of the China–Japan bilateral partnership.

Let us return to the original question. How does one evaluate the Chinese–Japanese relationship in recent years as well as its future trend? The answer lies in how to understand the meaning of the partnership.

In the mid-1990s, China and Japan faced four kinds of future scenarios for their bilateral relationship:

- The first was the worst-case scenario in which the two countries would fail to

104 *Jin Xide*

control or cease the political frictions between them such that their bilateral relations would become even worse.

- The second was to realise such preliminary goals as ceasing the frequent political frictions as in 1995 and 1996 and put their bilateral relationship onto a new track of stable and healthy development.
- The third was to accomplish an intermediate goal by shaping a new bilateral framework fitting the needs of the first decades of the twenty-first century.
- The fourth as well as the most idealistic scenario was to reach agreements on all of the disputed issues and establish a totally new and mature relationship.

Seeing the whole Chinese–Japanese relationship in the 1990s from the viewpoint of the above four scenarios, it can be said that the period of late 1998 was a turning point. The bilateral relationship had prevented the first scenario, achieved the second one and started the process of realising the third. I am rather optimistic about the future because I believe the Chinese–Japanese relationship has left behind the state of structural frictions of 1995 and 1996. On the other hand, China and Japan still have a long way to go before realising the intermediate goal and trying to challenge the higher and more ideal goal for their relationship.

In this chapter I am trying to make an overall observation on the readjustment process of the Chinese–Japanese relationship in the 1990s and to make an evaluation of the meaning, as well as the future fate, of the so-called China–Japan partnership. In doing so, I am focusing my analysis on the following three questions.

1 Why did the Chinese–Japanese relationship enter a new readjustment process in the 1990s?
2 What is the real meaning of the China–Japan partnership?
3 How do we foresee the future trend of the Chinese–Japanese relationship with the partnership at the core?

Structural changes of the Chinese–Japanese relationship in the 1990s

In the early 1990s, very few people had foreseen a change in the Chinese–Japanese relationship.[1] But in the period around 1992, people saw a positive shift, marked by the welcome first-time visit to China by the Japanese Emperor and Empress. However the relationship began to cool off after that, and in 1995 and 1996 fell into a state symbolised by a series of political frictions. The main reason for these frictions was the changing process of the general structure of the bilateral relationship in the post-Cold-War era.

1 The common basis of the strategic interests for China and Japan in defending themselves from the Soviet Union's threat had disappeared. Under the new East Asian regional security environment, China and Japan faced the

The background and trend of the partnership   105

need to re-define their strategic relationships. As the facts of recent years show, even now the two countries still have a long way to go to fulfil this process of redefinition.

2   In the early 1990s, the United States, which has become the only super-power, began to adjust its China policy away from friendship to confrontation, with China replacing the Soviet Union as the major ideological enemy and as a potential geo-political rival in the West Pacific zone. Such a policy change has exerted great impact on Japan's China policy in a negative way. This way of thinking, taking China as heterodox in ideology and social system, has increasingly influenced Japan's China policy.

3   In addition the great changes in the political and economic situations in both China and Japan in the 1990s have also accelerated the process of readjusting their bilateral relations. The recovery of the American economy, the long depression of the Japanese economy and the rising trend of the Chinese economy have changed the potential power balance, as well as the mentality of the three countries. Unlike the period of the early 1990s, Japan has to a large extent lost the confidence of being a major power. Japan began to rebuild its security system by strengthening both the Japan–US alliance and its own military capability on the assumption of the so-called potential China threat. This in turn has aroused great concern and a feeling of deep distrust in China.

4   Another influential factor was the change in Japan's political situation. The hard-liners toward China gained greater power in the post-Cold-War domestic political structure after the Social Democratic Party (*Shakaitō*) abandoned its progressive policy (*kakushin*), and the conservative (*hoshu*) tendency became the common direction of all the major political parties. Under such a domestic political situation, the hard-liners became more influential in Japan's policy-making towards China. They asked to change the model of the Japan–China relationship from a friendly relationship (*yūko kankei*) to a normal relationship (*futsū kankei*). On the most important and sensitive issues, history and Taiwan, the hard-liners gained power in the domestic political structure. All these tendencies in turn caused a reaction from the government of China and a readjustment of the Chinese–Japanese relationship.

5   By the change in generations, younger people of the post-WWII generation now occupy the main stream of political society both in China and Japan. The people of this generation are more assertive and nationalistic. Exchange channels between China and Japan have also been weakening with the fading out of the leaders of the older generation.

Pushed by the above-mentioned changes, the Chinese–Japanese relationship in the post-Cold-War era has been undergoing structural readjustments. Up to now this process can be roughly divided into the following stages.

The first stage covered the years from 1989 to around 1993. In this period, the so-called Soviet threat had disappeared. The United States, the only remaining superpower, began to readjust its China policy from a friendly one formulated in the 1970s and aimed at containing the Soviet Union, into a different one aimed at strengthening the pressure on China over the issues of human rights, trade and arms control, etc. These changes, especially the US policy transition, had exerted great influence on Japan's China policy. In this period China was in a relatively weak position economically as well as diplomatically while Japan was at the peak of its economic strength and political ambitions. The Japanese government had shown confidence at the G7 summit in 1989 by persuading the Western developed countries not to adopt a policy of isolating China. The well-received visit to China by the Emperor and Empress of Japan in 1992 marked a further improvement in bilateral relations. On the whole, the Chinese–Japanese relationship in this period can be taken to be on the same continuous track that was laid down in 1972.

During the second stage, from around 1994, the Chinese–Japanese relationship witnessed a series of new characteristics different from those of before, reflecting the accumulated influences of the changes that had taken place since 1989. Under the new conditions, political frictions frequently occurred between China and Japan. The following were the main issues causing these: the history problem, the Taiwan issue, the Japan–US security alliance, the Diaoyu (Senkaku) Islands dispute and the sanction on China by Japan by means of ODA. Throughout the whole process the issues concerning history and Taiwan were undoubtedly the most sensitive ones causing political friction between the two neighbouring countries. In this period the Chinese–Japanese relationship had become unstable and had fallen into a state of uncertainty, especially in the political and security realms.

The third stage began in 1997 as a reaction to the frequent frictions and setbacks of the Chinese–Japanese relationship during the previous period. The years of 1995 and 1996 were the worst in their bilateral relations since 1972, when the two countries normalised their relationship. Political frictions occurred frequently.

The continuous negative trend pushed the leaders as well as the people in the main stream of China and Japan to become aware of the necessity and urgency of improving relations with each other by taking certain positive actions.

At the time around 1996 and 1997, scholars in both China and Japan had been actively working on drafting possible blueprints for the Chinese–Japanese relationship in the years to come. They also exchanged views on future scenarios through various channels, such as interviews, bilateral symposiums, workshops and seminars. It was not difficult for an insider to discern the differences between Chinese and Japanese scholars in their attitudes to the future of the Chinese–Japanese relationship.

On the whole, Japanese scholars held more pessimistic views about the future, while Chinese views were relatively optimistic. Japanese scholars were more enthusiastic than their Chinese counterparts in making readjustments to the status quo and the basic framework of the Chinese–Japanese relationship formed in the 1970s. Japanese scholars seemed to hold an offensive position while the

The background and trend of the partnership 107

Chinese were being relatively defensive. Scholars of both sides showed changes in their approaches, from emotional ones to relatively rational ones, which were based on national interests and reality and the possible trend of the future Chinese–Japanese relationship.

In short, the China–Japan partnership was a result of the readjustment process of their bilateral relations. It was also an outcome of the mixed influences produced by various internal and external factors around the two countries in the 1990s.

Of course the final and decisive factor for reaching the agreement of a partnership lies in the governments of China and Japan, especially in the strong initiative of their top leaders. In a sense the partnership was a consequence of the 'diplomacy of leaders'.

The structure of the China–Japan partnership

The process toward the joint declaration of the partnership was a relatively long and tortuous one. It was influenced not only by bilateral factors but also by multilateral factors symbolised by various kinds of partnerships in the world, especially among big Asia–Pacific powers in the first half of the 1990s.

We all know that numerous kinds of bilateral 'partnerships' have been declared as the new frameworks for bilateral relations in the post-Cold-War world. One of the most important reasons for this phenomenon is the termination of the Cold War. In the totally new international environment, countries have felt an increasing necessity for building some kind of new framework for their bilateral foreign relations, different from the one that existed in the Cold War period and adaptable to the new trend of the world.[2] No matter how different these partnerships are, certain identical common features can be observed in various kinds of partnerships:

1   All of the partnerships seek to build a new model for bilateral relations different from that of the alliances that existed in the Eastern bloc and still exist in the West. Partnership is a kind of bilateral relationship looser in structure and lower in mutual goals than an alliance. Most of the partnerships declared in the post-Cold-War era belong to this category.
2   Building a partnership implies preventing confrontation and realising peaceful coexistence and cooperation between two countries. The partnership between Russia and America is the typical example of this.
3   A partnership means two countries build their relations on the basis of equal positions. A good example of this is the partnership Japan and America declared in the late 1980s and early 1990s.
4   The key function of the partnerships is peaceful coexistence and equal cooperation, unlike military allies whose aim is to resist a third party explicitly or implicitly.

Under the post-Cold-War international circumstances, during the middle of the 1990s, China and Japan had increasingly sensed the necessity and urgency for building some kind of partnership between themselves. Through 1995 and 1996, the policy-makers in China and Japan gradually became aware of the reality of the ongoing structural change in their bilateral relations. In addition, they also realised that a worsening of bilateral relations would be harmful for both of them, and it was deemed necessary to take decisive measures to improve them. On the other hand, it became clear that the Chinese–Japanese relationship could not simply go back to the position of the 1970s or 1980s.

Besides these considerations, the popularity of partnerships among other big Asia–Pacific powers in the first half of 1990 was a strong incentive for China and Japan to reach an agreement to build a partnership.

After preparations at various levels, especially the visit to China by Japanese Prime Minister Hashimoto Ryutaro in September, and the visit to Japan by Chinese Premier Li Peng in November 1997, President Jiang Zemin made a visit to Japan in late November 1998. It was on this occasion that China and Japan published the joint declaration on building a Partnership of Friendship and Cooperation for Peace and Development.

It can be said that the most important results of Jiang's visit to Japan included two aspects. One was the achievement of ending the structural political frictions which occurred in 1995 and 1996 and recovering a relatively stable state in Chinese–Japanese relations. The other was the achievement of the medium-term goal by determining the direction and a new bilateral framework for the Chinese–Japanese relationship in at least the first decade of the twenty-first century.

Although the China–Japan partnership has many common characteristics with other partnerships between many other countries, it also has its own typical features, basically reflected in the wording 'for Peace and Development' and 'Friendship and Cooperation'. The former has the function of being a precondition and orientation for the latter, and the latter are the means for realising the former.

During the two decades after 1972, the characteristics of 'peace' and 'friendship' had been the main stream in the development of Chinese–Japanese relations. In comparison the nature of 'development' and 'cooperation' were not in the main stream. Such bilateral relations reflected the reality of unbalanced political power and economic capability between China and Japan.

Throughout the 1990s, Japan's trend towards becoming a great political power and China's towards becoming a great economic power have been progressing simultaneously. These tendencies are laying a more solid foundation for a balanced Chinese–Japanese partnership. Of course it is true that a change in the balance of power often causes uncertainty and a readjustment of bilateral relations until a new stable structure is built. Therefore one should not neglect the possibility of new frictions originating from the actual or potential changes in the balance of power. It is the impact of these changes that will be the most important and delicate factor to be dealt with in the process of building the partnership between China and Japan.

The fact that China and Japan have reached an agreement for building a

The background and trend of the partnership 109

partnership is an important breakthrough for them in the process of readjusting bilateral relations. On the other hand, one has to remember that at present the partnership has not yet been realised, and is still merely a declaration and an ideal goal that is to be realised by joint efforts in the coming years. For China and Japan, the partnership will not be a natural process or an inevitable result. Both of them really have a long way to go. For them, it will be a challenging task.

Till now, before and after the joint declaration was published, many people have expressed their doubts about the necessity of using the word 'partnership' for defining the Chinese–Japanese relationship and even felt suspicious about the possibility and capability of building the partnership. Some Japanese scholars maintained that it was sufficient to use the words 'peace and friendship' to define the future framework of Japan–China relations.[3] Others considered it strange that Japan and China did not have any framework for partnership while among all the other big powers such relations already existed.[4] Someone even pointed out that China had been employing 'squeezing out' tactics by building partnerships with all the other big powers except Japan.[5] Within Japanese academic circle a debate on the issue of whether it was necessary to use the adjective 'strategic' as the defining word for the Japan–China partnership occurred. Most of the leaders of Japanese opinion felt the word 'strategic' was unacceptable. They regarded the term 'strategic partnership' mainly in the context of military allies. Therefore they were reluctant to adopt this word for Japan–China relations, fearing that it could cause conflict with the Japan–US military alliance.[6]

Whether or not to publish a joint declaration as the third document between China and Japan after the China–Japan Joint Statement in 1972 and the China–Japan Peace and Friendship Treaty in 1978 was another important issue. At first Japan suggested publishing an 'Action Plan' instead of a joint declaration. It was perhaps the idea of the Japanese government that the principles on the history and Taiwan issues had already been settled in the two documents in the 1970s, so what was necessary now was for the two countries to draft concrete measures for action. After consultations, the governments of China and Japan came to a consensus on the importance of formulating a third document for their bilateral relationship.

The governments succeeded in reaching the agreements of building a partnership. At this stage, little can be said with confidence about the future development of the partnership. Yet one thing is quite obvious: the agreed goal of a partnership reflected the most realistic and positive approach for both sides. It was the best result that could be expected in 1998. Generally speaking, it was a success and had advantages for both sides.

As the joint declaration and other documents show, the China–Japan partnership contains many facets which make up a whole bilateral structure on the following three levels:

- The first level is a general definition of the China–Japan partnership, namely the basic bilateral framework for future China–Japan relations defined as 'Partnership of Friendship and Cooperation for Peace and Development'.

110   *Jin Xide*

- The second level refers to the definition of the general range for bilateral cooperation between them including a series of principles and ideas on bilateral and multilateral issues basically accepted by both China and Japan.
- The third level contains thirty-three concrete cooperative projects fully reflecting the range and capacity of the two countries to cooperate with each other in this and coming years. These projects were declared in the 'China–Japan Joint Press Announcement'.

It would be appropriate here to make a few comments on some issues and events relating to President Jiang's visit to Japan in late 1998. Unlike the positive evaluation of both Chinese and Japanese governments, some people in both China and Japan regarded the visit as a failure in dealing with the history problem. Their appraisals had the same negative manner, while being completely opposite in approach. It has to be said that their observations were weak on two points. Firstly, they ignored the reality of serious structural frictions on the history issue in the middle of the 1990s, so that they tended to see the friction in Jiang's visit as the leaders' mistakes. Secondly, they concentrated so much on the history issue that they could barely accept the fact that the visit had succeeded on several levels. Another influential factor was the mass media. Some news reports orientated public opinion in a negative direction. In particular, some mistakes in the news reports produced very negative results.[7] Besides these issues, Japan's refusal to include the word 'apology' (*owabi* in Japanese and *daoqian* in Chinese) into the joint declaration, while the same word was included in the Japan–South Korean joint declaration, made the history issue much more sensitive.

Furthermore, President Clinton's visit to China in June 1998 also influenced Jiang's visit in a very complicated manner. Clinton's failure to stop in Japan on the way to China, and his remarks containing the 'three Noes' on American Taiwan policy, aroused opposition in a number of Japanese people. In addition, the Taiwan side also strengthened its lobbying on Japanese politicians and opinion leaders during this period. These factors pushed the government of Japan to harden its attitude toward the Taiwan issue. As a result, some friction occurred between the governments of China and Japan on the issue of whether the Japanese side should express the 'Three Noes' like President Clinton on the occasion of Jiang's visit.

In spite of the numerous obstacles and people's negative impressions, the visit was an important turning point, when the Chinese–Japanese relationship entered a new phase of realising a new bilateral framework with the partnership at the core.

The future trend of the China–Japan partnership

Generally speaking, the direction, content and degree of bilateral and multilateral cooperation have already been determined in the declared framework of the partnership. Specifically speaking, however, the process towards the realisation of such a partnership will face both opportunities and challenges. In

The background and trend of the partnership 111

the coming years, development of the China–Japan partnership will be continuously under the influence of multilateral factors as well as bilateral factors.

First of all, the triangular relationship between China, Japan and the United States will continue to be the most influential factor which can exert great influence, both positive and negative, on the process of building a partnership. It will be crucial for China and Japan to get rid of, or at least minimise, any negative impact of the Japan–US military alliance and to keep Chinese–US relations stable. Secondly, the readjustment of the relations between China, the US, Japan and Russia will have an impact on the China–Japan partnership. Meanwhile the development of regional multilateral economic and security cooperation will gradually play a greater role in influencing the bilateral partnership.

In the foreseeable future, the security dilemma originated by the so-called 'China threat' and the 'US–Japan alliance threat' will continue to be the major obstacle for China and Japan in building mutual confidence and trust. They will have to do their utmost to find a way to overcome these obstacles. It would be desirable if China and Japan could build a more harmonious triangular relationship with the US and at the same time push forward multilateral security cooperation in the East Asian region. As the precondition for this, a gradual increase in bilateral security dialogue and military exchanges will be the natural development for China–Japan relations.

In the coming years, one of the top issues for China and Japan is to adapt themselves to the changes in the balance of power between them, as well as to each other's style of diplomacy. The two countries will have to learn to accept the reality of the other side's becoming a greater power in the international structure, to acknowledge the other side's interests, and to cooperate in bilateral as well as multilateral issues on a broader range of issues.

In the economic field, Japan's superiority over China in capital and technology is not likely to change in the near future. China and Japan have complementary economic structures. Cooperation with gains for both sides will be the main feature in this area. Pushed by various factors, China and Japan will inevitably consult more and more on regional economic cooperation, such as an East Asian monetary system and a Northeast Asian economic zone, etc.

Under the above circumstances, the future development of the China–Japan partnership will presumably show the following trends. First of all, the framework of the 'Partnership of Friendship and Cooperation for Peace and Development' will be relatively stable because both China and Japan have vested interests in realising such a partnership. Secondly, the principles and ideas for bilateral and multilateral cooperation set forth at the joint declaration will be defined in more concrete terms, and practised in the process of interaction as well as patient cooperation between China and Japan.

People may easily see the differences between China and Japan in their understanding and interpretation of some of the principles and ideas of the joint declaration, even though they were included as a result of intense negotiations and bargaining by the two governments. For example, it is well known that big differences exist between the two countries in their general view of the new

112   *Jin Xide*

international order, the non-intervention principle, and the direction of UN reform, etc. Can we optimistically foresee that China and Japan will successfully lessen their differences on the interpretation of these principles and ideas? It has to be pointed out that there exists a large imbalance between economic and security aspects. In the former there is basically a common interest and structure from which both will gain; however, less so in the latter, so far.

Another difference between China and Japan lies in how to treat bilateral and multilateral cooperation. In the economic field the two countries can relatively easily reach consensus, but in the security area they have little experience of cooperation in international affairs up to now. As for the thirty-three cooperation projects, it can be foreseen that these will be implemented relatively smoothly. The following tendencies have been shown in carrying out these projects:

1   High-level exchanges between the leaders of China and Japan have entered a new stage of regular and close mutual intercourse and will hopefully be further deepened and matured in the coming period.
2   The China–Japan dialogue on security issues started early in the 1990s is now in a stage of readjustment.[8] Its further development will be continuously influenced by factors such as the direction of the Japan–US alliance, China–US relations and the Taiwan issue, etc.
3   As for the issue of disposing of the chemical weapons abandoned by former Japanese troops more than fifty years ago, the confirmed number is now approximately 700,000, and the government of Japan has reportedly formed an organ to deal with the issue and allocated an appropriated budget for it.[9]
4   The new China–Japan Fishery Agreement signed in 1997 had not come into effect by 1998,[10] although negotiations were progressing.[11] By the end of February 2000, the two countries completed ministerial consultations, which had lasted for more than two years.
5   Economic cooperation is and will continue to be the most developed and hopeful area for the two countries. Since 1997, the development of bilateral economic exchanges has tended to slow down.[12] Economic exchange will hopefully increase again in the near future.
6   Recently, cooperation on environmental protection has become one of the most important issues between China and Japan. From now on cooperation in this realm, especially supported by Japan's ODA, will hopefully be further developed.[13] The proportion of cooperation at the private company level in this field will also gradually increase.
7   Following the establishment of the bilateral framework of the partnership, cultural exchanges between the two countries will be pushed forward more actively by both governments in terms of quantity as well as quality. In particular the exchanges between the two countries' younger generation and scholars will hopefully develop further in the future.
8   From the aspect of international economic cooperation, the two governments have reached an agreement on the joint construction of a Eurasia Bridge, a railway connecting Asia and Europe.[14] The two countries have

The background and trend of the partnership   113

also finished negotiations on the issue of China becoming a member of the WTO. In addition, the two governments have held a meeting on the regional economy for the first time, a positive sign of strengthening cooperation on multilateral regional economic issues.

9   So far, cooperation in the area of regional security, international affairs and the issues concerning the UN, etc., has been the weak link. It is necessary for the two countries to push forward their cooperation in these areas more actively, but still cautiously, and with greater patience. Comparatively speaking, faster development could be expected on mutual cooperation in areas such as cracking down on international criminals.

Anyway, for China and Japan, the following will be the two basic preconditions for maintaining and pushing forward the process of building their partnership: (1) their common interest, and (2) a mutual friendly feeling. To a large extent, the future possibility for realising the partnership will depend on whether or not the people of the two countries can continue to build on these two preconditions.

Notes

1   Professor Tanaka Akihiko is one of the few persons who had foreseen the readjustment trend in Japan–China relations early in 1991. See Tanaka Akihiko, *Nicchū Kankei 1945–1990*, Tokyo, Tokyo University Press, 1991, p. 187.

2   Actually Koji Kakizawa, then Deputy Foreign Minister of Japan, suggested establishing a partnership between Japan and China early in 1992. See *Chuo Koron*, December 1992.

3   See *Asahi Shimbun*, 23 July 1998.

4   *Gaikō Forum*, November 1998.

5   *Sentaku*, August 1998.

6   See *Sekai Shūhō*, 24 November 1998.

7   The most typical examples include the following. Some newspapers in Japan wrongly reported President Jiang's clothes (*Jimminfuku* which means 'people's clothes' a word with negative connotations: the real name in Chinese for the clothes is *Zhongshanzhuang*, worn by China's leaders at the formal occasions), as being an expression of protest to Japan. Also some newspapers wrongly reported that the joint declaration had not been signed because of objections from the Chinese side.

8   Jijisha, 29 June 1999.

9   *Mainichi Shimbun*, 29 July 1998 and *Yomiuri Shimbun*, 25 August 1999. The government of Japan established the Office for Abandoned Chemical Weapons within the Prime Minister's Office on 1 April 1999. The governments of China and Japan signed the Memorandum of Understanding on the Destruction of Abandoned Chemical Weapons in China in Beijing on 30 July 1999. Also the government of Japan has appropriated 2826 million yen on the governmental draft of the FY2000 budget, following an appropriation of 809 million yen on the supplementary budget of FY1999.

10   *Sekai Keizai Hyōron*, October 1999.

11   *Asahi Shimbun*, 9 July 1999 and *Yomiuri Shimbun*, 25 August 1999.

12   *Chūbun Dōhō*, August 1999.

13   For Japan's ODA to China, see Jin Xide, *Riben Duihua ODA de Chengxiao Jiqi Zhuanzhe*, Ribenxuekan, Institute of Japanese Studies, CASS, no. 5, 1999.

14   *Nihon Keizai Shimbun*, 26 November 1998.

7 The role of ODA in the relationship

Marie Söderberg

Japan has advanced from being an aid recipient after WWII, to being the largest donor of foreign aid in the world. In fact, around one-fifth of all the Official Development Assistance (ODA)[1] from the industrialised countries today comes from Japan. As the world's second largest economy, Japan believes it has a responsibility to contribute to sustainable social and economic development in the world and hopes that such a contribution will win Japan the confidence and appreciation of the international community and ensure its own stability and prosperity.

For some years now China has been one of the main recipients of foreign aid. The largest contributor of all, in a class of its own, is Japan. Much of the Japanese aid to China has been in the form of financial support for economic infrastructure (such as roads, railways, ports, etc.). In the early days of Japanese aid to China, Japan maintained a policy of separating politics from economics (*seikei bunrei*), with recipients presenting projects that they requested aid for, but recently Japan has begun to attach a number of conditions to its aid. Now Japan formulates 'country assistance programmes' for all of its main recipients.

This change in ODA policy has made Japan's already complex relationship with China even more complicated. Japan's attempts to guide China on its path of development and using the freezing of aid as a tool to protest against certain Chinese actions, such as nuclear testing, has in fact turned ODA into another 'issue' between the two countries. A prolonged debate and difficulties in the formulation of a country assistance programme for China have revealed the depth of distrust and dissatisfaction that exist in their relationship. A recent Japanese report[2] suggests drastic changes in ODA policy towards China, turning aid from economic infrastructure towards 'soft' issues such as poverty alleviation and environmental clean-up. Considering Japan's own stagnant economy during the 1990s and the severe fiscal deficit, a general cut in ODA spending has also been announced,[3] although Japan will still be one of the major donors, if not the main donor. This cut is likely to be more severe towards China than towards most other countries.

Japan's ODA policy is, like that of most other donor countries, in a process of constant change. A considerable amount of research has been done about the different aspects of the policy-making process of Japanese ODA, such as the role of bureaucrats,[4] politicians,[5] the business community,[6] and external influences.[7] Others have looked at the rationale behind aid from strategic[8] as well as economic[9] viewpoints. Many researchers have evaluated Japanese aid, some concluding that it is 'bad'[10] and should be rejected and others concluding that it is 'good'[11] and should serve as a model for others to follow. Much of the literature on ODA is from a donor perspective but, as shown by me together with a group of other researchers,[12] aid is indeed a two-way process, especially at the implementation level, and has to be seen from both the donor's and the recipient's perspective.

China has its own way of treating aid, which differs from that of other countries. It also has its own way of treating aid from Japan. The debate around ODA has revealed a number of feelings and expectations that exist in the relationship between the two countries. The purpose of this chapter is twofold:

1   to analyse the policy changes suggested in aid for China and what will happen at the implementation stage;
2   to evaluate the future role of ODA in the Chinese–Japanese relationship.

To give a background for this analysis we will start with a short review of the history of Japanese ODA policy and the characteristics of Japanese aid. Next, the development and the characteristics of China as a recipient will be described. The Japanese–Chinese ODA relationship from past to present will be covered, and the present restructuring going on in Japanese aid policy to China will be analysed at the policy as well as the implementation level. Finally, the role of aid in the future relationship between Japan and China will be commented on.

The characteristics of Japanese aid

In 1994, Japan celebrated, according to the Foreign Ministry, the fortieth anniversary of its ODA programme.[13] But since the term ODA (see note 1) was first used by the OECD in 1969, one has to assume that Japan meant the fortieth anniversary of its foreign aid programme, or rather its programme of economic cooperation (*keizai kyō ryoku*), a terminology most commonly used in Japan. Economic cooperation is a wider concept, consisting of three parts, which besides aid (ODA) includes other official flows (OOF[14]) and private direct investment. It is within this framework that Japanese aid is firmly placed.

Japan's contribution of US$50,000 to the Colombo Plan in 1954, together with the war reparations agreements with Burma in 1954, the Philippines in 1956 and Indonesia in 1958, are seen as the origin of Japan's aid programme. The war reparations were given to build up what had been damaged during WWII. It was tied to procurement from Japanese companies, and in that way it also served the purpose of promoting exports from Japan. In 1957, the yen loans from the Export-Import Bank started. They went mainly to Asia, and besides filling certain needs in developing countries they also served the purpose of establishing Japanese industry in the area. Aid in the 1960s was almost exclusively directed

116 *Marie Söderberg*

towards Asia and overwhelmingly served Japan's commercial purposes. This pattern changed with the oil crisis of 1973 when a huge aid package began for the Arab world to secure the supply of oil. As a consequence of this crisis, a stable supply of natural resources became another ingredient of Japanese aid policy.

Trade was a prerequisite to obtaining resources, and Japan recognised its interdependence with developing countries and a certain amount of infrastructure was needed to conduct such trade. This is one of the reasons for the huge amount of aid money being spent on infrastructure development in Asia. It was seen as a necessary cost of achieving a secure and peaceful world, as well as Japan's own economic development. Humanitarian considerations, as a reason for aid, did not appear with any weight until the late 1970s.

In 1977, the first of a number of aid doubling plans was announced. The wish to be respected in the international community was another motive for these plans, which eventually turned Japan into a leading donor. It was also a way of improving Japan's image in Asia where Japanese businessmen had left far from favourable impressions of their country. This was the start of the gift-giving diplomacy (*omiage gaikō*), which Japanese Prime Ministers touring Asia have extensively used.

Since 1989, Japan has been the world's biggest donor of ODA in absolute terms. However, in terms of percentage of GNP the figures are much less impressive. Japanese ODA in 1998 was 0.28 per cent of GNP,[15] which was below average among DAC countries. Still it was a considerable increase compared with 1996 when it was only 0.20 per cent of GNP, one of the lowest figures among DAC countries. When it comes to the quality of aid (as measured in purely economic terms, by grant share and grant element), Japan has performed very poorly. This clearly demonstrates one of the peculiarities of Japanese aid: it is to a large extent based on loans and the recipients are expected to repay them although the loans come with a long grace period and a low interest rate.

A significant difference between Japanese loan aid and that distributed by others (mostly multilateral organisations) is its limited staff numbers. The OECF, the organisation distributing Japanese ODA loans in the 1990s, used to have a staff of around 300 people. The World Bank with loans slightly more than double those of the OECF, has a staff of around 6000.[16]

Another characteristic of Japanese aid is its heavy emphasis on Asia. In 1998, 62.4 per cent of all bilateral aid went to Asia. Asian countries receive the main part of their aid in the form of loans, receiving a total of 91.5 per cent of all the loan aid. The number 1 recipient on a cumulative basis is Indonesia. China has a much shorter history of receiving aid but is quickly catching up and was the largest recipient during much of the 1990s.

A comparison of the content of Japanese ODA with that of other countries clearly shows an emphasis on economic infrastructure development (39 per cent of the total). Within the category of economic infrastructure, transport receives the largest amount of ODA. A total of 23.5 per cent of Japanese ODA is in this sector.

In the 1990s, Japanese ODA, at least verbally, became more politicised and

The role of ODA in the relationship   117

more environmentally conscious. The 'ODA Charter', which was adopted in 1992, called for the consideration of the following principles in aid implementation:

1   Environmental conservation and development should be pursued in tandem.
2   Any use of ODA for military purposes or for aggravation of international conflicts should be avoided.
3   Full attention should be given to trends in recipient countries' military expenditure, their development and production of weapons of mass destruction and missiles, and their export and import of arms.
4   Full attention should be given to efforts for promoting democratisation and the introduction of a market-oriented economy, and to the situation regarding the securing of basic human rights and freedoms in the recipient country.

These principles were well in line with the policy of other major donors at the time. That Indonesia and China have remained the main recipients of Japanese ODA after the adoption of this charter makes it very clear that it is not the performance in these areas that is decisive in Japan's decision to extend aid or not. It is the trends in these areas that the Japanese authorities claim they are watching. The validity of the first principle as such can be questioned, as Japanese ODA has a strong emphasis on economic infrastructure development and such projects usually imply a certain amount of environmental destruction. The third principle has been applied, to a certain extent, in connection with Chinese nuclear tests, which led to a temporary halt of a minor part of the aid flow (see below).

In its latest five-year medium-term policy document on ODA, announced in August 1999, the future approach and priority issues are outlined. Japan will emphasise the DAC's 'Development Partnership Strategy' in which the improvement of the living standards of all humankind is the main objective of development cooperation. A number of specific goals for social development are also formulated. They include a reduction by one-half in the proportion of people living in extreme poverty, provision of universal primary education, and the elimination of gender disparity in education. The key to realising these goals lies in self-help efforts, as developing countries work towards economic take-off. The importance of improving the environment for private-sector activities and inflow of private funds is emphasised, as are increased opportunities for Japanese business to participate in ODA projects, as well as further coordination between the different forms of economic cooperation (that is, ODA, OOF and private investment).

According to the new policy document, special 'country assistance programmes' are to be formulated for major recipients. This is to be done through the coordination of the pertinent ministries and government agencies. The programmes will specify the significance of the assistance provided by Japan, its

118   *Marie Söderberg*

basic objectives, the priority issues and fields and the forms of assistance to be deployed. These programmes will take into account coordination with other donors as well as the private sector.

This is a considerable change from the earlier policy of approving ODA on a request basis. It will further strengthen the Japanese influence on how its aid money will be used and therefore it might not be so popular among the recipients. It also implies that there will be stronger cooperation between the two implementing agencies: JICA (which deals with the grant aid and technical assistance) and the newly formed JBIC[17] (which is in charge of the loan aid as well as OOF).

The characteristics of China as a recipient

Being the 'Middle Kingdom' with a long cultural tradition and the largest population in the world has led to the way the Chinese view the world and their own role. From the communist takeover in 1949 until the end of 1978, the People's Republic of China followed a policy of 'self-reliance'. Under this policy all foreign borrowings and acceptance of outside assistance were denounced as humiliation of the country and in most cases rejected.[18]

It was only after China declared its economic reform and open-door policy in 1978 that multilateral organisations and various OECD countries began to give aid in 1979. The amount of aid steadily increased but with the military crackdown on the pro-democratic demonstrations on Tiananmen Square in June 1989, economic sanctions were introduced and foreign aid was temporarily stopped.

This served as a reminder to the Chinese that there are two sides to every coin. With the benefits that aid had brought there was also the possibility of foreign influence and that such aid could be withdrawn if other countries did not like what China was doing. There was also the problem of accumulating international debt. The Chinese debt problem grew after June 1989, when private capital was withdrawn due to political uncertainties.

Economic sanctions and withdrawal of foreign aid in 1989, however, gave new impetus to the policy of 'self-reliance' or, at least, showed the importance of not being too reliant on others. To keep control is an important component of Chinese policy and one that they are implementing in the field of their own development. Although they accept aid from abroad the Chinese government have made it clear that they do not want any external agent to coordinate or control aid to China. As a result they have decided not to join the World Bank's consultative group or the UNDP (United Nations Development Programme) donor round-table discussions.

The Chinese government, wanting to keep control, have also made all types of coordination between bilateral donors almost impossible by constructing an administrative process of aid reception that effectively prevents coordination. Different Chinese ministries, departments, or divisions within them handle contacts with and aid from different donor countries. All these bodies tend to have their own interpretation of national development policy. This makes any form of cooperation extremely difficult. Each donor also has to deal with several counterparts depending on the type of aid extended. China has one system for receiving grant aid and technical assistance, and another for loan aid. The State Science and Technology Commission handles all grant aid and technical assistance while the State Planning Commission handles loan aid. They are the ones who decide the total amount of money that China is allowed to borrow from abroad. To be able to receive external financing for any project the ministry responsible or the provincial planning committees must first apply for permission from the State Planning Commission.

The State Planning Commission has some idea of the level of funding that can be expected from different sources and compiles a list of projects that it considers should be financed with foreign loans. It also decides which source of finance would be suitable for which project and what proportion of that project that should be covered by foreign sources. The list of projects is then submitted to the State Council for its approval.

After this the State Planning Commission gets back to the different Chinese ministries, departments and divisions, which are the opposite numbers of the foreign donors. In the case of Japanese loan aid the matter is handled by the Foreign Financing Administration, Division 1 of the Finance Department at the Ministry of Finance. Together with the State Planning Commission they start consultations with Japanese government officials and an Exchange of Note between the two governments is then signed.

As the implementing agency of Japanese loan aid the Chinese Ministry of Finance signs all loan agreements on behalf of other Chinese provincial entities or ministries, such as the Ministry of Railways or the Ministry of Communications. These bodies in turn have special departments dealing with Japanese loan aid and they are in frequent contact with Japanese officials from JBIC. Formally it is the Chinese central government which is responsible for guaranteeing the repayment of ODA loans but in practice they make the end users (often provincial governments) bear the responsibility.

Usually the proportion of the cost of a project to be covered from abroad is not more than 50 per cent. That means the Chinese are still in control of each and every project. From the Japanese side there have been complaints that this makes their aid invisible. No project is their own, although they partially participate in the various projects.

Figures from the OECD[19] show that the People's Republic of China was the single largest recipient country of ODA in 1998. It received 2.4 billion US dollars, 6.7 per cent of all ODA. Although it is a huge sum it amounted to only 0.2 per cent of Chinese GNP, which is quite low.

The Japanese–Chinese ODA relationship from past to present

War reparation from Japan was never paid to the People's Republic of China although they suffered under Japanese aggression. After WWII both the People's Republic of China and Taiwan renounced reparations. The Japanese Peace

120   *Marie Söderberg*

Treaty was not signed by the People's Republic of China in 1951 and a year later Japan, an ally of the United States, signed a treaty with Taiwan. From the inception of its aid programme, Japan extended assistance to Taiwan. This continued until the initiation of Japan's diplomatic relations with the People's Republic of China in 1972.

An ODA programme to the People's Republic of China commenced after the declaration of an open-door policy and Prime Minister Ohira Masayoshi's visit to China in 1979. Since that time ODA has grown enormously. Between 1982 and 1986, China was the single largest recipient of ODA from Japan. The incident at Tiananmen Square in 1989 led to a temporary cessation of ODA, but aid was soon resumed, Japan being the first nation to restore friendly relations with China.[20] In August 1989 it lifted the freeze on ongoing projects and in October that year the World Bank resumed its lending to China for humanitarian aid. After that, Japan extended grant aid and in July 1990 it announced that all aid would gradually be resumed. Soon after that other industrialised countries followed one after another. Since then China has remained as one of the major, if not the top, recipient of Japanese aid.

On a bilateral level Japan has been the largest contributor of ODA to China. It has usually contributed twice as much as the second donor and often more than the largest multilateral donor, IDA of the World Bank (see Tables 7.1 and 7.2).

The largest part of the aid is given in the form of loans. This has made up 75 per cent of the total aid (see Table 7.3). The loans have been announced in the form of four packages of five years each,[21] matching the Chinese five-year plans. In fact, Japanese loan aid has been provided only to projects included in China's own plans. This is a wide deviation from Japan's regular budgetary procedures of annual commitments. This is special treatment that has been extended only to China.

The five-year packages have all been orally announced by Japanese Prime Ministers to Chinese leaders on different occasions. This can be seen as a proof of the political importance of ODA loans to China. Such matters are not delegated to the bureaucracy to handle but are presented by Japanese Prime Ministers in connection with meetings where other matters are also discussed.

The first two packages of ODA loans (1979–84: 331 billion yen and 1984–9: 540 billion yen) were characterised by the fact that financing for transportation infrastructure projects, particularly for coal transportation was emphasised. In

Table 7.1 Bilateral ODA donors to China by size (disbursement in millions of US$)

Year	1	2	3	4	5
95	Japan (1380)	Germany (684)	France (91)	Austria (66)	Spain (56)
96	Japan (861)	Germany (461)	France (97)	Britain (57)	Canada (38)
97	Japan (576)	Germany (381)	France (50)	Britain (46)	Australia (36)
98	Japan (1158)	Germany (321)	Britain (55)	Canada (52)	France (30)

Source: *Waga Kuni no Seifu Kaihatsu Enjo*, Gekkan, 2000, p. 80.

The role of ODA in the relationship   121

Table 7.2 Multilateral ODA to China by size (disbursement in millions of US$)

Year	1	2	3	4	5
95	IDA (798)	UNDP (38)	CEC (33)	WFP (21)	UNICEF (20)
96	IDA (790)	CEC (35)	UNDP (29)	WFP (22)	UNICEF (18)
97	IDA (687)	UNDP (43)	WFP (38)	IFAD (26)	UNICEF (21)
98	IDA (554)	CEC (22)	UNICEF (18)	UNDP (14)	IFAD (13)

Source: *Waga Kuni no Seifu Kaihatsu Enjo*, Gekkan, 2000, p. 81.

Note: CEC, Commission of European Communities; IFAD, International Fund for Agriculture Development; UNICEF, United Nations Children's Fund; WFP, World Food Program.

Table 7.3 Japanese ODA to China (disbursement in millions of US$)

Year	Grant aid	Technical assistance	Loan aid	Total
94	99.42 (7)	246.91 (17)	1133.08 (77)	1479.41 (100)
95	83.12 (6)	304.75 (22)	992.28 (72)	1380.15 (100)
96	24.99 (3)	303.73 (35)	533.01 (62)	861.73 (100)
97	15.42 (3)	251.77 (44)	309.66 (54)	576.86 (100)
98	38.22 (3)	301.62 (26)	818.33 (71)	1158.16 (100)
99	65.68 (5)	348.79 (28)	811.50 (66)	1225.97 (100)
Accumulated	821.88 (6)	2944.91 (20)	10711.98 (74)	14478.69 (100)

Source: *Waga Kuni no Seifu Kaihatsu Enjo*, Gekkan, 2000, p. 80.

the third package (1990–5: 810 billion yen) the scope was somewhat broader, as was the number of projects. In addition to transportation projects there were water supply and sanitation projects, gas supply projects, communication projects to link together several cities, fertiliser plant projects and infrastructure projects in economic development zones.

The concession by the Japanese to accommodate the Chinese five-year plans has a number of practical implications. One is that the amount of aid for specific projects is based on rough estimates and is, therefore, imprecise. Another one is that the amount of aid has been decided in advance, irrespective of the total amount of Japanese ODA, as this is decided on a yearly basis. The five-year commitment also means that it has been difficult to make major changes during this period even if the priorities of Japanese ODA policy change.

When the Japanese ODA Charter was adopted in 1992 it could not be applied to the content of the third yen loan package as this had already been approved. That is one of the reasons why the Japanese side has now decided to abandon the five-year package system and provide Japanese ODA on a yearly basis from 2001.

The Chinese nuclear testing in 1995, which was in direct violation of article 3 of the ODA Charter, led to a temporary freeze of Japanese grant aid. This was partly due to strong public opinion in Japan against the testing. As grants are only around 6 per cent of the total aid, it did not affect the amount of aid to China in any major way. The freeze was ended when the testing was over in 1997. The withholding of aid while China was making nuclear tests created a lot of ill will in China. The Chinese saw this as a major change from the days when aid was given partly for geo-political reasons, such as a strong Japanese interest in Chinese natural resources and its market, and partly as a compensation for the war reparations that were never paid.[22] It was also a deviation from the old Japanese policy of trying to separate politics from economics. Looking at ODA strictly from an economic cooperation point of view there would have been no necessity to freeze aid, but the aid was frozen because certain conditions had been attached to the aid and there was a strong opinion in Japan that it should take some action against China.

Similar actions have not been taken on other occasions, although there have been some instances that could be seen as violations of basic human rights, as stipulated in principle 4 of the ODA Charter. For example, the treatment of dissidents and the detention of members of the religious Falun Gong group can be regarded as violations of principle 4 of the charter, which concerns the situation regarding the securing of basic human rights, but there has been no strong Japanese public opinion pushing the government to take action against China in this field.

In a Japanese climate where foreign aid, and especially that directed towards China, is being questioned for a number of reasons (see below), there have been attempts to use ODA to put pressure behind Japanese demands in other areas. The most recent example is the special yen loans for the Beijing Urban Railway Construction Project and the Xi'an Xianyang International Airport Terminal Expansion Project (17.2 billion yen). Agreement was supposed to be reached in the summer of 2000, but although there was no formal freeze, procedure was slowed down due to opposition raised in the ruling Liberal Democratic Party's foreign affairs committee. The main reason for the opposition was that these were strictly economic infrastructure projects, which were no longer a priority area for Japanese ODA. However, there were also opposing voices due to the increase of Chinese naval activities in Japan's exclusive economic zone, which were perceived as a military threat.[23] Foreign Minister Kono Yohei brought up this issue during his visit to China in August and at that time the two countries agreed to set up a formal notification mechanism for naval vessels entering their respective exclusive economic zones. On 7 September the foreign affairs panel members approved the loans, and final signing took place in Beijing on 10 October 2000, just before Chinese Prime Minister Zhu Rongji's visit to Japan.

This new tendency of using aid as a leverage in the discussion of other issues is likely to lead to friction in the future. During his visit the Chinese Prime Minister warned Japan against using ODA to China as a diplomatic card.[24] In China, such actions are seen as an attempt to intervene in their domestic affairs.

The present situation and suggested policy changes

The fourth yen loan package (1996–2000: 580 billion yen for the first three years and 390 billion for the following two), in addition to the economic infrastructure

The role of ODA in the relationship   123

undertaken so far, emphasised the environment and regional development of the inland areas.

Environmental preservation, put forward as a priority area for Japanese ODA in general, received a share of 16 per cent of the yen loans. Rapid Chinese economic development has led to considerable environmental problems, and to abate air pollution Japan launched the Environmental Development Model Cities Concept. Three cities were chosen (Guiyang, Chongqing and Dalian) and a number of measures to improve the environment are being undertaken there.

In the agriculture field, ODA loans are supporting, among other things, the Zipingpu Dam construction in Sichuan province that is to deal with water shortages and the Yellow River Delta Comprehensive Agricultural Development Project that has the purpose of increasing agriculture production. A majority of the projects in the last two years of the fourth yen loan package, eighteen out of twenty-eight, are directed at the inland areas.

Japan is the main provider of ODA to China at present. Since the establishment of the JBIC in 1999, the bank has become the major source of financing from foreign official sources for the Chinese government. In 1999, Japan provided a total of 280,937 million yen[25] (ODA 192,637 and OOF 88,300), which is approximately US$2.5 billion. As for the World Bank, China has become non-eligible for loans from IDA (which handles the most favourable loans) since June 1999. The total amount of the loans from the World Bank to China that year amounted to US$2 billion (IDA 422 million and IBRD 1674 million).

A problem with Japanese ODA to China is that it is not very popular in Japan. Neither is ODA in general. Recently, Shizuka Kamei, policy chief of the Japanese Liberal Democratic Party, suggested a 30 per cent cut, referring to Japan's heavy debt situation where fiscal spending has been used as a means to improve the economic situation during the 1990s.[26] Actually there were already plans for substantial cuts in Japanese foreign aid some years before, but this changed with the financial crises in Asia in 1997 after which ODA increased again. For the fiscal year 2001 a decision has been taken for a 3 per cent general cut of the overall budget.[27] Aid to China has been at the centre of the debate. Articles like the one by Komori Yoshiki in Chūō Kōron[28] have pointed out how it has been used to build luxurious subways that very few people in Beijing use whereas people in Tokyo have to put up with old and very crowded ones. He compares Beijing airport with its fifty-one elevators with the much smaller crowded Narita airport in Tokyo, suggesting that the Japanese government should think of their own taxpayers rather than wasting money on China. Others have also suggested substantial changes in Japanese aid to China.[29]

According to the latest plan for ODA, Japan is to formulate a 'country assistance programme' for all the major recipients. MOFA (the Ministry of Foreign Affairs) is in charge of formulating such a programme and it started to do so for China two years ago. Due to severe criticism of aid to China in the mass media, and the political debate on aid to China even within the governing LDP party (for the increasing strength of the Taiwan lobby see Chapter 5), the framing of the programme was stopped.[30] The main points of criticism were that:

124 *Marie Söderberg*

- China itself is an aid-providing country and does not need to be a recipient country.
- Japan's aid to China is not visible to the Chinese people.
- Aid projects are not properly evaluated.
- Aid allows the Chinese government to allocate more of its budget to a military build-up.
- China must take its own initiative in solving problems such as poverty.

Suggestions from the round-table conference

To solve the deadlock over the country assistance programme to China a round-table conference composed of fifteen people from academia, the private sector and non-governmental organisations was organised to give advice. In their report published in December 2000[31] they suggested radical changes to Japanese ODA.

The report points out how conditions have changed since the initiation of the yen loans in 1979, when loans were given to support the Chinese policy of opening up and reform. China's economy has grown enormously since then and Japanese ODA has played an important part in that development.

The report emphasises that ODA is still important in the building of a good relationship between the two countries and that the understanding of this has to be enhanced in Japan. There is a warning against an increase of nationalism in both countries that has to be countered by an adjustment of ODA to the new needs in China. ODA should be effective and of the kind that the Japanese people can agree to. In the long run China's own capital and foreign direct investment should play a more important role in its development. Japan should, besides ODA, also use OOF and promote private investment in China. It is important for Japan to help China to integrate with the world economy and make it a responsible member of the international community. All aid that could be connected with military purposes or that are in violation of the ODA Charter should be strictly avoided.

Aid decisions should be made according to the conditions at the time and how well the project matches development priorities in the country assistance programme. This is a radical change that the report suggests. Before the change China, as well as many of the other recipient countries in Asia, has known roughly how much money to expect every year. Now China has to come up with suggestions that are considered interesting enough for Japan to support and they cannot take it for granted that they will get a certain support.

Concerning the priority areas, the report suggests a move from infrastructure development in the coastal areas towards more environmental and social infrastructure in inland areas. There has, as shown above, already been some change in that direction during the fourth yen loan package, although a number of traditional economic infrastructure loans still remain. According to the report the focus on inland areas and the environment should be sharpened, and if each item is judged separately the traditional economic infrastructure in the coastal areas is then likely to be neglected.

The role of ODA in the relationship 125

There is also a general suggestion for more 'soft' aid, such as help to strengthen the legal framework for economic transactions as well as good governance. Other priority areas are an increase of mutual understanding through an increase in exchanges on a number of levels, poverty alleviation and different measures to support Japanese business interests in China. Money should also be put aside for the specific purpose of making Japanese aid visible in the form of advertisements, etc.

What will happen at the implementation level?

The round-table discussion group issued their report to help the Japanese government get the stalled process of formulating a country assistance plan for China going again. That is probably why it argues to such an extent from the Japanese side (why Japan should assist China) rather than from the Chinese side (what is needed for social and economic development in China).

From the Chinese perspective, a Japanese country assistance programme will not be very useful. China has made it quite clear that it intends to stay in control of its own development process and set its own priorities. Only to the extent that the Japanese programme follows Chinese priorities, such as the development of inland areas, which is also a Chinese priority, will it be of any use. Otherwise the only purpose such a programme could have is to make it clear in which areas it might be worth looking for Japanese ODA.

Another problem with Japanese ODA to China is that it consists mainly of loans (75 per cent). This fact puts a limit on the type of project it can be used for. If the projects are not likely to generate a reasonable return and the deals are not good enough according to Chinese evaluation, they will refrain from accepting it and try to find finance through other sources. Many of the 'softer' projects are likely to fall into a category where the Chinese will not be willing to spend money.

The Chinese implementing agency that signs all the loan agreements with JBIC is the Chinese Ministry of Finance. The Ministry is very careful in its choice of projects. Most often it, in its turn, will put the responsibility of repaying the loan on to a lower level of government. Take the Environmental Development Model Cities as an example. The Ministry of Finance authorised the initiative, yet it is Guizhou province that will be paying for Guiyang, the Chonqing municipality (under the direct control of the central government) in the case of Chongqing and the Dalian municipal government in the case of Dalian.

The aspiration is that these three cities will act as a model for other Chinese cities to follow. It will be difficult for poorer provinces to do so, however. These provinces have other more urgent matters and generally give greater priority to economic growth than environmental investment.

Another problem with 'softer' aid is that it will need a totally new organisation and a considerable increase in staffing at the implementation level. As shown above, Japanese loan aid has been handled by a very small number of people distributing large amounts of money. A prerequisite for this has been that they work with large projects (such as economic infrastructure) where big amounts

126 *Marie Söderberg*

are dispensed at one time. It is one thing for a limited number of people to handle a limited number of big projects and quite another if they are to divide their time between a huge number of smaller ones.

A turn towards a 'softer' type of aid will also require people with different educational backgrounds and experience. To distribute big loans, knowledge of economics and administrative skill are needed, whereas for softer types of aid one would need knowledge of developmental work in general as well as knowledge of the specific conditions of the Chinese countryside. In order to make a careful evaluation of the numerous projects Japanese aid officials will need to travel to a number of small villages in inland areas where there might not even exist infrastructure in the form of roads to take them there or decent hotels where they can stay. It will also make the aid officials much more involved in local politics where there might be a debate about which solutions that are the best and where different vested interests pull in different directions and corruption is commonplace. This type of aid is very time-consuming and labour-intensive. It is also a field where Japan must be considered as lacking in education and experience. This is something that takes a long time to build up and where one cannot expect any quick results.

Softer aid would probably not apply to the type of projects that the Chinese government would want to borrow money for. It would have to be in the form of grant aid and technical assistance, which does not have to be repaid. This will be more costly for the Japanese government, which already has a huge budget deficit.

It is unlikely that the Japanese government will be able to make any quick change in the type of aid extended to China, at least not without substantial cuts in the amount distributed. It could stop most loan aid, but it will not be able to substitute that with other forms of aid if it wants to keep it on the same level as now. The capital-intensive infrastructure projects cannot easily be exchanged for a softer type of aid.

The role of aid in the future relationship

As far as ODA to China is concerned, it seems that the Japanese government is now trying to take the initiative over what projects its aid money is used for. Up to now the decisions with regard to the most important projects for economic development have been made by the Chinese government. Now there is a new thinking that it is Japan that should set the priority areas according to their own policy and that Japan's own national interests also should be taken into consideration.[32] One sign of this is the cessation of the five-year loan aid packages coordinated with the Chinese five-year plans. Another is the emphasis on environment and anti-poverty measures, the areas that are not necessarily the main priorities of the Chinese government.

On the political level, ODA will continue to be of importance in the two countries' relationship. Japanese Prime Ministers are likely to continue with their gift-giving diplomacy in connection with meetings with Chinese leaders where

The role of ODA in the relationship 127

other matters are also discussed. In a sense ODA will have the function of being the glue that keeps the relationship together.

The positive way of using ODA, by using it as the proverbial carrot, will still be important. The negative use, such as freezing grant aid in connection with Chinese nuclear testing, is likely to cause friction. The Chinese continued the testing according to its own schedule and the freeze of aid only created a lot of ill feeling and a sense of distrust. The prolonging of the procedure for the special yen loans in the summer of 2000 is an example of how public opinion at home can make Japanese politicians use ODA to make their protests against Chinese behaviour heard. This way of using aid is quite risky, however, as it might cause anti-Japanese feelings. The internal debate in Japan on ODA to China has also clearly revealed Japanese sentiments towards China.[33] To a certain extent ODA has already become another 'issue' between the two countries.

Japan has strong motivations for wanting to integrate China into the world community and help it prosper rather than trying to isolate it and impose sanctions. First, Japan is one of the main holders of Chinese debt; second, a policy of isolation would most likely also hurt Japanese business interests; and, third, it might create instability in China, which is something Japan would not like.

Still, there is a great need for capital in China as there are many projects that need financing. Japanese ODA loans have been one of the most favourable available on a large scale, since IDA of the World Bank stopped theirs. This makes it likely that the Chinese will read the Japanese country assistance plan carefully and try to squeeze some of the projects they already have in the pipeline into the different priority areas so that they will be eligible for aid. To a certain extent they will agree to Japanese ODA loans even for projects that might not be their highest priority. Chinese interest in Japanese aid is likely to decrease as conditions for the way the aid is used increase, however, and in no way will they let Japan govern their development process.

In the future there is likely to be a decrease of ODA, considering the policy changes and the severe fiscal situation in Japan, as well as the fact that China has reached a higher developmental level itself. Foreign direct investment and trade will grow in importance and there will be an increase in OOF instead of ODA. This will be the case especially in the coastal areas, which are not a priority area of ODA any longer, but where there is a great interest from the Japanese business community. Conditions might be less favourable for OOF than for ODA, but this is a field where there is less transparency and Japanese business interests can more easily be promoted.

Notes

1 Aid will be defined here according to the same rules as ODA within the OECD's Development Assistance Committee, which means that it should consist of (1) resources provided by official agencies or by their executing agencies; (2) the main objective being the promotion of the economic development and welfare of developing countries; (3) its concessional character is due to the effort to avoid

128   Marie Söderberg

placing a heavy burden on developing countries, and thus consists of a grant element of at least 25 per cent.

2 21Seiki ni Muketa tai Chū Keizai Kyōryoku no Arikata ni Kan Suru Kodankai. Their proposal can be found at http://www.mofa.go.jp/mofaj/gaiko/oda/seisaku/seisaku_1/sei_1_13_4.html

3 According to *Asahi Shimbun*, 12 December 2000, the budget for 2001 will be cut by 3 per cent.

4 Alan Rix, *Japan's Economic Aid: Policymaking and Politics*, London, Croom Helm, 1980.

5 Suzuki Kenji, *Kokusaiha Giin to Riken no Uchimaku*, Tokyo, Yell Books, 1989.

6 David Arase, *Buying Power: The Political Economy of Japan's Foreign Aid Power*, Boulder CO, Lynne Rienner, 1995.

7 Robert M. Orr Jr, *The Emergence of Japan's Foreign Aid Power*, New York, Columbia University Press, 1990.

8 Dennis Yasutomo, *The Manner of Giving: Strategic Aid and Japanese Foreign Policy*, Lexington, Lexington Books, 1986.

9 Nishigaki Akira and Shimomura Yasutami, *Kaihatsu Enjo no Keizaigaku*, Japan, Yuhaikaku, 1993, or Margee Ensign, *Doing Good or Doing Well? Japan's Foreign Aid Program*, New York, Columbia University Press, 1993.

10 See, for example, Sumi Kazuo, *ODA Enjo no Genjitsu*, Tokyo, Iwanami Shinsho, 1989, or Murai Yoshinori, *Musekinin Enjo Taikoku Nihon*, Tokyo, JICC, 1989.

11 See, for example, Hanabusa Masamichi, 'A Japanese Perspective on Aid and Development', in Shafique Islam (ed.), *Yen for Development: Japanese Foreign Aid and the Politics of Burden-Sharing*, New York, Council of Foreign Relations Press, 1991, pp. 88–105.

12 Marie Söderberg (ed.), *The Business of Japanese Foreign Aid – Five Case Studies from Asia*, London, Routledge, 1996.

13 Foreign Ministry, *Waga Kuni no Seifu Kaihatsu Enjo 1994*, p. 1, as well as the OECF, *Annual Report 1994*, p. 3.

14 Different kinds of official flows that have conditions that are not concessional enough to make them qualify as ODA.

15 The following figures are from Foreign Ministry, *Waga Kuni no Seifu Kaihatsu Enjo 1999*.

16 Marie Söderberg, op. cit., pp. 53–4.

17 JBIC, Japan Bank of International Cooperation was created through a merger in 1999 of the Japan EXIM Bank, which used to deal with OOF and OECF, the Overseas Economic Cooperation Fund that was the implementing agency for the ODA loans.

18 Tong Xiangao, 'Japan's ODA and the Peoples Republic of China: Strategic Aid?', in Chulacheeb Chinwanno and Wilaiwan Wannitikul (eds), *Japan's Official Development Assistance and Asian Developing Economies*, Institute of East Asian Studies, Bangkok, Thammasat University, 1991, pp. 175–217.

19 OECD, *The DAC Journal Development Cooperation 1999 Report*, vol. 1, no. 1, 2000.

20 For a detailed account of this see Quansheng Zhao, *Japanese Policymaking: The Politics Behind Politics – Informal Mechanisms and the Making of China Policy*, Oxford and New York, Oxford University Press, 1995, pp. 161–85.

21 The fourth package was divided into three plus two.

22 See, for example, Jin Xide, 'Chū nichi Seiji Masatsu no Koozu, Genin Oyobi sono Sū sei', in *Senshū Daigaku Shakaikagaku Kenkyūjo Geppō*, no. 430, Tokyo, 1999.

23 *The Daily Yomiuri*, 9 August 2000.

24 *Japan Times*, 9 October 2000.

25 JBIC press release.

26 *Asahi Shimbun*, 15 November 2000.

27 *Asahi Shimbun*, 12 December 2000.

28 Komori Yoshihiki, 'Machigaidarage no Chūgoku Enjo', *Chūō Kōron*, March 2000, pp. 94–109.

The role of ODA in the relationship   129

29 See, for example, Miyamoto Yūji, 'Tai Chū Keizai Enjo Dō Suru ka', in *Gaiko Forum*, 8, 2000, pp. 78–82.

30 Interviews at JICA in Tokyo, June 2000.

31 Op. cit., 21Seiki ni Muketa tai Chū Keizai Kyōryoku no Arikata ni Kan Suru Kodankai.

32 See, for example, OECF, *Japan News Letter, Special Report on China*. Their proposal can be found at http://www.mofa.go.jp/mofaj/gaiko/oda/seisaku/seisaku_1/sei_1_13_4.html, March 1999.

33 A recent example of this is Tomoyuki Kojima's, 'Chūgoku o "Skekinin aru taikoku" ni suru tame', *Gaikō Forum*, 2 February 2001.

8 Economic relations

What can we learn from trade and FDI?

Hanns Günther Hilpert and Nakagane Katsuji

Introduction: why is the Sino-Japanese relationship so important?

Japan and China – in spite of their distinct differences – are economically the largest and most important countries of East Asia (see Table 8.1). Still the economic superpower Japan dwarfs the upcoming challenger China: by economic size Japan is four to five times as big as China; by level of income (i.e. GDP per capita) Japan outdoes China by nearly fifty times.

However, the sustained rapid economic growth of China contrasts with the economic stagnation of Japan in the 1990s. If China keeps growing at the same rate as it did in the 1990s (10.3 per cent in average), and if Japan keeps growing at the low average yearly rate of 1.2 per cent, as it did in the 1990s, China will surpass Japan in the year 2020 and become the second largest economy in the world. However, the extrapolation of present economic trends into the future is a very unreliable prognosis technique. Over the next twenty years Chinese growth rates may be considerably lower, as in the late 1990s they had already fallen below 8 per cent. On the other hand, Japanese growth rates could possibly be higher, once the current process of structural adjustment has been accomplished. These caveats notwithstanding, we can realistically expect that the size of the gap between Japan and China will narrow considerably and eventually disappear.

Certainly the rapid catching-up of China will not only alleviate poverty and improve economic welfare in China, but will also be beneficial to the outside world, including Japan, as the opportunities for profitable economic exchanges increase. By neo-classical reasoning the economic rise of China is not at somebody else's loss, but rather to everybody's gain. Japan more than any other country should profit from China's rise by virtue of the complementarity of the two countries. China is abundant in natural resources and in cheap labour and it has a huge market. These are all factors which Japan needs for its economic security. Japan, on the other hand, possesses all the capital, technology and human skills China needs for its modernisation and industrialisation. Japan may also utilise Chinese resources for the manufacturing of low-cost products for the world market. Furthermore the increasing supply of low-cost Chinese products improves the terms of trade of Japan in world trade. Hence, by virtue of

Economic relations 131

Table 8.1 Japan and China compared (1999)

	Unit	Japan	China
GDP	billion US$	4,847	991
GDP per capita	US$	38,313	782
Share of East Asian GDP (98)	%	66	15
GDP growth 1980–90	%	4.1	9.5
GDP growth 1990–9	%	1.2	10.3
Foreign exchange reserves	billion US$	287	158
Foreign trade volume	billion US$	730	361
Share of world trade	%	6.4	3.2
Population	million people	127	1,267
Land area	sq.km	377,829	9,560,770

Source: IMF, *International Financial Statistics, International Trade Statistics*, own calculations.

complementary economic patterns, both Japan and China can enhance their welfare, if they trade more bilaterally and if they intensify their economic integration. Certainly the economic growth of China ought to be welcomed unreservedly. So should Japan have any reason to worry, when the centre of economic gravity within East Asia shifts from the Japanese archipelago to the Chinese continental shelf?

The rise of a large economy from the status of a developing country to the rank of a fully developed industrialised nation does not occur without tensions, just as the example of Japan's past political and economic relationship with the West has shown explicitly. Starting out from this parallel, the occurrence of Sino-Japanese conflicts should be anticipated. On the micro-economic firm level Japanese companies will be challenged by Chinese firms' low wages and imitation strategies and the Japanese agricultural sector has to compete against cheap Chinese food imports. On the other hand, Chinese companies have to face more severe competition at home from foreign, including Japanese, firms. Thus on the industrial level the incidence of displacement competition can be expected. In the political economy arena a shift of bargaining power in trade negotiations and a shift of geo-political weight may take place.

There will be both benefits and conflicts in the Sino-Japanese relationship. But which aspect of the relationship will prevail? Can the conflicts be resolved? If so, how will the benefits be distributed? What is a realistic scenario for the future relationship? For both Japan and China the other country looms large in economic and political strategic thinking. At times the bilateral relationship is regarded as the key not only to mutual prosperity, but also to the peace and development of the whole region. No doubt, the relationship is very important and deserves a closer look into its inherent nature.

Obviously the commanding elements in the bilateral relationship are foreign trade and foreign direct investment (FDI). Although Japan has provided China with a tremendous amount of ODA and loans, it is above all trade and FDI that stimulate the development and industrialisation in China's outward-oriented

132 *Hanns Günther Hilpert and Nakagane Katsuji*

development strategy. Furthermore, it is trade and FDI which may or may not lead to the eventual increase of mutual economic interdependence. Henceforth bilateral trade and investment are at the focus of the analysis of this paper. First we shall enquire into the quantitative dimensions and the economic functions of trade and FDI. The results of these analyses and the structures revealed may allow a prognosis into the future developments of bilateral trade and investment flows. In the concluding section the analysis will be extended from pure economics into the realm of political economy by the presentation and the assessment of four possible scenarios for the Sino-Japanese relationship.

Bilateral trade

Trade volumes in absolute values

Table 8.2 shows the development of Sino-Japanese trade by its absolute volume values from 1980 to 1999. It can be seen that over the last twenty years both Japanese exports to and imports from China have surged. However, the rise has not always been smooth. After 1985 China restricted imports on Japan in order to cut down its trade deficit and to reduce its unilateral import dependency on Japan, most notably in the case of vehicles and consumer durables. Only after 1990 did Japanese exports to China start to increase again. On the other hand, Chinese exports to Japan did not really take off before 1986. As a result, Japan's bilateral trade balance with China turned into the red in 1988 and has remained there ever since.

Statistical issues and the role of entrepôt trade through Hong Kong

From a closer look on Table 8.2 one can easily make out the fairly large differences between Japanese and Chinese statistical records: in the trade statistics of both Japan and China the bilateral import figures are considerably higher than the respective export figures of the trading partner. This can partly be explained by the well-known discrepancies between FOB-based (= free on board) registered exports and CIF-based (= cost, insurance and freight) registered imports. The transport share of the traded goods' value is only recorded at the import statistics side. A further inflation of Chinese import values occurs because Chinese import statistics are overstated by over-invoicing, which is a convenient way of evading foreign exchange control.

The principal cause for the distortion of the Chinese trade statistics is the uneven registration of entrepôt trade through Hong Kong. A large volume of the bilateral Sino-Japanese trade is trans-shipped and marketed though Hong Kong. Unfortunately this trade appears only partly in the bilateral trade statistics. To be precise, it appears only in the import statistics. Whereas both Japan and China regard their bilateral imports through Hong Kong correctly as imports, their bilateral exports through Hong Kong are considered as exports to Hong Kong. Thus both Japan and China understate their bilateral exports, but record

Economic relations   133

Table 8.2 Japan's and China's bilateral trade, 1980–99 (in millions of US$)

Year	Japan's trade with China[1]			China's trade with Japan[1]		
	Exports[2]	Imports	Trade balance	Exports[2]	Imports	Trade balance
1980	5109	4346	763	4032	5169	−1137
1985	12,590	6534	6056	6091	15,178	−9087
1988	9486	9861	−375	8046	11,062	−3016
1990	6145	12,057	−5912	9210	7656	1554
1992	11,967	16,972	−5005	11,699	13,686	−1987
1993	17,353	20,651	−3298	15,782	23,303	−7521
1995	21,934	35,922	−13,988	28,466	29,007	−541
1997	21,692	41,827	−20,135	31,820	28,990	2830
1998	20,182	37,079	−16,897	29,718	28,307	1411
1999	23,450	43,070	−19,620	32,399	33,768	−1369

Source: IMF, *Direction of Trade Statistics*, Japan and China Tables.

Notes
1   Exports are registrated on FOB basis (free on board), imports CIF basis (cost, insurance and freight).
2   Both Japanese and Chinese imports include imports through Hong Kong, but Japanese and Chinese exports through Hong Kong are not included. The latter are recorded as exports to Hong Kong.

correctly their bilateral imports. Consequently both Japan and China overstate their bilateral trade deficits or understate their bilateral trade surpluses.

The distortion in the Sino-Japanese trade can be corrected if both countries' indirect exports (i.e. through Hong Kong) are included in the bilateral trade records. Fortunately the Hong Kong Census and Statistics Department provides fairly detailed data on the territory's re-exports, from which the annual volume of Japan's indirect exports to China and of China's indirect exports to Japan can be roughly estimated. Adding the estimated values of Japan's and China's indirect bilateral exports to bilateral direct exports leads to the values of Japan's and China's total bilateral exports. The adjusted bilateral export figures in the Sino-Japanese trade are higher and are much closer to the respective import figures. Still they do not match.

From the analysis of Hong Kong's trade figures it can be recognised that the entrepôt assumes a symmetric role in the Sino-Japanese trading relationship. Hong Kong is about as important for Japanese exports to China as it is for Chinese exports to Japan. In this respect Sino-Japanese trade is markedly different from Sino-US trade, in which the Hong Kong entrepôt trade assumes an unsymmetrical role.

Relative trade shares

What is the relative importance of China for Japan's trade? What is the relative importance of Japan for China's trade? At present Japan is China's most important import source and, following the US and Hong Kong, its third largest

134   Hanns Günther Hilpert and Nakagane Katsuji

export market. When China's indirect exports are included, Japan is actually China's second largest export market. However, the relative importance of Japan for China's exports and imports has decreased somehow in the course of China's foreign trade expansion in the 1980s and 1990s (Table 8.3). From the Japanese perspective trade with China has grown increasingly important in the last two decades. At present imports from China are only surpassed by imports from the US. As a destination for Japanese exports China is the number 3 location – after the US and closely behind Taiwan (Table 8.4).

Bilateral trade interdependence

For an assessment of the trade interdependence between the two countries, both trade volumes in absolute values and relative trade shares are rather poor indicators. Trade shares are always dependent on the world market share of the respective trading partner. To put it in more concrete terms: as Japan is the third largest trading nation worldwide, you would expect the country to assume a prominent role in the Chinese export trade. Nevertheless, it may be possible that China still fails to assume its proportional share in Japan's world imports. On the other hand, Japanese exports to China could have grown rapidly compared to Japan's exports, or compared to world trade, but could still have failed to keep pace with China's rapidly increasing share of world imports.

Therefore the more adequate indicators of trade interdependence are the so-called trade intensity indices, which measure quantitatively the relationship between a trading share and the world market share of the trading partner.[1] They give a measurable assessment of the extent of trade biases towards a particular trading partner relative to the assignment of trade across all partners. The value of that index is unity, if the trade relationship is just average. That is, the trade intensity index of any country with the world is unity. When the value of the index exceeds unity, it indicates the existence of a positive trade bias between the countries considered. In other words, country A trades with country B more intensively than B trades with the rest of the world.[2]

Table 8.5 shows the development of the index of trade intensity of Japan's export trade with China, East Asia and the US from 1980 until 1999. In 1999 the intensity index of Japanese exports to China amounted to the high value of 1.85. If Japan's indirect exports to China via Hong Kong are included, the index value at 2.75 is still higher. Japan is exporting nearly three times as much to China as it

---

Export trade intensity index:

$$I_{ab} = EX_a / IM_b$$

EX_a = the share of country B in country A's exports.
IM_b = the share of country B in the world import market.

Economic relations 135

Table 8.3 China's trade by export destinations and import sources, 1980–99

EXPORTS

Trade partner	1980 %	1985 %	1990 %	1995 %	1999 %
US/Canada	6.2	9.4	9.2	17.6	22.8
US/Canada (adj.)[1]	7.1	11.7	19.6	37.4	40.4
EU-15	13.7	8.6	10.0	12.9	15.5
East Asia[2]	52.8	58.8	64.8	55.9	47.1
Japan	22.2	22.3	14.3	19.1	16.6
Japan (adj.)[1]	22.9	23.1	17.1	24.2	20.4
Hong Kong	24.0	26.2	43.2	24.2	18.9
Hong Kong (adj.)[1]	22.4	23.0	29.9	9.2	5.3
NIEs-3[3]	2.3	7.5	4.4	8.9	8.3
ASEAN-4[4]	4.3	2.7	2.9	3.7	3.2
Rest of world	27.3	23.2	16.0	13.6	14.6

IMPORTS

Trade partner	1980 %	1985 %	1990 %	1995 %	1999 %
US/Canada	23.8	14.9	15.0	14.2	13.2
EU-15	15.7	15.6	17.0	16.1	15.3
East Asia[2]	32.8	49.6	51.4	54.6	55.4
Japan	26.5	35.7	14.2	22.0	20.4
Hong Kong	2.9	11.2	27.0	6.5	4.2
NIEs-3[3]	1.0	0.6	6.2	21.5	24.6
ASEAN-4[4]	2.4	2.1	4.0	4.5	6.2
Rest of world	27.7	19.9	16.6	15.1	16.2

TOTAL TRADE

Trade partner	1980 %	1985 %	1990 %	1995 %	1999 %
US/Canada	15.3	12.8	11.8	16.0	18.4
US/Canada (adj.)[1]	16.1	13.7	17.4	26.5	27.9
EU-15	14.7	12.9	13.2	14.4	15.4
East Asia[2]	42.4	53.0	58.8	55.4	50.9
Japan	24.4	30.4	14.4	20.4	18.3
Japan (adj.)[1]	24.8	30.8	16	23.2	20.4
Hong Kong	13.1	17.0	35.7	15.9	12.1
NIEs-3[3]	1.6	3.3	5.2	14.9	15.8
ASEAN-4[4]	3.3	2.3	3.4	4.1	4.6
Rest of world	27.6	21.3	16.2	14.2	15.3

Source: IMF, *Direction of Trade Statistics, Hong Kong External Trade* (monthly).

Notes
1 Exports include indirect exports via Hong Kong.
2 East Asia: Japan, Hong Kong, Macao, NIEs-3, ASEAN-4.
3 NIEs-3: Korea, Singapore, Taiwan.
4 ASEAN-4: Indonesia, Malaysia, Philippines,Thailand.

136 Hanns Günther Hilpert and Nakagane Katsuji

Table 8.4 Japan's trade by export destinations and import sources, 1980–99

EXPORTS

Trade partner	1980 %	1985 %	1990 %	1995 %	1999 %
US/Canada	26.3	40.2	34.0	28.9	32.7
EU-15	15.2	13.1	20.4	15.9	17.8
East Asia[1]	25.8	24.1	29.6	42.2	35.9
China	3.9	7.1	2.1	5.0	5.6
China (adj.)[2]	4.1	7.8	2.6	7.7	8.4
Hong Kong	3.7	3.7	4.6	6.3	5.3
Hong Kong (adj.)[3]	3.5	3.0	4.1	5.0	4.0
NIEs-3[4]	11.2	9.1	15.2	18.8	16.3
ASEAN-4[5]	7.0	4.2	7.7	12.1	8.6
Rest of world	32.7	22.6	16.0	13.0	13.6

IMPORTS

Trade partner	1980 %	1985 %	1990 %	1995 %	1999 %
US/Canada	20.8	23.7	26.1	25.8	24.3
EU-15	7.1	7.8	16.2	14.5	13.8
East Asia[1]	22.3	25.6	23.2	31.8	37.6
China	3.1	5.0	5.1	8.1	13.9
Hong Kong	0.5	0.6	0.9	0.8	0.6
NIEs-3[4]	4.7	7.1	10.1	11.5	11.0
ASEAN-4[5]	14.0	12.9	7.1	11.4	12.1
Rest of world	49.8	42.9	34.5	27.9	24.3

TOTAL TRADE

Trade partner	1980 %	1985 %	1990 %	1995 %	1999 %
US/Canada	23.4	33.2	30.5	27.6	29.1
EU-15	11.0	10.9	18.5	15.3	16.1
East Asia[1]	24.0	24.7	28.7	38.7	36.6
China	3.5	6.2	3.5	7.4	9.1
China (adj.)[2]	3.6	6.6	3.8	9.0	10.7
Hong Kong	2.0	2.4	2.9	3.9	3.3
Hong Kong (adj.)[3]	1.9	2.0	2.6	3.1	2.6
NIEs-3[4]	7.9	8.2	12.9	15.6	14.1
ASEAN-4[5]	10.6	7.9	8.9	11.8	10.1
Rest of world	41.6	31.2	22.3	18.4	18.2

Source: IMF, *Direction of Trade Statistics, Hong Kong External Trade* (monthly).

Notes
1   East Asia: China, Hong Kong, Macao, NIEs-3, ASEAN-4.
2   Exports include indirect exports via Hong Kong.
3   Exports exclude re-exports to China.
4   NIEs-3: Korea, Singapore, Taiwan.
5   ASEAN-4: Indonesia, Malaysia, Philippines, Thailand.

Economic relations 137

Table 8.5 Japanese export intensity index,[1] 1980–99

Year	Trading partner			
	China	China (adj.)[2]	East Asia[3]	US
1980	3.62	3.07	3.08	1.72
1985	2.94	3.35	2.26	1.83
1988	1.67	2.03	2.17	1.91
1990	1.30	1.66	2.31	2.01
1992	1.57	2.03	2.18	1.88
1993	1.64	2.60	2.03	1.73
1995	1.80	2.79	2.22	1.71
1997	1.94	3.07	2.25	1.68
1998	1.98	3.13	2.26	1.75
1999	1.85	2.75	2.27	1.62

Source: IMF, *Direction of Trade Statistics, Hong Kong External Trade* (monthly), own calculations.

Notes

1 The Japanese export trade intensity index is the ratio of the share of Japanese exports to a specific trading partner (i.e. Japan, East Asia, US) in the total of Japanese exports to the share of the trading partner's imports in the world import market.

2 Japanese exports to China including indirect exports via Hong Kong.

3 East Asia = China, NIEs-4, ASEAN-4, Macao.

does on average to the rest of the world. In the course of the last two decades the Japan–China export intensity index first fell (from 1980 to 1990) and then rose (from 1990 to 1999). When China was a closed economy there were apparently special links between Japan and China and the very little trade China had was extremely biased towards Japan. When China opened up to the world, her trade became more diversified. Consequently the bias towards Japan came down. Moreover in 1985 China restricted its imports from Japan and an abrupt fall of the index can be observed. But in 1990 a turnaround occurred and since then the index has been converging with the East Asian average. If Japan's indirect exports to China via Hong Kong are included, the intensity of Japanese exports to China is already from 1993 higher than the intensity of Japanese exports to the rest of East Asia. Furthermore it is notable that since 1992 the Japanese export bias to China is higher than to the US.

Table 8.6 shows the development of the index of trade intensity of China's export trade with Japan, East Asia and the US from 1980 until 1998. In 1999 the intensity index of Chinese exports to Japan amounts to the unusually high value of 3.01. If China's indirect exports to Japan via Hong Kong are included, the index value rises to 3.50. Thus China is exporting more than three times as much to Japan as it does on average to the rest of the world. The index was already as high as that in 1980, but in the course of China's trade diversification it fell substantially. Again, in 1990 a turning point can be noticed. Since then the China–Japan export intensity index has been rising steadily. In 1993 it was above the China–East Asian export intensity index, which has been on a continuous declining trend since 1980. The development of the intensity index of Chinese

138 *Hanns Günther Hilpert and Nakagane Katsuji*

Table 8.6 Chinese export intensity index,[1] 1980–99

Year	Trading partner					
	Japan	Japan (adj.)[2]	East Asia	East Asia (adj.)[4]	US	US (adj.)[3]
1980	3.03	2.68	4.01	3.63	0.41	0.44
1985	3.16	2.68	3.85	3.18	0.44	0.48
1988	2.45	1.95	3.33	2.94	0.42	0.59
1990	2.15	1.64	3.23	2.46	0.57	0.85
1992	2.23	1.66	2.94	2.14	0.69	0.99
1993	2.63	1.96	1.81	1.45	0.13	1.55
1995	2.84	2.11	2.05	1.54	1.08	1.47
1997	2.85	2.33	2.13	1.64	1.11	1.43
1998	3.16	2.58	2.26	1.92	1.20	1.47
1999	3.01	2.45	2.11	1.79	1.16	1.23

Source: IMF, *Direction of Trade Statistics, Hong Kong External Trade* (monthly), own calculations.

Notes
1 The Chinese export trade intensity index is the ratio of the share of Chinese exports to a specific trading partner (i.e. Japan, East Asia, US) in the total of Chinese exports to the share of the trading partner's imports in the world import market.
2 Chinese exports to Japan including indirect exports via Hong Kong.
3 Chinese exports to the US including indirect exports via Hong Kong.
4 East Asia = Japan, NIEs-4, ASEAN-4, Macao. Chinese exports to East Asia include indirect exports via Hong Kong.

exports to the US is a mirror image of the China–Japan export intensity index. From a low value in 1980 (0.48) it rose (1993: 2.03) and then went on in a second phase to decrease again. The bias of Chinese exports to the US has never become higher than the respective bias towards Japan.

To sum up: following the opening up of China, the trade interdependence between Japan and China first fell considerably due to the diversification of China's trade. However, since 1990, the mutual bias has been rising again and has already attained a level higher than both partners' trading relations with the rest of East Asia and the industrialised world (i.e. the US, but also – not shown here – the EU and Canada).

Dynamics of Sino-Japanese trade

The above analysis of Sino-Japanese trade shows an increasing bilateral trade in absolute volumes, an increasing share for China in Japan's trade, a decreasing share for Japan in China's trade and, since 1990, an increasing bilateral trade interdependence. From this analysis it is safe to say that cooperation rather than conflict prevails in the Sino-Japanese economic relationship. Judging from the dynamics of Sino-Japanese trade there are good reasons to believe that trade will expand further.

This empirical analysis brings up the question of the driving forces behind Sino-Japanese trade: why did the interdependence grow so quickly in the 1990s?

Economic relations 139

Why were the growth rates of Sino-Japanese trade higher than the growth rates of Japan's and China's trade with the rest of East Asia and with the industrialised world? There seem to be four major factors, which are driving the dynamics of Japan–China trade: (1) the competitive advantage of Chinese products in the Japanese import market, (2) the competitive advantage of Japanese products in the Chinese import market, (3) the inflow of Japanese FDI into China and (4) the role of politics.

1   In the course of the opening up and liberalisation of its foreign trade, China's export trade pattern and international comparative advantage changed fundamentally from agricultural and natural resource-intensive goods to labour-intensive goods.[3] The commodity structure of China's exports to Japan changed accordingly. Whereas in the 1980s Japan imported mainly raw materials such as oil, coal, foodstuffs, cotton, silk and the like from China, Chinese exports to Japan now look quite different. They consist predominantly of industrially manufactured goods, such as processed food, textiles and apparel, footwear, toys and games, video and sound equipment, cameras, etc. Manufactured goods from China are cheap and their quality has improved markedly over the last few years. They dominate the Japanese import market in an increasing range of products. Apparently China is capable of supplying resource- and labour-intensive products, which are in high demand in Japan's industrial and consumer markets, but cannot be manufactured in Japan at low cost. Since most Chinese exports to Japan are traded through Japanese production and distribution networks, they seem not to be affected by structural import impediments. There is also a difference between the trade relations between China and Japan and the trade relations between the rest of East Asia and Japan. The current industrial upgrading process in China is markedly more rapid than elsewhere in the region. No other country except oil-rich Brunei and Indonesia has been able to attain a sustainable trade surplus with Japan. China has achieved what Western industrialised exporting countries have tried to do in vain over the last twenty years: turning a bilateral deficit with Japan into a surplus.

2   Since the 1970s Japanese companies have been successfully supplying the emerging markets of East Asia with industrial manufactured goods. Thus it comes as no surprise that Japanese suppliers have become very competitive in the emerging China market, too. The competitive situation in China is more severe due to the greater presence of US and European firms. However, Japanese companies seem to have a competitive edge in capital- and technology-intensive products such as general industrial machinery, iron and steel, and specialised machinery and vehicles.

3   Japanese FDI into China is driving the bilateral trade. Japanese FDI, mostly located in eastern and in north-eastern China, is a source of Chinese imports in the form of industrial plant and machinery, industrial components and other intermediate products. In return, Japanese companies and their local

joint venture partners are increasingly producing consumer goods for the Japanese market.[4] Based on the relative importance of the Japanese market for Chinese exports, Japan seems to have played a positive role in China's outward-looking growth strategy.[5]

4   In spite of certain protectionist tendencies by Japan in 2001, both in Japan and in China there seems to be a special interest in the expansion of bilateral trade and the promotion of economic cooperation. A supportive role from both Japanese and Chinese politicians at the national and the local level has been rising along with the liberalisation of the Chinese economy and a shift from a centrally planned system to an international rules-based framework.[6] Here are various examples of promotional activities:

- the active promotion of Japanese FDI into China by the Chinese and Japanese governments after 1990, not to mention promotional measures at provincial and local level;
- an active role for Sino-Chinese institutions: apart from the quasi-official Japan–China Trade Expansion Council (1985) and the Japan–China Investment Promotion Organisation (1990), there are about 100 different Sino-Japanese associations that promote bilateral trade, investment and technology transfer at the private level;
- an active Japanese foreign policy to promote the integration of China into the world economy and in its regional and multilateral institutions (APEC, WTO, G8);
- Japan's retreat from planned protective measures to curb surging Chinese imports of textiles and apparel in 1995.[7]

Japan's foreign direct investment in China

Foreign direct investment (FDI) differs from trade in several senses, particularly for developing countries. FDI is an activity, which has a rather long-term economic impact, while trade is basically for short-term gains. FDI involves the import of new things from abroad, such as capital, advanced technology and managerial know-how, culture, access to the world market, etc., while trade basically only absorbs foreign currencies.[8] Moreover, FDI often has political implications for host countries, while trade does not. China, for instance, rejected any type of FDI throughout the Maoist era, when they insisted on 'self-reliance' and FDI was regarded as 'domination by foreign [imperialist] capital'. When China opened its doors to the world in the late 1970s, it implicitly recognised the success of the outward-looking development strategy of some of its neighboring countries, especially the NIEs, which had attracted an enormous amount of foreign capital. China dramatically changed its former stance of 'self-reliance' and adopted a more active FDI absorption policy. In the following section we shall enquire into the trends, the features and the motives of Japan's direct investment flows to China in recent years, and how it contributed to the economic growth of China.

FDI in China: volumes and major investor countries

China's FDI inflows from the world are shown in Table 8.7. It can be seen that foreign direct capital inflows to China reached a peak in 1993, on the basis of contracts, both in terms of value and number of projects. However, the peak of actually invested foreign direct capital in China came in 1998. In 1997, FDI in China (on contract base) sharply decreased due to the Asian currency crisis and its aftermath. Since 1993 the relative shares of Hong Kong and other major investor countries have been declining. This trend implies that China's inward FDI has been dispersed. The relative share of Japan has also decreased over the 1990s and has thus fallen to almost the same level as the share of Taiwan and the United States, but it is still an indispensable part of China's FDI inflows as a whole.

Japanese FDI outflows to China and the world

Table 8.8 shows the relative importance of China as a location for Japanese investment abroad. There is a high degree of yearly fluctuation in Japanese direct investment in China. It sharply increased in the middle of the 1980s, then reached a peak in the middle of the 1990s after a few years of stagnation. Since 1995 it has been declining, whether relative to Japan's FDI in Asia or to the total amount of its investment worldwide, which were increasing at least until 1997. On the one hand, this shift seems to suggest that Japanese investors' interest gradually moved away from China to other regions in the late 1990s. On the other hand, the trend may just reflect the rebounding effect of the 'China FDI boom' in the early 1990s, when many Japanese small and medium-sized firms reportedly rushed to China without much preparation. No wonder some of them retreated from their business in China.[9] Whether Japan's FDI is biased in favour of China or not can be measured by the 'FDI intensity index'.

If this index is greater than 1, Japanese investors favour investment in China over investments in other locations. Table 8.8 indicates that the index is

Table 8.7 Foreign investment in China by major source countries, 1983–99

Year	Total contract value US$ million	Total actual value US$ million	Major investor countries %			
			Hong Kong	Japan	Taiwan	US
1983	1723	636				
1985	5932	1661	48.9	16.1		18.3
1990	6596	3487	54.9	14.4	6.4	13.1
1993	111,436	27,512	62.8	4.9	11.3	7.4
1995	91,282	37,521	53.4	8.5	8.4	8.2
1998	52,102	45,463	40.7	7.5	6.4	8.6
1999	41,223	40,319	40.6	7.4	6.4	10.5

Source: *Statistical Yearbook of China*, various issues.

142 Hanns Günther Hilpert and Nakagane Katsuji

Table 8.8 Japanese foreign direct investment to China, 1980–99

Year	Share in Japan's FDI to Asia %		Share in Japan's total FDI %		FDI intensity index
	By items	*By value*	*By items*	*By value*	
1980	0.93	1.01	0.25	0.26	
1985	17.23	6.97	4.52	0.82	
1990	11.01	4.94	2.81	0.61	0.371
1993	47.36	25.47	20.07	4.71	0.356
1995	47.27	36.23	26.89	8.71	0.807
1998	20.86	16.31	7.01	2.61	0.406
1999	14.39	10.49	4.44	1.13	0.241

Source: Japanese Ministry of Finance: *Zaisei Kin-yū Tōkei Geppō* (Fiscal and Financial Statistics Monthly), various issues.

Notes
1 Original figures are those that Japanese firms and individuals reported to the Ministry of Finance.
2 The FDI intensity index is the ratio of the share of Japanese (outward) FDI to China in the total of Japan's (outward) FDI to China's share in the world total FDI flows.

FDI intensity index:

$$I_{ab} = FDI\ flow_a\ /\ FDI\ world_b$$

$FDI\ flow_a$ = the share of country B (= China) in country A's (= Japan) outward FDI.

$FDI\ world_b$ = the share of country B (China) in the world total FDI flows.

---

generally lower than 1, implying that Japanese investors do not necessarily favour China as their investment destination. Even during the China investment boom, it was below 1. In 1999 it had declined to 0.24.[10]

Statistical issues

Just as Japan's exports to China do not match China's imports from Japan, the volume of Japanese capital outflows to China is not necessarily equal to China's inflows of Japanese capital, as reported in the different national statistics. These statistical discrepancies have several causes. It may partly be due to statistical leakage or error, as the Japanese statistics cover only large-scale investments of more than 100 million yen (before 1994 more than 300 million yen). The Japanese Ministry of Finance's (MOF) data of FDI outflows are based on notifications by investing companies. The Chinese data are based on the notifications to the local investing authorities. Thus, some firms may make inaccurate reports of their investments to the Ministry, while some provinces in China may exaggerate their performance of accepting FDI for certain political purposes. The statistical discrepancy may further result from a difference in the statistical basis. For example, some projects that have been reported to the Japanese ministry may have proved abortive or were not realised. But the most important cause for statistical discrepancies lies in the fact that reinvestment by Japanese companies is counted as a foreign investment by the Chinese statistical standard, while it is not recorded at all in Japanese statistics. Therefore, the Chinese figures of Japan's capital inflows tend to overestimate and the Japanese figures tend to underestimate Japanese direct investment into China. Both the Chinese and the Japanese statistical reports show a similar trend until the middle of the 1990s, but move quite differently after Japan's investment boom in China was over. According to the Japanese MOF statistics, Japan's Chinese investment reached its highest level in 1995 followed by a steep decline until 1999. According to the Chinese statistics it gradually declined after 1993.

A comment on China's FDI inflows from Hong Kong, as reported by the Chinese statistics, may be in order. Investment by any Hong Kong company is counted as a Hong Kong investment, even though it is a subsidiary of a foreign company. For example, Hong Kong Sanyo, a subsidiary of Sanyo Japan, legally owns a factory in Shenzhen, and its investment is treated as Hong Kong investment. Furthermore many Chinese or foreign-owned companies channel their (domestic) Chinese investment via Hong Kong in order to reap valuable tax concessions. Thus, it is safe to say that Hong Kong's investment in China is overestimated. It includes many FDI flows made by non-Hong Kong, multinational firms.

Features of Japan's FDI in China

What are, then, the main characteristics of Japanese direct investment in China compared to other major countries? We may summarise some features of Japan's investment in China as follows:

1   Industry: Generally foreign capital is invested in the manufacturing sector in China, and Japanese investment in particular has been biased towards this sector. In contrast, relatively few Japanese firms have ever tried to enter the Chinese service and real estate markets (see Table 8.9), where Hong Kong and other overseas Chinese capital has invested relatively more.
2   Export: Japan's FDI in China is more or less export-oriented. The sectors and industries that absorb Japanese capital are likely to export their products back to Japan or to other export destinations, thus contributing heavily to China's exports. In 1996, 40.8 per cent of China's exports were made by foreign enterprises. In contrast to Japanese investment, it is believed that more US and EU capital came to China in order to supply the domestic market. Japanese investors are also interested in the Chinese market, but they are more risk averse.

144 *Hanns Günther Hilpert and Nakagane Katsuji*

Table 8.9 Japanese investment in China by industrial sector (%)

	By number of projects	By value
Primary industries[1]	3.94	2.38
Construction	3.16	2.82
Food and tobacco	10.70	6.63
Textiles and clothing	17.65	10.05
Chemicals	8.82	9.95
Ceramics	3.12	5.91
Metals	5.07	5.31
Electrical machinery	8.28	20.01
Precision machinery	2.30	4.29
Other manufacturing[2]	15.84	8.97
Wholesale and retail	7.69	3.54
Real estate	1.93	6.88
Other services[3]	11.49	13.23

Source: Own calculation from the investment data for twelve provinces and cities in: Mitsubishi Research Institute 1999, *Chūgoku Shinshutsu Kigyō Ichiran* (List of Japanese Firms in China), Sōsōsha.

Notes
1 Farming, forestry, fishing, mining.
2 Timber processing and furniture, papermaking, publishing, leather, general machinery, transport equipment and other manufacturing.
3 Utilities, transport and communications, finance and insurance, rental services, hotels, recreational services and other services.

3 Firm size: A majority of Japanese investors in China are small or medium-sized enterprises. The low average firm size of Japanese investors is reflected in the relatively low average amount of capital invested by Japanese firms, in sharp contrast to US and EU investment in China.

4 Implementation: Compared to investors from other countries the 'implementation ratio' of investment contracts undertaken by Japanese firms is high.[11]

5 Geographical location: Like most other FDI in China, Japanese capital is concentrated in the coastal areas, because in these places infrastructure is more developed. Japanese FDI is concentrated in the northern and central part of China, while the focus of investment by overseas Chinese is on Guangdong, Fujian, Zhejiang and Jiangsu provinces, which are the location of their ancestors' homes. Whether certain agglomeration effects inherent in FDI, which we shall refer to below, bring about this geographical bias itself is open to question (see Table 8.10). There are relatively many Japanese enterprises investing in Dalian in Liaoning province, a city with a historical link of the Japanese in prewar China.

Motives for Japanese FDI in China

There are various objectives behind foreign direct investment in developing countries. The subjective motives of Japanese firms' direct investment in China can be found through systematic surveys at the firm level (Table 8.11). The table

Economic relations 145

Table 8.10 Regional dispersion of Japan's investment in China

	Projects Number	%	Enterprises Number	%
South China[1]	567	10.9	1138	10.8
Greater Shanghai[2]	1723	33.2	3668	34.9
Bohai Rim[3]	1750	33.7	2760	26.3
North-east China[4]	622	12.0	2114	20.1
Inland provinces	532	10.2	828	7.9
Total China	5194	100.0	10,508	100.0

Source: Zhu Yan, *Chūgoku no Kokuyūkigyō Kaikaku to Nihon no Taichū Tôshi* (China's SOE Reform and Japan's Investment in China), FRI Research Report, no. 45, Tokyo, 1999.

Notes
1 Guangdong, Guangxi, Fujian Hainan.
2 Shanghai, Jiangsu, Zhejiang.
3 Beijing, Tianjin, Henan, Shangdong.
4 Liaoning, Jilin, Heilongjiang.

Table 8.11 Investment purposes of Japanese investors by region in 1999 (%)

	China	ASEAN-4	US/Canada	EU	Average
Maintenance and expansion of existing markets	68.8	64.4	74.5	70.6	67.1
Opening up a new market	48.4	42.4	45.5	45.1	44.3
Export to third countries	20.3	35.6	9.1	5.9	18.0
Development of goods suited to host countries	14.1	16.9	21.8	19.6	15.8
Utilisation of cheap labour	29.7	33.9	0.0	0.0	15.5
Supply of parts to assembly makers	14.1	23.7	18.2	15.7	15.5
Overseas dispersion of production sites	14.1	27.1	10.9	9.8	14.9
Export to Japan	23.4	25.4	5.5	2.0	13.6

Source: JBIC, *Kaihatsu Kin-yū Kenkyūsho Hō* (Institute of Development Finance Report), January 2000.

Note
Figures indicate percentage of investment purposes based on multiple answering method.

shows that the major purpose of Japanese foreign investment is generally market-related, whether keeping existing markets or seeking a new market in host countries. Investment in China is no exception. When it comes to investment in developing countries like China and ASEAN-4, utilising cheap labour and exporting products to Japan or other foreign markets are the second most important purposes. Japanese companies investing in China do not only seek to enter and expand their market, they also want to enjoy the local comparative advantages, including low wages.

This finding can be confirmed by estimating Japanese FDI functions. If we regress the number of cases of Japan's FDI in China on (a) the wage differential between Japan and China, (b) the future prospects of the Chinese economy represented by its growth rate, and (c) the openness of China represented by the export/GDP ratio, then we can obtain good results.[12] In other words, Japanese investors have always had at least three motives for investment in China. First they have been attracted by the low wages in China, particularly after the drastic appreciation of the Japanese yen. Second, they were looking at the expanding Chinese market and at seemingly bright future prospects. Third, the openness of the Chinese economy has definitely been conducive to Japanese capital inflows. As mentioned above, Japanese FDI in Chinese manufacturing industries is characterised by its export orientation. Japanese companies invest in China primarily in order to export the products manufactured there. The more China exports, the more FDI will be attracted to China. Therefore, there seems to exist a mutual and close relationship, at least potentially, between Japanese FDI and China's export growth.

Externality effects as well as agglomeration effects may also work inherently in the investment decisions of Japanese companies in China. Putting it in another way, the more investment is accumulated, the more likely is continuing investment in China. As shown in Table 8.10, Japanese investment is dispersed across China, but it is concentrated in some specific regions. Japanese FDI in China in general, and in the textile and clothing industry in particular, is said to have demonstrated stronger agglomeration effects than US direct investment in China. In the electronics and electric machinery industry, US presence in a region increases the possibility that Japanese investors will select the same region for their investment.[13] Such effects seem to have played a role during the aforementioned China investment boom.

Japanese FDI and its contribution to China's economic growth

FDI accelerates economic growth in developing countries, directly or indirectly. Four major contributions of FDI to economic growth in developing countries are commonly referred to in the economics literature:[14] (1) FDI helps to improve human resource capacities, whether entrepreneurial, technological, or managerial, by way of education and training as well as by the creation of employment opportunities. (2) FDI carries new technology to host countries. In China foreign-owned firms have a higher productivity than state-owned and other domestic firms. (3) FDI brings capital from abroad, which adds to domestic capital formation in host countries. Whether FDI is a substitute for or a complement to domestic savings is a matter of empirical test, but in the case of China we can find no substitutability between these two types of capital. (4) FDI can contribute to economic growth in developing countries by promoting their international trade. Many empirical studies, contrary to Mundell's hypothesis,[15] support the view that FDI generates more exports rather than replacing them, at least in the initial stages. In our view, the fourth channel is quite significant in the

Chinese context. As Japanese FDI is a major source of Chinese FDI it also contributes to China's economic growth, through the above four channels, at least to the same extent as, but probably more than, its share. Japanese capital has promoted Chinese exports, which in turn has attracted more Japanese capital.

Conclusions

Basic assumptions on Sino-Japanese economic relations

Based on the reviews and analyses of trade and FDI in previous sections, we shall now analyse future prospects for the Sino-Japanese economic relationship in a wider context. Before proceeding, we make three basic assumptions:

China's entry into the WTO will promote the globalisation of the Chinese economy

As China enters the WTO it can be expected that its foreign trade will be further developed, more foreign investment will be brought in and its capital flows will be more liberalised. However, the WTO cannot settle all trade and investment disputes between member countries. Disputes will continue thus: China might seek regional arrangements to protect its own industries in face of, say, hardening US pressures to open its domestic grain market, and China will oscillate between the two poles of internationalism – globalism versus regionalism. China's entry into the WTO will also encourage Japan to develop more intense economic relations with China. It can be assumed that Japan will continue to contribute to the economic development of China through trade, FDI and probably also ODA.

China's development strategy remains basically the same

At present China is moving its development focus from the eastern coast to the west. As much ODA and FDI as possible shall be brought to this area. Domestic investment, induced by an enormous amount of infrastructure construction, is also attracted to the underdeveloped west. Although it is still uncertain how effective this new development focus will be, it is quite probable that China will adopt a relatively more inward-oriented policy. Nevertheless the existing interregional gaps will remain or may even widen further. Moreover, China will go on pursuing its existing industrial policy in order to establish a comprehensive, modern industrial structure. In other words, China will not adopt a market-guided industrial policy based on the comparative advantage theory for the foreseeable future.

Political and international stability will stay intact

Although it is impossible to predict political change over the next twenty years, we simply assume that China's political stability will be sustained. Serious

148 *Hanns Günther Hilpert and Nakagane Katsuji*

international conflicts concerning Taiwan or other neighbouring countries will be avoided and China's domestic stability will be maintained.

Four scenarios for the future of the Sino-Japanese economic relationship

Given the above assumptions, it seems that we can write the following four possible scenarios of the Sino-Japanese economic relationship in terms of two forces, namely coordination mechanism (market versus state) and psychological distance (sympathy versus hostility).

Rivalry

As we can assume from the estimation of economic growth, China will become a big economic power in Asia by the year 2020. On the basis of this economic strength China could display political leadership in international affairs. Then the two big economies of Asia would be rivals for hegemony in the Asian economy. In this case the state rather than the market is the main actor coordinating the interrelationship. The governments of both nations might try to establish their own regional groupings, which would be driven by some sort of mutual antagonism.

Dependence/domination

An environment where the market mechanism basically determines the bilateral economic relations may also lead to an antagonistic result. In this scenario, as a consequence of the unrestricted activity of foreign investors, China's major capital- and technology-intensive industries, such as steel, chemicals, automobiles and semiconductors, would be dominated by Japanese (and other foreign) financially strong companies. On the other hand, China would dominate the Japanese markets for labour-intensive products, e.g. textiles, apparel, electric appliances, etc. Trade conflicts would characterise the bilateral relationship. It is true that economic domination does not mean political control, but if one country dominated the market of the other, certain hostile feelings would be nourished by the people in the economically dominated country, as a result of bankruptcy, unemployment and a sense of humiliation.

Regionalism

In this scenario the state governments of the two economies would agree on a cooperative economic arrangement like a 'free trade zone'. This zone might also include neighbouring countries such as Korea and Taiwan. In this case a close economic relationship between these nations, based on an intensifying linkage of trade and investment, would give a push to a new trend of regionalism on a global scale. Furthermore, an Asian Monetary Fund might be created in spite of fierce US opposition. In this scenario certain ideological underpinnings such as 'Asianism' would play a role.[16]

Economic relations 149

Competition

In the world of the globalisation of production and markets every country, whether in Asia or somewhere else, is exposed to ever increasing competition in the global market. If current Chinese industrial policies are continued, China will be an increasingly strong competitor on the world market. However, the rising strength of Chinese suppliers does not preclude the industrial involvement of companies from Japan, the US, Europe or Korea in China's development. Foreign investors are engaging in infrastructure projects and in joint ventures in China. At times these companies form international alliances, because market competition forces them to cooperate. In this scenario both Japan and China would take an active part in the global economic network and thus contribute to the deepening of the international division of labour. However, it cannot be excluded that the coordination by market mechanisms might result in a one-sided dependence of either country in the bilateral relationship.

Bilateral trade, Japanese FDI and economic growth in China

The dynamic development of Chinese exports to Japan, Japanese FDI to China and the economic growth of China does not seem to be a mere coincidence. There seems to be a dynamic relationship between these three factors. Given the huge disparities in wages between China and Japan, the expanding market in China is increasingly attracting Japanese (and other foreign) capital. This capital contributes to China's increasing exports (to Japan and to other countries) and to its economic growth, which in turn stimulates more capital inflows to China. Yet the virtuous circle of these factors is not endless and may be subject to external or systemic shocks. If the Chinese economy happened to halt its growth, e.g. because of transformation failures, financial market turbulences or a WTO shock, foreign investors would retain its capital. Then exports would not increase any further and economic growth would be even more seriously affected. Thus the virtuous cycle would turn in a vicious one, as in the case of the Chinese economy in 1998–99.

Assessment of the Sino-Japanese economic relationship

Figure 8.1 shows the position of the four possible scenarios in a diagram, in which the coordination mechanism (state versus market) forms the vertical axis and the psychological distance (sympathy versus hostility) the horizontal axis. Which is the more likely scenario? Which is the most desirable one for the future of the Sino-Japanese economic relationship? Since it is difficult to predict which of the two coordination mechanisms will prevail in the future and what exactly the psychological distance between Japan and China will be, for a first appraisal the analysis of bilateral trade and investment flows may be useful.

The analysis of trade data not only shows a fast-growing bilateral trade, but – more importantly – unusually high values of bilateral trade interdependence.

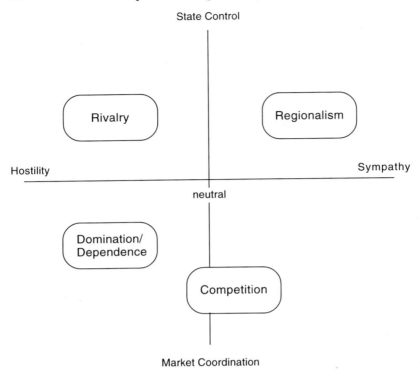

Figure 8.1 Four possible scenarios of Sino-Japanese economic relations

Thus in Sino-Japanese trade cooperation clearly prevails over conflict. As other bilateral economic transactions, notably foreign direct investment and ODA, are complements rather than substitutes for trade, it seems to be justifiable to generalise the predominance of a cooperative pattern to the overall economic relationship. The Chinese economy continues to integrate into the world economy and Japan is assuming a prominent role in this process. In the end the Japanese economy will be linked increasingly closely with China. Although the total volume of Japanese FDI in China seems to be disappointingly low in relative terms, it should not be forgotten that Japanese investing firms cherish China as the most important investment location worldwide. According to the yearly survey by the Japan Bank for International Cooperation (JBIC), almost two-thirds of the enterprises surveyed regard China as the most promising country for their FDI from a long-term point of view (Table 8.12). Hence the more Japanese companies are investing in China, the more intense the horizontal relationship of labour between the two countries will be, and the more neatly both countries will be interwoven into the network of global production. This development will bring about a dynamic, but very delicate relationship between the two economies. From the empirical data we can conclude that rivalry, which would imply a disintegration of the bilateral economic relationship, is the most

Economic relations 151

Table 8.12 The most promising country for Japanese FDI

Ranking	1995 Survey			1999 Survey		
	Country	Number of enterprises	Share %	Country	Number of enterprises	Share %
1	China	215	78	China	170	66
2	Vietnam	113	41	US	77	30
3	India	98	36	India	71	27
4	US	83	30	Thailand	61	24
5	Indonesia	66	24	Vietnam	47	18
6	Thailand	66	24	Indonesia	46	18
7	Myanmar	40	15	Brazil	36	14
8	Malaysia	35	13	Malaysia	20	8
9	Philippines	31	11	Philippines	20	8
10	UK	16	6	Mexico	17	7
	Total	274	100	Total	259	100

Source: JBIC, *Kaihatsu Kin-yū Kenkyūsho Hō* (Institute of Development Finance Report), January 2000.

Note
Figures indicate percentage of investment purposes based on multiple answering method.

unlikely scenario of the four. Of course the existence of economic conflicts between Japan and China cannot be denied. Various incidents prove this. But economic conflicts are obviously not at the centre of the Sino-Japanese economic relationship. The conflicts are rather the consequence of very fruitful and beneficial relations, which generate large gains from cooperation to both sides. The conflicts, however, arise from time to time on the distribution of these gains. The outcome of market processes, the result of negotiations on the micro level, may not be acceptable to the parties involved under some circumstances. Therefore private business or special-interest groups, represented and supported by politicians, may sometimes interfere to change market results in their favour. There are many examples to hand: market access negotiations, anti-dumping charges and import restrictions resulting from them, the grant of investment licences, the employment of ODA, etc. The simple issue is, who is getting what?

Now we shall ponder on the future psychological distance between Japan and China and ask whether the economic growth and the industrial maturing of China will have a political impact on the bilateral relationship. It is obvious that when the Chinese economy grows to become another giant in Asia, Japan may cherish some ambivalent feelings about China. It is not just a partner, which Japan should help to develop, but it is a tough competitor in the world market. As long as China pursues its dream of building a 'prosperous and strong great nation' (*fuqiang daguo*), it will seek a comprehensive industrial structure, with the result that it will have to or it will be able to compete with Japan in a wide range of industries. On the other hand, Japan will not reduce its manufacturing capacities, although it has lost its comparative advantage. Neither will Japan give up agriculture. Thus China will blame Japan for delaying unavoidable industrial

152 *Hanns Günther Hilpert and Nakagane Katsuji*

restructuring to the detriment of China's industrial development. Both for Japan and for China the growing economic interdependence becomes problematic in the event of displacement in competition. In addition to the well-known political conflicts – the unresolved legacy of Japanese war atrocities, the Japanese wariness of China's rising military capacities – economic relations may also be a reason and a trigger for a bilateral conflict.

In order to prevent a hostile relationship, it does not seem appropriate to rely on market coordination. The state will have to come in and a certain coordination mechanism may be required. Beyond multilateral institutions like the WTO or APEC there is a need for bilateral arrangements or bilateral institutions to resolve disputes or to tackle special contentious issues. A prime example is the much-needed Sino-Japanese cooperation for improvement in the environmental field. In particular, the handling of China's CO_2 emissions, which produce negative spillovers into China and in Japan, should be dealt with bilaterally. Yet it is difficult to imagine that Sino-Japanese cooperation will be developed so far as to establish a regional trading arrangement with China as an indispensable partner. Free trade between Japan and China would be more likely to fuel than curb the existing bilateral economic conflicts.

As rivalry and regionalism are rather unlikely development scenarios, it seems to us that Sino-Japanese economic relations will pass to a phase of competition and cooperation. In our view this is also the most desirable scenario for both of them. As the Chinese economy develops, Sino-Japanese relations will have to evolve from an era of 'special relations' into a new one. The relationship has been special in the sense that one country, China, maintained a psychological superiority over the other country, Japan, because it renounced the right of war reparations to the latter. By 2020, a new period will have arrived, in which the two economies will be basically subject to an unprecedented scale of globalisation.

Notes

1 For a detailed discussion of the use of the trade intensity index in bilateral trade analysis, see Kym Anderson and Hege Norheim, 'History, Geography and Regional Economic Integration', in Kym Anderson and Richard Blackhurst (eds), *Regional Integration and the Global Trading System*, New York and London, Harvester-Wheatsheaf, 1993, pp. 23–4, 47–8; Peter Drysdale and Ross Garnaut, 'Trade Intensities and the Analysis of Bilateral Trade Flows in a Many-Country World', *Hitotsubashi Journal of Economics*, 1982, pp. 62–84.

2 The world import market must not include imports from country A, because a country cannot export goods to itself.

3 For a thorough analysis of China's export trade pattern, see Zhang Xiao-guang, *China's Trade Patterns and International Comparative Advantage*, Houndsmill, Basingstoke, Macmillan, 2000.

4 For the connection between Japanese investment in China and the bilateral trade, see Thomas Chan, Noel Tracy and Zhui Wenhui, *China's Export Miracle, Origins, Results and Prospects*, Houndsmill, Basingstoke, Macmillan, 1999, pp. 136–9.

5 Nakagane took up the well-known theme in development economics, whether trade is an 'engine' or a 'handmaiden' of growth, and applied Shims' causality test to the

special case of China. This test made clear that for the data of the magnitude of exports during the period 1978–95 the handmaiden hypothesis was supported, but when one looks at the growth rate of exports neither of the hypotheses can be denied, or a dual causality can be identified. See K. Nakagane, *Chūgoku Keizai Hattenron (Economic Development and Transition in China)*, Tokyo, Yūhikaku, 1999, pp. 295–7.

6 For an institution-based explanation of this argument, see D. D. Zhang, *China's Relations with Japan in an Era of Economic Liberalisation*, New York, Commack, 1998, pp. 87–93, 119–67.

7 In April 2001 Japan introduced import safeguards against three agricultural products from China, namely, scallions, shiitake mushrooms and rushes to make tatami mats.

8 Needless to say, trade carries technology and information indirectly from abroad, because new technology, for example, is usually embedded in capital goods imports. Certain types of consumer goods, too, would bring new fashions or ways of life to developing countries.

9 A Japanese businessman tells a vivid story of why his company had to retreat from China. See Y. Akamatsu, *Nicchū Gōbenkigyō Funtōki* (Memoirs of a Japanese Joint Venture Struggling in China), Tokyo, Sōsōsha, 1999.

10 A caveat must be added to this result. Contrary to trade data, FDI data is hardly internationally comparable. Counting methods and definitions of FDI differ from country to country. For example, no recognised standard has yet been established to fix a minimum capital volume or to treat the re-investment of profits, the fund raising in the host country or in financial offshore centres, or the disinvestments. Taking into account the statistical issues raised in the following section one may expect Japanese investment in China to be somehow higher than FDI intensity indices.

11 A Japanese firm investing in China has told us, 'A Japanese company's behaviour is different from that of other nations. We respect marriage rather than just engagement.'

12 For the regression, see Nakagane Katsuji, 'Sino-Japanese Economic Relations: FDI, Trade and China's Economic Development', a paper presented at a workshop on the Chinese–Japanese relationship organised by the European Institute of Japanese Studies and the Swedish Institute for International Affairs, Stockholm, 17–19 August 2000.

13 Ding Jianping, 'Agglomeration Effects in Manufacturing Location – Are There Any Country's Preferences?', *Economia Internazionale*, vol. 52 (2) (1998), pp. 59–78. He analyses the agglomeration effects of Japanese and American investment in China, based on the conditional logit analysis.

14 A. Bende-Nabende, *FDI, Regionalism, Government Policy and Endogenous Growth*, Aldershot, Ashgate Publishing Company, 1999.

15 R. Mundell, 'International Trade and Factor Mobility', *American Economic Review*, vol. 47 (1957), pp. 321–35. He shows that an increase in trade impediments stimulates factor movements, while an increase in restrictions to factor movements stimulates trade.

16 For example Morishima proposed the idea of establishing a Northeast Asian version of the 'European Union', though it looks absolutely unfeasible. See M. Morishima, *Naze Nihon-wa Botsuraku-suruka* (Why Will Japan Fall?), Tokyo, Iwanami Shoten, 1999.

9 Japanese firms in China
What problems and difficulties are they facing?

Hu Xinxin

Japan has been one of the most important economic partners for the People's Republic of China since 1979, when China's economic reform and opening up started. By the end of 1999, the Chinese authorities had approved nearly 19,000 FDI projects from Japan, with a total contractual value of more than US$35 billion, of which, US$25 billion had been actually invested (Table 9.1).

Japanese firms in China are playing an important role in the Sino-Japan economic relationship. This is not only because Japan is one of the most important FDI (foreign direct investment) source countries for China, but also, as recent statistics prove, these Japanese firms have become the leading forces in China's exports to Japan.

According to questionnaire surveys by the Japan Bank of International Cooperation (JBIC), many Japanese firms consider China to be the most promising FDI destination over a medium and long-term period. However, firms that made earlier investments in China have not been very satisfied with the outcomes, particularly in terms of profitability and sales. The government's (Ministry of Finance of Japan, or MOF) statistics also indicated a sharp reduction in the FDI flow from Japan from 432 billion yen in 1995 to 84 billion yen in 1999.

This paper will focus on the problems and difficulties that Japanese firms are actually facing in China. Some Japanese organisations or institutions, such as the Japan External Trade Organisation (JETRO),[1] JBIC[2] and the Japan–China Investment Promotion Organisation (JIPO)[3] have conducted general surveys on the issue. What I intend to do here, however, is to discuss this issue in detail and to provide my independent opinions from a Chinese researcher's point of view. To make my research more solid, I have conducted my own survey by interviewing Chinese and Japanese business persons involved in a dozen Japanese-funded firms in China. I then intend to compare the results of these interviews with my previous surveys conducted in earlier years, and discuss some successful cases.

This paper is organised into four sections. In the first section I will try to draw a rough picture of Japanese FDI and the general background of Japanese firms in China. The second section will discuss the problems and difficulties that Japanese firms are facing in China. The third section will illustrate a few successful cases, and finally, in the fourth section, I will discuss the subject further and make suggestions as the summary of this research.

Japanese firms in China   155

Table 9.1 Top ten investors in China by the year-end 1999 (US$100 million)

	Projects		Contracted value		Realised value	
	Number	*Share %*	*Amount*	*Share %*	*Amount*	*Share %*
Accumulated total	341,538	100.00	6137.17	100.00	3076.31	100.00
Hong Kong	184,824	54.12	3109.57	50.67	1547.94	50.32
US	28,702	8.40	526.10	8.57	256.48	8.34
Japan	18,769	5.50	351.34	5.72	248.86	8.09
Taiwan Province	43,516	12.74	437.74	7.13	238.63	7.76
Singapore	8500	2.49	333.49	5.43	148.20	4.82
Virgin Islands	2031	0.59	204.05	3.32	93.95	3.05
Korea	12,726	3.73	163.20	2.66	88.37	2.87
UK	2554	0.75	161.41	2.63	75.84	2.47
Germany	2128	0.62	93.35	1.52	48.11	1.56
Macao	6418	1.88	93.09	1.52	36.36	1.18

Source: Ministry of Foreign Trade and Economic Cooperation (http://www.moftec.gov.cn/).

General background: Japanese FDI and Japanese firms in China

Foreign investment and foreign-funded firms have played an important role in Chinese economic development in the past two decades. It is reported that there were more than 20 million people employed by foreign-funded firms in the PRC in 2000. The government tax revenue from foreign-funded firms made up 15 per cent of the country's industrial and commercial tax revenue, while the trading volume by foreign firms made up half of China's total imports and exports.[4]

FDI flow from Japan is an important element in China's FDI. According to the data from the Ministry of Foreign Trade and Economic Cooperation (MOTFC), China had approved more than 341,000 FDI projects with a total contractual investments value of about US$614 billion, of which, US$308 billion had actually been used by the end of 1999. The main stake of FDI was the investment by overseas Chinese from Hong Kong and Taiwan.[5] Among the foreign source countries, Japan ranked second next to the US, with a 5.5 per cent share of total projects, 5.72 per cent in contractual value and 8.09 per cent in accumulative totals of realised value (Table 9.1).

Although the Chinese government had approved almost 19,000 FDI projects from Japan by 1999, it is difficult to know exactly how many Japanese firms are actually doing business in the PRC. Some of them are no longer visible in the Chinese market for a number of reasons, such as withdrawal, merger or acquisition and suspension of operations. Mitsubishi Research Institute (MRI) collected various references issued in China and enlisted 12,000 firms in its 1998 listing. This listing probably does not cover all Japanese firms in China. The Japanese-funded firms are heavily concentrated in the coastal cities and areas such as Shanghai, Liaoning, Jiangsu, Shandong, Beijing and Guangdong. Seventy per cent of the firms in this listing are in these six coastal cities or provinces (Table 9.2). We can also learn from the statistical data that most of the Japanese FDI is made in manufacturing industries, especially in the sectors of textiles and electrical machinery.

156 *Hu Xinxin*

Table 9.2 Japanese-funded firms by region in the PRC

	No. of firms	%
Shanghai	2305	19.8
Liaoning	2006	17.3
(Dalian)	(1289)	(11.1)
Jiangsu	1288	11.1
Shandong	951	8.2
Beijing	871	7.5
Guangdong	770	6.6
Total for the above six cities/provinces	8191	70.49
Total for the coastal areas	10,218	87.93
Other parts	1402	12.07
Total for the country	11,620	100.00

Source: Chūgoku Shinshuto Kigyō Ichiran, Mitsubishi Research Institute, Sōsōsha, 1998.

Joint venture is the most common format for Japanese investments in China. According to the JBIC data, more than 62 per cent of Japanese FDI in China consists of joint ventures. This is far larger than the ratios of joint ventures in other countries or regions. However, the ratio was reduced by ten percentage points during the past five years, from 72.3 per cent in 1995 to 62.3 per cent in 1999, while the ratio of solely owned companies was increased from 31.4 per cent to 41.4 per cent (Table 9.3).

Since it is difficult to find general information to evaluate the performance of Japanese firms in China, we have to quote questionnaire surveys conducted by some Japanese organisations. JETRO conducted a survey in March 2000. According to this survey which covers 275 companies in the cities of Beijing, Dalian and Shanghai, and the Guangdong province, nearly 69 per cent of the responding companies increased their sales in 1999, and more companies are expecting further increases in 2000 (Table 9.4). In 1997, only 40 per cent of the companies reported profits. In 1999 the percentage rose to 56.7 per cent (Table 9.5), and in FY 2000, 64.7 per cent of the companies are expecting an improvement in their balance sheet (Table 9.6).

JIPO also conducted a survey at the end of 1999, which covered more than 500 Japanese companies. According to the survey, the average sales turnover of the responding companies had increased by 15 per cent in 1999. Seventy per cent of the companies managed to make profits in 1999.

As mentioned earlier, FDI flow from Japan into mainland China has been sharply reduced since 1996. Although a large number of Japanese companies still consider China the most promising FDI destination over the medium and long term, the latest available survey by JBIC which covers 786 Japanese manufacturing companies with three or more overseas affiliates shows that the percentage of companies still in favour of investing in China has dropped in the past few years from 71 per cent in 1994 to 55 per cent in 1999 (over the medium term) (see Table 9.7). The reasons for the decline of Japanese FDI flow into China and the

Japanese firms in China   157

Table 9.3 Patterns of Japanese FDI in China, 1995–9 (%)

	1995	1997	1999
100% ownership	31.4	30.4	41.4
Joint venture	72.3	77.2	62.3
Mergers and acquisitions	5.8	2.5	0.6
Equity participation			4.9

Source: Kaburagi Shinji, Noda Hidehiko and Ikehara Satoshi, 2000 (JBIC's survey).

Table 9.4 Performance in sales of Japanese firms in China

	1998		1999		Expectation of 2000	
	Number of firms	Ratio %	Number of firms	Ratio %	Number of firms	Ratio %
Increase	157	57.1	190	69.1	205	74.5
No change	36	13.1	34	12.4	44	16.0
Decrease	58	21.1	41	14.9	19	6.9
Not clear	24	8.7	10	3.6	7	2.5
Total	275	100.0	275	100.0	275	100.0

Source: JMA Research Institute Inc., 2000 (JETRO's survey).

Table 9.5 Profitability of Japanese firms in China

	1997		1998		1999	
	Number of firms	Ratio %	Number of firms	Ratio %	Number of firms	Ratio %
Profitable	110	40.0	123	44.7	156	56.7
Balance	22	8.0	20	7.3	34	12.4
Loss	118	42.9	122	44.4	76	27.6
Not clear	25	9.1	10	3.6	9	3.3
Total	275	100.0	275	100.0	275	100.0

Source: JMAR, 2000 (JETRO's survey).

Table 9.6 Expected profitability of Japanese firms over FY, 1999–2000

	1999		2000	
	Number of firms	Ratio %	Number of firms	Ratio %
Better	175	63.6	178	64.7
No change	39	14.2	55	20.0
Worse	51	18.5	32	11.6
Not clear	10	3.6	10	3.6
Total	275	100.0	178	100.0

Source: JMAR, 2000 (JETRO's survey).

158   Hu Xinxin

Table 9.7 Promising FDI destinations over the medium and long term
(multiple response)

Medium term (next three years)

1994 238 firms	No.	%	1997 342 firms	No.	%	1999 278 firms	No.	%
1 PRC	169	71	1 PRC	219	64	1 PRC	153	55
2 Thailand	75	32	2 US	126	36	2 US	108	39
3 US	72	30	3 Indonesia	97	28	3 Thailand	76	27
4 Indonesia	58	24	4 Thailand	84	25	4 India	42	15
5 Malaysia	57	24	5 India	77	23	5 Indonesia	41	15
6 Vietnam	34	14	6 Vietnam	66	19	6 Vietnam	30	11
7 Singapore	33	14	7 Philippines	47	14	7 Malaysia	25	9
8 Taiwan	23	10	8 Malaysia	46	13	8 Philippines	25	9
9 UK	19	8	9 Brazil	28	8	9 UK	25	9
10 Philippines	14	6	10 Taiwan	28	8	10 Brazil	21	8
11 India	14							

Long term (next ten years)

1994 238 firms	No.	%	1997 269 firms	No.	%	1999 259 firms	No.	%
1 PRC	169	71	1 PRC	169	64	1 PRC	170	66
2 Thailand	75	32	2 India	98	36	2 US	77	30
3 US	72	30	3 US	83	28	3 India	71	27
4 Indonesia	58	24	4 Vietnam	64	25	4 Thailand	61	24
5 Malaysia	57	24	5 Indonesia	57	23	5 Vietnam	47	18
6 Vietnam	34	14	6 Thailand	44	19	6 Indonesia	46	18
7 Singapore	33	14	7 Brazil	30	14	7 Brazil	36	14
8 Taiwan	23	10	8 Philippines	29	13	8 Malaysia	20	8
9 UK	19	8	9 Malaysia	25	8	9 Philippines	20	8
10 Philippines	14	6	10 Myanmar	14	8	10 Mexico	17	7
11 India	14							

Source: Kaburagi Shinji, Noda Hidehiko and Ikehara Satoshi, 2000 (JBIC's survey).

diminishing interest may vary. However, the overall performance of Japanese
business activities in China is obviously not considered satisfactory.

Problems and difficulties that Japanese firms encounter in China

The JBIC survey, which was conducted by a questionnaire format, provides data
on how Japanese companies have evaluated the performances of their business
activities in various countries. The responding companies give very low points to
their performances in China. The self-evaluation of the overall performance in
China, as well as of profitability and sales, are all among the lowest in the world
(Table 9.8). Furthermore, the points have become lower over the past few years
(Table 9.9).

Table 9.8 Self-evaluation of FDI performance by region

	Overall performance	Profit-ability	Sales	Local-isation	Technology transfer*	Contribution to export*
PRC (223 companies)	2.72	2.61	2.59	3.01	2.93	3.03
NIES (289)	3.23	3.07	3.12	3.45	3.38	3.23
ASEAN-4 (525)	2.96	2.74	2.89	3.27	3.10	3.21
US/Canada (314)	3.19	2.97	3.21	3.57	3.46	3.21
EU (218)	3.09	2.78	3.00	3.50	3.35	3.29
Latin America (101)	2.87	2.67	2.81	3.31	3.03	3.03
Central Europe (14)	3.00	2.94	2.82	2.88	3.12	3.18

Source: Kaburagi Shinji, Noda Hidehiko and Ikehara Satoshi, 2000 (JBIC's survey), supplemented by data from EXIM Japan FY 1998 Survey (data from 1997, published in *Journal of Research Institute for International Investment and Development*, vol. 25, no. 1, 1999).

Scale: 1. Insufficient; 2. Somewhat insufficient; 3. In between; 4. Somewhat sufficient; 5. Fairly sufficient.

*Figures from EXIM Japan FY 1998 Survey (1997 data).

Table 9.9 Changing self-evaluation of FDI performance in China, 1995–9

	Overall performance	Profitability	Sales	Localisation
1995	2.85	2.75	2.76	2.96
1996	2.82	2.55	2.72	2.95
1997	2.85	2.65	2.70	2.94
1998	2.81	2.67	2.74	2.89
1999	2.72	2.61	2.59	3.01

Source: Kaburagi Shinji, Noda Hidehiko and Ikehara Satoshi, 2000 (JBIC's survey).

Scale: 1. Insufficient; 2. Somewhat insufficient; 3. In between; 4. Somewhat sufficient; 5. Fairly sufficient.

What caused such a low self-evaluation by Japanese businesses in China? In other words, what problems and difficulties are Japanese firms facing in China? Let us first look at the results of the questionnaire surveys conducted by JBIC, JETRO and JIPO.

The JBIC's survey puts the spotlight on what Japanese investors are mostly concerned about while undertaking FDI in various countries, and indicates that major concerns about China are frequent, and abrupt changes in the local legal system (64.7 per cent of the responding companies), ambiguous application of local legal systems (60.8 per cent), local infrastructure (53.6 per cent) and frequent and abrupt changes in local taxation systems (53.6 per cent) (Table 9.10).

The JETRO's survey examines what kind of problems Japanese-funded firms encounter when operating in China. According to the survey conducted in March 2000, the top ten problems are: (1) complicated administrative procedures (48.7 per cent of the responding companies); (2) changes in yen/dollar exchange rates (45.5 per cent); (3) difficulty in obtaining materials/parts from the local market

160   *Hu Xinxin*

Table 9.10 Concerns in undertaking FDI in China (multiple response)

	1	2	3
1998	Local legal system	Local infrastructure	Local taxation
1999	(Frequent and abrupt changes in) local legal system (64.7%)	(Ambiguous application of) local legal systems (60.8%)	Local infrastructure (53.6%)
			(Frequent and abrupt changes in) local taxation systems (53.6%)

Source: Kaburagi Shinji, Noda Hidehiko and Ikehara Satoshi, 2000 (JBIC's survey).

(41.8 per cent); (4) delay in getting the credit back after the sales of products (39.3 per cent); (5) high customs duty (37.1 per cent); (6) competition with other companies (33.1 per cent); (7) quality control (29.8 per cent); (8) recession of the Japanese economy (28.7 per cent); (9) complicated tax system (25.8 per cent); and (10) the condition of the local market in China (23.3 per cent).

JIPO has recently examined the problems in the business operation of Japanese firms, compared with the results of its survey in 1997. A large number of companies still consider marketing/distribution, personnel/labour supervision and changes in government policies toward foreign investment as the most serious problems, while the relationship with the government had become more important than two years previously (Table 9.11).

The above-mentioned surveys are very informative, although they sometimes give us slightly different figures due to the different approaches and questions set in their questionnaires. They cannot, however, give us more information about the background to the various companies that are carrying out businesses in various industries and in various areas. To obtain more detailed and solid information, I visited more than a dozen Japanese-funded firms and business organisations in Beijing, Shanghai, Tianjin and Guangdong province during the period June 1999 to July 2000. I tried to cover different types of companies: manufacturers and non-manufacturers, joint venture companies and solely owned Japanese ones, big ones and smaller ones, successful ones and not very successful ones.

In my survey, I interviewed Japanese managers at eight companies and Chinese managers at six companies. There were nine manufacturers and three non-manufacturers. The patterns of the investment were joint venture (eight companies), Japanese solely funded (two companies) and cooperative joint venture (one company; another company was a business representative office). Among the nine joint venture or cooperative joint venture companies, the Japanese have majority ownership with more than 51 per cent shares in five companies (four of them with the Japanese shares of more than 80 per cent), while the Chinese parties have majority ownership in only two companies.

Japanese firms in China 161

Table 9.11 Changes in problems for Japanese business in China (multiple response)

	December 1999		December 1997	
	Rank	*Ratio*	*Rank*	*Ratio*
Marketing and sales	1	33.9	1	43.2
Personnel/labour supervision	2	30.2	3	34.5
Changes in foreign investment system and policies	3	29.8	2	35.7
Relationship with the government	4	26.0	9	17.5
Material/parts supply	5	25.8	4	30.7
Changes in exchange rate	6	21.4	5	29.3
Financing	7	17.3	7	21.3
Relationship with shareholders and their representatives	8	14.2	10	14.1
Rising prices and costs	9	12.7	6	26.1
Underdevelopment of infrastructure	10	7.9	8	20.9
Quality control and production supervision	11	5.0	11	12.7

Source: Japan–China Investment Promotion Organisation, 2000.

The most serious concerns of Japanese business in China seemed to be government-related issues, such as government administration, policies, regulations and laws. Their complaints can be roughly classified into two categories: government-administration-related issues and law/policy-related issues.

Government administration

The government-administration-related issues were mentioned by half of the companies. The main complaints were as follows:

1   Foreign companies still have to face various business restrictions in China, especially when a company plans to develop its marketing/retail outlets, or tries to import some products from other countries. A Japanese manager of a consumer goods manufacturer commented: 'to make our product combination well coordinated at our retail outlets, we sometimes need to import a small quantity of products produced in our factories in other countries, but we were told that this was not allowed'. Some Japanese top managers told me that their companies had not been permitted to open their own retail outlets in the country. A manager of a Japanese solely owned pharmaceutical company stated that the public health administration had not given the company approval to begin production, despite the fact that the company had already got a production licence from the industrial and commercial administration.

2   Foreign companies have to wait for a long time and get through various complicated administrative procedures to obtain their business licences.

Things are particularly difficult for the cosmetic and pharmaceutical companies. I was told that it took more than six months to get government approval (the longest case was about twelve months), and it still takes three to six months nowadays.

3 Rules and administrative procedures in various cities and provinces are all different from each other, and some responsible officials in local governments examine business applications according to their personal preferences, instead of the laws and rules. Thus, a good relationship (or friendship) with government officials is essentially needed in many cases, and sometimes is even more important than the regulations and rules. This may cause corruption.

4 Some government departments, especially at local level, issue business licences only when the foreign investor accepts certain conditions for a contract. For example, a company planned that it would import some materials to guarantee the quality of its product at the beginning of the operation, and would later shift to locally produced materials once they found the proper import-substitute sources. But the government officials told them that they had to use locally produced materials from the beginning, otherwise they would not be allowed to start the production.

5 Government at various levels did not provide necessary information and statistical data to foreign investors. Some Japanese managers and business representatives complained that they were not able to collect the basic data and statistics related to the industries which they were serving. The manager of a cosmetics company which opened many retail outlets in various cities told me that the company had great difficulties when they tried to obtain information on administrative procedures and schedules in these localities, and they had to go to every locality to learn what was happening and what things were really like there.

6 Foreign companies are suffering from the low efficiency of government administration and lack of well-regulated operation processes and standards, and yet it is very hard to find a place to complain. A Japanese manager told me the following story: when they asked the government official in charge of their affairs why the company had not been able to get through the administrative procedures faster, they were told that there had not been enough staff to cope with all applications. When a head of a certain department was out of the town, all the other officials would just wait for her/his return. So the whole procedure would be suspended for days or even weeks.

7 Some Japanese managers complained that the authorities at the various local levels had tried to force them to do things they did not want to do. One of the Japanese managers at a retail company told me that his company had been 'supervised' by too many authorities such as the police, the Department of Public Health, the Fire Department and so forth. Another Japanese manager complained that when the company was planning to build a new entrance, the local transportation authority tried to force the company to hire a local firm to do the job.

Law and policy issues

Laws and policy issues were also the most frequently mentioned problems in my interviews. Here are some examples:

1   In China, rules, regulations and laws as well as government policies change frequently and in a very abrupt way without giving any prior notice to foreign companies. This makes the foreign companies seriously concerned because they are not sure whether the government will do what they have promised to do. Recently, the Chinese government has tried to encourage foreign companies to invest more in the central and western part of the country and has promised some favourable policies. However, some Japanese managers told me that they did not believe in it, because they had learnt from past experience that the more favourable treatment the government promises, the more easily the policy changes.

2   Although China has tried to strengthen the legislation system for years, laws and regulations are still not uniformly accessible to the public, nor strictly enforced. Chinese managers told me that one of the good things about their Japanese partners was that they abide by the laws. However, some Japanese managers told me that their Chinese employees told them that if they obeyed the rules and laws, they would be regarded as foolish in China.

3   There are inconsistencies of policies and regulations between the lower local authorities and the upper-level governments, and among the various governmental departments. Furthermore, laws and regulations are not consistently interpreted among various localities. For example, a Japanese manager of a company that has established a number of subsidiaries in the country told me that one of his subsidiaries could easily send its profits back to Japan while another (in another city) was not allowed to do so.

4   Some Japanese managers believe that there are still some defects in Chinese laws. For example, a Japanese manager said that he thought 'The Law of the People's Republic of China on Joint Ventures with Chinese and Foreign Investment' could not protect the rights of the big shareholders. He also complained that, according to Chinese labour law, the company was not able to fire employees with more than ten years working experience with the company even if they behave badly.

5   Although the government had created many policies to encourage foreign investment, a number of Japanese managers indicated that governments at various levels in China were not providing the necessary public services for foreign investors so as to help them to solve their problems, such as labour disputes and intellectual property problems, and to keep the laws and rules observed.

Among other problems related to the policy issues, a few Japanese managers complained that foreigners' income tax was unfairly high. Some complained about the problem of imposition of miscellaneous fees (*Luan Shou Fei*), although most of the Japanese managers agreed that the situation has been largely

164   *Hu Xinxin*

improved in the past few years. Only one company complained about high customs duty.

In addition to the government administration and law/policy issues, there were other problems concerning partnership with Chinese counterparts, infrastructure and business environment, labour/employee issues and the relationship with mother companies.

Partnership

The second most important concern for Japanese firms in China is the relationship with their Chinese partners. The most common problem is the difficulty in communication, mostly because of the different ways of thinking. Disagreement and differences in various respects, from the development strategy of the company and the profit divide policy to more detailed matters, often occur. Among the companies I have visited, almost half of the Japanese managers have had some trouble with their Chinese partners, although only one company suffered seriously. Most of the Chinese managers stated that they enjoyed a good partnership with the Japanese. One of the Chinese managers told me that they were happy with their Japanese partners, while another said they had had some trouble with a Japanese manager, because he never told his Chinese colleagues a word about what he was thinking, but after the Japanese manager was removed, everything became all right. A few Chinese managers had complaints, although none felt that they had serious trouble with their Japanese partners.

The following are complaints I have heard from the Japanese side:

1   Some of their Chinese partners were more interested in taking money and advanced technology from the Japanese side and less interested in developing a long-term cooperative relationship. Thus, after they get the money and technology, they want to get rid of the Japanese.
2   The Chinese tried to force the joint venture companies to hire managers that were obviously not qualified.
3   A company had suffered badly from the relationship with a Chinese manager who was neither cooperative nor friendly. The Japanese manager said this Chinese manager even built up his own 'black organisation' within the company to enable him to control the Chinese employees, despite the fact that the Japanese side had the majority share in the company's capital.
4   A Japanese accounting manager complained that, in his company, the Chinese party kept a part of the company's welfare/pension funds in a secret way and never let the Japanese party know how they handled the money.

Complaints from the Chinese side were as follows:

1   Japanese usually consider the joint venture company not as an independent enterprise but only a factory or a production base affiliated to the mother

company in Japan. The Japanese never trust the Chinese managers, and they only trust the Japanese staff sent from the mother company.

2   The Japanese party insisted in importing expensive equipment from Japan, and refused the suggestion from the Chinese party that the company should import similar equipment of better quality and better price from another country.

3   Since some of the joint venture manufacturing companies are export-oriented, and in most cases the Japanese parties handle and control the import–export channels, they like to offer a higher (than usual) price when they import materials and a lower price when they export the products. This is obviously unfair to the Chinese party and the joint venture itself, but only benefits the Japanese mother firm.

Infrastructure and business environment

One of the most serious problems is counterfeiting. Among manufacturers I have visited, at least half suffered from this problem. This concern was most serious for the pharmaceutical companies. Another trouble was the credit problem. According to a recent survey by the Japan–China Investment Promotion Organisation, a large number of Japanese manufacturing companies have had trouble in getting their credits back after the sales of their products. This problem seemed to be caused by the underdevelopment of the credit system and the financial system in China.[6]

Other problems mentioned were logistical problems, especially for the retail companies and pharmaceutical companies which need their products transported in refrigerated conditions.

Labour/employees

Some Japanese managers indicated that the quality of Chinese labour is basically better than in many other Asian developing countries. But others complained that they had difficulties in finding qualified staff. Some Japanese managers were unhappy with the disloyalty of some Chinese staff, who were educated and trained at the company but later moved to other companies that offered higher pay and better positions.

Most of the Japanese managers agreed that the Chinese employees worked hard, although they were very different from the Japanese in the way they thought and behaved. For example, the Japanese managers found that the Chinese employees were more sensitive to economic incentives, so some companies had introduced the system of efficiency wages, which means every worker receives her/his pay according to her/his own performance and results. Some Japanese managers found that it was hard to train the Chinese employees to adapt to the Japanese way of cooperating and exchanging information with their colleagues, and to propose creative ideas to improve the company's efficiency, as Japanese employees would usually do in Japan.

166 *Hu Xinxin*

Relationship with the Japanese mother company

Some Japanese managers have complaints about their mother companies. The most frequently mentioned problem is the centralised system in Japanese companies, under which the local companies are not allowed sufficient autonomy and right to make important decisions. This makes the company's operation rather difficult. Another problem pointed out by Japanese managers was that Japanese companies had not established global standards in company management. Thus, many of them have not adapted to the expansion of international business in a flexible way.

Other findings from my interviews were:

1 All of the manufacturing companies I visited had introduced production technology from Japan, and almost all of them were applying the Japanese way of supervising the production process and Japanese quality control.
2 Meanwhile, about half of the Japanese managers stated that they had introduced or were considering introducing Chinese methods to supervise the local employees.
3 Some Chinese managers indicated that they had learnt many things from their Japanese colleagues, although very few Japanese seemed to have the intention of learning from the Chinese.

Successful cases

Although Japanese companies complain about the countless problems and difficulties they are facing in China, I have found some successful ones among the companies I visited. I have to state in advance that the standards I set to judge a company's success are simple and not very academic. They are based on only two points: (1) whether the company is making a profit; (2) if it is a joint venture, whether the company is enjoying a good partnership. I have chosen four companies for my discussion (this of course does not mean that the other firms are not successful). The following description is based on my interviews with the managers, rather than on any in-depth investigation.

Guangdong Meizhi Compressor Co. Ltd

The Guangdong Meizhi Compressor Co. Ltd is a joint venture company established in 1995 with a 60 per cent share by Toshiba of Japan and a 40 per cent share by the Guangdong Marco Group (*Wanjiale*). The company produces compressors and supplies them to air conditioner manufacturers in China. In October 1998, the Guangdong Midea Group (*Meidi*) took over the share of the Marco Group and asked Toshiba for another 20 per cent share. At present the company is under the management of the Midea Group, which holds a 60 per cent share in the company's capital.

The company had losses on its balance sheet for every year from 1995 to 1998.

The main reason for the losses was that the amount of the investment was too large, therefore causing too many debts. Before Midea's takeover, the three sides had worked on clearing the company's debts, and re-evaluated the company's equipment. When the company started under Midea's operation, it began to make a profit.

In the days under Toshiba, most of the important positions at the company were held by Japanese managers and staff. Now only two technicians from Toshiba are working there. At present, the company is operated under the sole management of the Midea Group.

When I visited the company at the end of May 2000, I could only interview some Chinese managers because the Japanese staff were out of town. They described the situation as follows:

When the company was under the management of Toshiba, everything was carried out in the Japanese way. It was like a workshop of Toshiba, and not an independent enterprise with its own strategy and development planning and marketing activities. However, after Midea obtained a majority share of the company, the Chinese managers tried to establish a company culture and enterprise spirit of their own. The top management introduced Chinese ways of operating the company, and kept the Japanese way of supervising the production and controlling the quality of the products. Since Midea is a company without any governmental background that has survived through the difficult time of China's transition from a planned economy to a market economy, it is well adapted to China's recent market. This makes Midea very strong in marketing and operation. Furthermore, since the early 1990s, Midea itself has introduced many technology projects from Toshiba and has gained a lot of experience through cooperation with Toshiba.

From the business management point of view, Midea has tried to apply various measures to improve the company's efficiency and performance. The most important measures were as follows:

1   They enlarged the sales department and tried their best to strengthen the company's marketing function. Now the company has twenty-seven marketing staff, which is more than twice that of the Toshiba era. In 1999, it managed to sell 1.69 million sets of compressors, compared to 0.93 million sets in 1998. During January–May 2000, the company had already sold 1.28 million sets.
2   The Chinese managers from Midea have introduced a system of efficiency wages. This has given more incentives to the employees.

The Chinese managers of the company told me that, at the beginning of the Midea era, some Japanese staff had worried about the relationship between the two parties. However, as time went on, the two parties, through communication, established a good partnership. The Toshiba technicians are working very hard to keep the production level and check the quality of the products seriously. In this way they have gained a good reputation as well as friendship. The company

168 *Hu Xinxin*

has benefited from Midea for its flexible style of management and from Toshiba for its high-level technology. This is apparently the key to its success.

Beijing Nantsune Meat Machinery Joint Venture Co. Ltd

The Beijing Nantsune Meat Machinery Joint Venture Co. Ltd was established in 1986, with a 30 per cent share from the Beijing Electronic Machinery Research Institute, a 20 per cent share from the China International Trust and Investment Corporation (CITIC), a 45 per cent share from Nantsune Tekko of Japan, and a 5 per cent share from the Fuji Bank (the shareholders were changed in 1994 when the Beijing Electronic Machinery Research Institute withdrew). It is a small manufacturing company with fifty-two employees and a capital of $1 million at present. The company produces meat-processing machines and sells them in both local and international markets.

The strength of the company is the good quality of its products. This has brought the company a good reputation in the local market and enabled it to survive severe competition. The company's sales was RMB 0.38 million in 1986, which then increased to RMB 4.34 million in 1990, RMB 15.1 million in 1995, and RMB 24 million in 1999. In 1988, output was only 500 machines, and now it is about 3000. During the period from 1986 to 1998, the company earned net profits of more than RMB 37.92 million. It was awarded a number of honours by the Beijing municipal government for its excellent performance.

I visited this company in 1990. What impressed me most at that time was the remarks made by the Japanese general manager on how satisfied he was with the company and the business, and how he enjoyed his life in Beijing. When I visited the company again in July 2000, the old Japanese manager had retired, and all day-to-day business at the company was handled by the Chinese deputy general manager who has been serving the company from its establishment. The Chinese manager summarised the reasons for the company's success as follows:

1   As the most populated country in the world and with a culture of enjoying food, China is a huge market for meat-processing machines. The company introduced advanced technology and imported the most important parts from Japan. This guaranteed the quality of the products.

2   The Chinese and Japanese parties of this company have established good working relations. Both sides have made great efforts to cooperate with sincerity. Compared with those Japanese firms that like to bring old over-priced machines as part of their investment, the Japanese partner of this company is more honest. While there have been disagreements and friction, the two parties have managed to solve their problems by discussion and consultation.

3   As for operation, one of the most important things with joint venture companies is localisation. For this reason, it is important for the company to trust and make good use of the local managers and staff. Some Japanese companies do not like to trust their local employees, but the latter are more

familiar with Chinese laws and policies and the behaviour of government officials, as well as the customers in their own country. In this company, the Chinese managers handle the day-to-day operation and local marketing, while the Japanese party provides technology and key parts and takes responsibility for import–export business and technical training. Having the division of functions as such, the company is operated more effectively.

4   Another important factor for the joint venture companies is the qualified managers, who must be knowledgeable and experienced. The Japanese partner of this company trusts the Chinese managers because the latter have the quality and ability to run the company well. If a company cannot obtain qualified staff, things will be very difficult.

At present, the company is planning to build a new factory, which is four times bigger than the current one.

NEC–CAS Software Laboratories Co. Ltd

This is a joint venture company established by NEC of Japan and the Institute of Software of the Chinese Academy of Sciences (CAS). NEC originally planned to form a joint venture company with the Chinese Academy of Sciences, but this intention failed because, as a national academic research institution, CAS was not allowed to establish a company with a foreign firm. As a result, NEC turned to a software company affiliated to the Institute of Software at CAS.

The company has 160 employees at present. Most of them are software engineers, engaged in software research and development. In most cases, its products are the middle-software which is part of a big system that NEC is engaged in. At the beginning, there were only forty employees working for the company. Most of them came from the Institute of Software at CAS. The company started making a profit after two-year losses on its balance sheet. It is now considered to be among the most successful companies in China that NEC has invested in, with a consistent profit rate of about 7–8 per cent in recent years.

I visited the company in July 2000. It was located in a new modern building shared with many other IT companies. The vice-president of the company, a man from the Institute of Software of CAS, explained the factors in the company's success in the following way:

1   The top management of both sides communicated and cooperated very well. Although NEC is the majority shareholder with 90 per cent of the company's capital, it has never regarded the company as only one of the software R&D bases attached to it. Rather, it considers the company as an independent enterprise. The company's first president from NEC has said many times that this company was not a Japanese company but a Chinese corporation registered in China. This enables the company to enjoy its own autonomy.

2   The Japanese party made great efforts to improve the operation of the

company. NEC has sent the company its high-ranking managers. They are friendly and cooperative, and very serious about their jobs.

3 The company has invested in training for its employees. At the beginning, most of the engineers came from the institute of CAS. They were not adapted to a commercial environment. The company has tried to establish an enterprise culture of its own, and has paid great attention to training and education, while trying to help the employees to change their ways of thinking and develop their consciousness.

4 The marketing channel is guaranteed as the company gets orders from NEC.

5 NEC has helped the company in many aspects. It helps the company to formulate its plan and budget, to evaluate the level and quality of the software that the company creates, and suggests improvements. This has greatly promoted the company's efficiency and the quality of its products.

6 The company did not expand aggressively. It has developed in a steady way and managed to avoid unnecessary risks and losses.

The vice-president mentioned the problems and difficulties the company was facing. For example, as in IT industry in general, engineers and researchers move from one company to another frequently, and this makes the company's operation difficult. The company was also concerned about its lack of marketing power and defects in product planning. To solve these problems and meet future challenges, the company is considering a new policy that will encourage the employees to stay longer. They also plan to develop software with their own copyright and to strengthen the company's power of local marketing. The company has also established an R&D base at a university in Xi'an, with sixty engineers currently working there.

TF Tianjin Industrial Co. Ltd

The company was established in December 1987. It is a manufacturing company that produces stainless steel flexible metal hose and unit assemblages. Most of its products are for export.

After two years of losses, the company turned to profit in 1990. Its sales and profits have increased rapidly since then. In 1988, the company's sales turnover was RMB 0.385 million. In 1990 it soared to RMB 10.56 million and then jumped to RMB 50.66 million in 1995 and RMB 66.86 million in 1999. Profit was RMB 0.73 million in 1990, which increased to RMB 4.23 million in 1995 and RMB 5.21 million in 1999. During this period, the company has increased its registered capital as well, from 250 million Japanese yen in 1987 to 561 million Japanese yen in 1998.

I first learnt about this company from an article in the periodical called JETRO Center (no. 5, 2000). According to this article, the Japanese president of the company indicated that the primary reason for the company's success was that the Japanese party had been able to find the right partner. The president gave the

Following advice to Japanese companies which plan to invest in China: (1) you must make clear why you are investing, (2) you need to find the right partner, and (3) you have to send a capable person, who is flexible enough, to run the company at the local level and give him/her decision-making autonomy.

I visited the company at the end of July 2000. Unfortunately, the president was then back in Japan and I could only talk with two Chinese managers. The following is their explanation of the reasons for the company's success:

1   The most important reason is that the products are very competitive. The company has made great efforts to guarantee the product quality as well as the quantity and the date of delivery.
2   As an export-oriented company, it has enjoyed the benefits of low cost in China.
3   The Chinese and Japanese parties have cooperated in a sincere and honest way. They both wanted to develop the company further.
4   The company tries to hire employees with a relatively long term contract and never fires them for minor reasons. This makes the company attractive to employees.

Of course, there have been some problems. Of those the managers mentioned, there were communication problems caused by the different ways of thinking and the different purposes of investment between the two parties. However, these kinds of problems can usually be solved with efforts on both sides. There are only two Japanese working at the company at present, and the Chinese managers are carrying out most of the day-to-day business. During my visit there, I found the offices, factories and campus very clean and everything was in order.

Further discussion and suggestions

In connection with the problems and difficulties faced by Japanese-funded firms in China, one can find big differences between the past and the present. When I visited Japanese-funded firms in Shenzhen seventeen years ago, the Japanese managers were complaining about bad living conditions, the slow development of infrastructure and the inactivity of the Chinese employees. When I conducted my survey in Amoy and Beijing in 1990, most concerns were about political and economic uncertainty, in addition to problems associated with business partners (some Japanese managers complained that their business partners had not honoured their contract in the way it should have been honoured). The problems with infrastructure remained.

In my recent survey, political and economic uncertainty and infrastructure were no longer the most serious concerns, though problems associated with business partners and operations (contract, credit, loyalty, counterfeiting and so forth) have increased. The most serious problems for Japanese business in China at present, however, are centred on inefficiency and lack of discipline in government administration, and law/policy-related issues.

172   *Hu Xinxin*

Compared with my previous surveys, the new findings of my recent survey are as follows:

1   Never before have a large number of Japanese-funded companies faced such intensive competition in the Chinese market. This makes it more difficult to operate for some local market-oriented companies.
2   Some Japanese managers working in China have become increasingly aware of the shortcoming of Japanese management and have begun to advocate the importance of the localisation of management. They are appealing to their home companies for a global standard of operation and greater right of decision-making.
3   More Chinese managers have begun to believe that a joint venture company should apply more Chinese ways in supervising local employees, and carrying out marketing activities, while keeping the Japanese way of supervising the production process and quality control.[7]

Generally speaking there are three basic problems faced by Japanese-funded firms in China: (1) they encounter great difficulties when dealing with government administration and officials at various levels; (2) they have trouble with their business partners such as vendors and users, who lack the necessary respect for contract, credit, etc.; and (3) some of them have had difficulties in establishing a good relationship with their joint venture partners.

One can find that these problems exist not only in Japanese-funded firms but also represent concerns for all foreign businesses in China.[8] As for the first and second problems, I have to say that Chinese companies have suffered even more, because a lot of domestic companies (with local capital only), particularly the privately owned ones, have been treated even less favourably by the government. The first and second problems relate to the underdevelopment of the market economy and lack of functional systems and order that are essential to a modern society. Therefore, it is important for foreign companies to appeal to the government for administrative efficiency and the establishment of economic order. For the Chinese government, it is necessary to pay more attention to the voices of investors and to make greater efforts to improve its ethics and efficiency as well as to establish more functional systems and rules in order to serve both domestic and foreign enterprises better. However, the development of a market economy and a modern political and social system will take a long time. There is very little an individual can do. Therefore, in my view, the most important thing for Japanese companies to do at present is not to complain, but to improve themselves.

From the surveys I conducted in 1990 and recently, I have learnt some key factors for the success of a joint venture company. The points are: (1) correct strategic choices, including choices of the project, the location of investment, partner, and target market, etc.; (2) honesty and sincerity to the cooperative partners, e.g. to work for mutual benefit rather than the benefit of one side is especially important for a joint venture; (3) establishment of a basic reliable relationship, i.e. to trust and be faithful to each other is essential for business cooperation; (4) sufficient communication between the cooperative partners, e.g. frequent communication will help to solve the problems caused by different cultures and ways of thinking; and (5) qualified personnel with good educational background and experience in international communication.

The recent findings by a research team at the Development Research Centre of the State Council of China suggests that some American multinational companies (usually more decentralised than the Japanese firms) are more successful in the respect of (3), (4) and (5), by employing a large number of the Chinese staff (mostly with educational backgrounds in Western countries) and putting them in important positions, both in joint ventures or American solely owned companies.[9] In the second section I discussed a number of successful cases. I have found a common feature in these companies where Chinese managers play relatively important roles while the numbers of Japanese managers are rather small. Referring to the practices of successful companies from Japan and other countries, I believe that localisation (particularly of the personnel) is one of the most important tasks for Japanese firms in China.[10]

As Japan is a one-race one-language homogeneous nation, the Japanese people are proud of their own culture and tradition, and have a tendency to avoid or even to exclude people and things that are foreign to them. This attitude may hinder the Japanese from localising management in their companies in China. In this regard, both Chinese and Japanese business partners need to put efforts into promoting localisation with the objective of achieving better performance.

Appendix: list of the companies and organisations I visited

Companies

Shanghai Friendship Seiyu Co. Ltd
Establishment: October 1996 (withdrew 1999)
Feature of the company: joint venture
Capital: $5 million (Seiyu, Japan 45 per cent; SSV, Japan 5 per cent; Shanghai Friendship Group Co. 50 per cent)
Location: Shanghai
Number of employees: 200 (including part-time workers)
Scope of business: supermarket

Huatang Yanghuatang Commercial Co. Ltd
Establishment: October 1997
Feature of the company: joint venture
Capital: $65 million (China Candy and Spirits Group Corp. 51 per cent; Ito-Yokado, Japan 36.7 per cent; Itochu, 10.58 per cent; Itochu (China) 1.67 per cent)
Location: Beijing
Number of employees: 500
Scope of business: general merchandise

174 *Hu Xinxin*

Guangdong Meizhi Compressor Co. Ltd
Establishment: 1995
Feature of the company: joint venture
Capital: $55.27 million (Guangdong Media Group Co. 60 per cent; Toshiba, Japan 40 per cent)
Location: Shunde, Guangdong
Number of employees: 1200
Scope of business: production and marketing of compressors
Main products: compressors

Shanghai ZODOS CITIC Cosmetics Co. Ltd
Establishment: February 1998
Feature of the company: cooperative joint venture
Capital: $18.8 million (Shiseido, Japan 80 per cent; CITIC, Shanghai 20 per cent)
Location: Pudong, Shanghai
Number of employees: 480
Scope of business: production and marketing of cosmetics
Main products: cosmetics

Sumitomo Chemical Co. Ltd
Location: Beijing
Scope of business: representative office

Beijing Nantsune Meat Machinery Joint Venture Co. Ltd
Establishment: 27 February 1986
Feature of the company and shareholders: joint venture
Capital: $1 million (Nantsune Tekko, Japan 45 per cent; Beijing Xi Hai Co. 23 per cent; CITIC 20 per cent; Beijing Dong Feng Meat Machinery Factory 7 per cent; Fuji Bank, Japan 5 per cent)
Location: Beijing
Number of employees: 52
Scope of main business: production and marketing of meat-processing machines
Main products: meat-processing machines

Beijing Wacoal Co. Ltd
Establishment: January 1986
Feature of the company: joint venture
Capital: $3.5 million (Wacoal Co. Ltd., Japan 60 per cent; Beijing Hongdu Group Co., 36 per cent; Beijing Tourist Product Group Co. 4 per cent)
Location: Beijing
Number of employees: 698
Scope of business: production and marketing of underwear and clothing
Main products: underwear for women

Omron (China) Co. Ltd
Establishment: 1994

Feature of the company: solely invested by Omron Corporation, Japan
Capital: $43.895 million
Location: Beijing
Number of employees: 23
Scope of business: holding company (deals with Omron's investment in China, takes care of the invested companies and provides technical and consulting services for Omron users nationwide).

Daiichi Pharmaceutical (China) Co. Ltd
Establishment: 29 November 1995
Feature of the company: solely invested by Daiichi Pharmaceutical Co. Ltd, Japan
Capital: $8 million
Location of headquarters: Beijing
Number of employees: 200
Scope of business: development, production and marketing of pharmaceuticals
Main products: pharmaceuticals

Daiichi Pharmaceutical (Beijing) Co. Ltd
Establishment: 19 May 1998
Feature of the company: joint venture
Capital: $23.8 million (Daiichi Pharmaceutical Co. Ltd, Japan 95 per cent; Beijing Pharmaceutical Group Co. Ltd 5 per cent)
Location: Beijing
Number of employees: 60
Scope of business: production and marketing of pharmaceuticals
Main products: pharmaceuticals

NEC-CAS Software Laboratories Co. Ltd
Establishment: 18 June 1994
Feature of the company: joint venture
Capital: 150 million yen (NEC 90 per cent; Institute of Software, Chinese Academy of Sciences 10 per cent)
Location: Beijing
Number of employees: about 160
Scope of business: software research and development
Main products: software

TF Tianjin Industrial Co. Ltd
Establishment: December 1987
Feature of the company: joint venture
Capital: 560.5 million Japanese yen (Technoflex, Japan 83.05 per cent; CITIC Tianjin 16.95 per cent)
Location: Tianjin
Number of employees: 278

176 *Hu Xinxin*

Scope of business: production and sales of stainless steel flexible metal hose and unit assemblages
Main products: stainless steel flexible metal hose and unit assemblages

Organisations

Beijing Representative Office, Japan External Trade Organisation (JETRO)
Beijing Representative Office, Japan–China Investment Promotion Organisation

Notes

1 Kaburagi Shinji, Noda Hidehiko and Ikehara Satoshi, 'The Outlook of Foreign Investment by Japanese Manufacturing Companies – Prospects of Overseas Business Operations after the Asian Economic Crisis', *JBIC Review*, no. 1, 2000, pp. 3–38.
2 JMA Research Institute Inc., *99 Nendo JETRO Nikkei Seizougyō Jittai Chōsa, Chūgoku Zentai Hen* (*A JETRO Survey on the Condition of Japanese Manufactures in China, Fiscal Year 1999*), Japan External Trade Organisation, 2000.
3 Japan–China Investment Promotion Organisation, *Nikkei Kigyō Ankieto Chōsa Shūkei Bunseki Kekka* (*Result of General Analysis of the Questionnaire Survey on Japanese Companies*), Japan–China Investment Promotion Organisation, 2000.
4 See Xie Shusheng 'Work Hard and Render Good Services to Foreign Investment Utilization and Economic Development', *Foreign Investment in China*, vol. 87, no. 2, 2000, pp. 7–9.
5 There is some argument about FDI from Hong Kong: for example, Hal Hill and Prema-chandra Athukorala indicate: 'It is generally believed that the overall importance of Hong Kong FDI is over-stated in official statistics. Hong Kong trading companies have formed joint ventures to obtain foreign trading privileges in China, rather than to profit from the joint venture ostensible business. Other Hong Kong firms have formed multiple joint ventures to benefit from tax holidays, which overstated the number – but, not the value – of HK projects.' (Foreign Investment in East Asia: A Survey, *Asian-Pacific Economic Literature*, vol. 12, no. 2, 1998).
6 Hattori Kenji, the Beijing chief representative of Japan–China Investment Promotion Organisation, emphasised this point during my interview with him.
7 This viewpoint is supported by the recent JIPO survey, which shows that the profit rates of the joint ventures and cooperative joint ventures are higher than the Japanese solely owned companies among the local market-oriented companies. The report suggests that this implies that joint ventures have benefited from their Chinese parties in marketing and sales activities. See Japan–China Investment Promotion Organisation (2000).
8 According to a survey conducted by AmCham-China through a questionnaire, many responding companies cite market access restrictions, high taxes and customs duties, high costs, and slow market development as the top barriers to profitability. In addition to challenges caused by government policies, 72 per cent of responding companies feel that corruption in China is unacceptably high and most do not believe that corruption in business is decreasing (American Chamber of Commerce, People's Republic of China, *White Paper 2000*, American Business in China, 2000). However, some Japanese managers told me that they felt the level of corruption had actually decreased in recent years.
9 Research Team on Environment and Policy for Foreign Investment in China, 'Comparison of Cases of Some Multinational Companies', *Foreign Investment in China*, vol. 80, no. 7, 2000.
10 Meanwhile, I think some export-oriented companies may be more likely to take the form of 100 per cent ownership.

10 Managing the global–local dilemma

Problems in controlling Japanese subsidiaries in China

Jochen Legewie

One of the most striking characteristics of Japanese firms is their high reliance on expatriates in running their overseas subsidiaries – a management practice for which they have been both praised and criticised worldwide. In China, this approach only fits well for some firms. According to a recent survey by the Japan–China Investment Promotion Organisation, Japanese export-oriented affiliates in China are quite profitable, with only 15 per cent turning in losses.[1] Among local market-oriented affiliates, by contrast, more than 40 per cent are operating in the red. Unlike Western firms, the majority of Japanese companies in China are still export-oriented. However, the trend is clearly turning towards a stronger local market orientation forcing more and more Japanese firms to address the issue of low profitability. Can this issue of profitability be related to expatriate management or, in more general terms, what role do control and coordination mechanisms that are specific to Japanese firms play?

All multinational companies (MNCs), regardless whether they are from Japan, Europe, the US, or elsewhere, face the task of an effective and efficient control and coordination of their overseas subsidiaries. Defined as a means to achieve common organisational goals, such international management control (IMC) directly relates to the general global–local dilemma of internationally active companies. MNCs must find the optimal mix between centralised and decentralised decision-making and employ an optimal mix of the various control and coordination mechanisms.

To solve this dilemma, recent international management theory suggests that MNCs should move toward a kind of loosely coupled network organisation.[2] The final outcome is often described as a 'transnational' company.[3] Within such an organisation, the management of human resources is obviously very important. Coordination shifts from formal to more informal and subtle mechanisms.[4]

The employment of expatriates plays a crucial role within such indirect control and coordination systems.[5] Authors like Child, Edström and Lorange, Kobrin, Daniels and Radebaugh, and Roth and Nigh refer to the observations of Edström and Galbraith who were among the first to find different patterns of expatriate employment in the overseas subsidiaries of otherwise similar MNCs.[6] Echoing Wiechmann,[7] they see expatriates as an alternative to formal control

178　*Jochen Legewie*

mechanisms and centralisation creating a coordination system which is based on socialisation and informal communication.[8]

Japanese MNCs are well known for the concentration of expatriates in their overseas subsidiaries.[9] Referring to the numbers of expatriates alone, authors like Harrison et al. or Jain and Tucker claim that Japanese MNCs show a high degree of centralisation in decision-making by international standards.[10] By contrast, other studies have arrived at the exact opposite conclusion, i.e. most US and European MNCs tend to exert relatively more centralised and formalised control over their overseas affiliates.[11] Ferner offers a key to understanding these contradictory findings. He describes the Japanese approach as 'strong but informal centralised co-ordination of foreign operations, highly reliant on establishing an international network of Japanese expatriate managers'.[12] Japanese expatriates obviously play an important role within the typical Japanese international management control (IMC) system. But we do not have sufficient knowledge about the real degree of formality and centralisation of the Japanese IMC system and its specific suitability in different environments. This paper aims to fill that gap.

However, this paper does not aim to tackle the problem of a global–local dilemma in a general manner. Rather we will focus our analysis on the control and coordination of Japanese subsidiaries in China. Drawing both on empirical research in China and Japan and the relevant secondary literature, this chapter presents an overview of the expatriate-based control system Japanese MNCs currently employ in China and an evaluation of its organisational fit. The analysis here concentrates exclusively on Japanese firms. It identifies areas of incongruity and explains the underlying reasons for problems with this specific IMC model in China. This chapter demonstrates that the Japanese expatriate-based control system in China continues to be characterised by a special kind of ethnocentrism, or – in other terms – by an insider–outsider mentality. We argue that this form of ethnocentrism hinders a fast shift to international operations in the 'transnational' sense.

There are several reasons for the exclusive focus on Japanese operations in China. First, China confronts Japanese MNCs with a unique business environment. Firms face both a high uncertainty and instability (typical for many developing countries) and a huge domestic market potential and a sophisticated industrial structure in certain areas (typical for many developed countries). This presents a unique combination that comes with special requirements for IMC systems. Second, besides its generally growing importance, China is of special significance to Japanese firms. Being an Asian country and thus lying in the Japanese 'backyard', Japanese firms cannot afford to lose out to Western competitors in China if they want to stand against them on a global level. Third, with regard to this special challenge in China in terms of requirements and importance, a closer analysis of the current situation in China promises the most telling country study to arrive at deeper insights into the general functioning of Japanese IMC and its problems, and eventual ways to overcome them. Thus findings derived here might offer results applicable to Japanese operations elsewhere, too.

Managing the global–local dilemma   179

The structure of this chapter is as follows: the next section starts with a typology of international control and coordination mechanisms and places the Japanese IMC system in international perspective. The following section outlines the characteristics of the business conditions in China that require foreign firms simultaneously to emphasise local flexibility and cross-border organisational learning. The subsequent main part describes the current state of Japanese IMC systems in China and analyses their most common problems. The final section summarises the findings and offers an outlook on future development in various industries.

Typology of international management control systems

If we want to put the Japanese IMC system into international perspective we need a typology of control mechanisms. Harzing[13] is offering such a classification scheme, which accommodates other typologies that have been developed to date, including those of Martinez and Jarillo, Mintzberg, Ouchi, Edström and Galbraith, Galbraith, Lawrence and Lorsch as well as March and Simon.[14]

Harzing uses two dimensions – 'personal/impersonal' and 'direct/indirect' – to generate four distinctive groups of control mechanisms employed by MNCs. These four groups are defined as follows (also see Table 10.1):

1   *Personal centralised control* designates the idea of hierarchy. This control mechanism relates to decisions that are taken at the centre or top level of companies and that are followed by a direct personal surveillance of their execution.
2   *Bureaucratic formalised control* is the other direct behaviour control mechanism. By contrast, it is of an impersonal nature. Written manuals that prescribe ex ante the behaviour expected of employees standardise the course of action.
3   *Output control* (or management by objectives) resembles the market mechanism by focusing on outputs rather than on behaviour as the other three mechanisms do. The firm measures outputs such as production, sales or financial data. By comparing these outputs with pre-specified goals, the final result is evaluated and controlled, rather than controlling inputs, i.e. the behaviour of single employees.
4   *Control by socialisation and networks* refers to all other control mechanisms – in other words, mechanisms that are not hierarchical, bureaucratic, formal or output-oriented. There are three main sub-categories: (a) socialisation by sharing organisational values and goals, (b) informal and horizontal exchange of information with an emphasis on non-hierarchical information flows between all managerial levels, and (c) temporarily formalised cross-departmental relations taking the form of task forces or cross-functional teams.

Personal centralised control and bureaucratic formalised control aim at controlling behaviour directly and explicitly; the two other groups do so indirectly and implicitly. Similarly, personal centralised control and control by

180 *Jochen Legewie*

Table 10.1 Typology of control mechanisms

	Personal/cultural	*Impersonal/bureaucratic/technocratic*
Direct/explicit	Personal centralised control	Bureaucratic formalised control
Indirect/implicit	Control by socialisation and networks	Output control

Source: Harzing, 1999, p. 21.

socialisation and networks are based on personal exchange and social inter-action. The other two are clearly of an impersonal and bureaucratic nature.[15]

The four control mechanisms do not work in isolation but rather in close interdependence to each other.[16] One might see, for example, a combination of the first two groups in situations characterised by environmental stability, a low level of technological development and transparent transformation processes. There would be an emphasis on personal, centralised control in smaller companies and bureaucratic, formalised control in larger companies. By contrast, a combination of output and social/network controls is better suited to situations with high environmental instability, complex technology, and limited knowledge of transformation processes. There would be an emphasis on output control if there were measurable outputs and on socialisation and networks if there were not.[17]

Expatriates are deliberately excluded by this typology of control mechanisms. They are rather regarded as an alternative, though one that can ultimately perform crucial functions. The use of expatriates as a control measure usually takes two different forms. It can strongly substitute or complement personal, centralised control by headquarters and it can assist in the cultivation of shared values and thus facilitate control and coordination through socialisation and networks.[18] Both functions are especially important for Japanese MNCs, as we will see later.

International management control of Japanese MNC in international comparison

In 1995/96 Harzing conducted a far-reaching international survey based on the above typology that identified similarities and differences in the subsidiary control mechanisms of MNCs from the US, Europe and Japan.[19] The results of the study offer a good empirical base for comparisons of the various patterns of IMC employed by multinationals of different countries, from different industries, and with different organisational models.[20]

To identify characteristics of Japanese firms, we will focus here only on country-of-origin effects and compare Japanese MNCs to companies of three other countries in Harzing's study: the US, Germany, and Sweden (Table 10.2). These three countries have been selected as each stands for a distinctively different IMC model. At first sight we notice a distinctive feature of the Japanese IMC

Managing the global–local dilemma 181

Table 10.2 Use of control mechanisms in subsidiaries of firms from different countries

	Japan	*US*	*Germany*	*Sweden*
Personal centralised control	Medium	Medium	Very high	Low
Bureaucratic formalised control	Low	Very high	Medium-high	Medium
Output control	Very low	Medium-high	High	Medium
Control by socialisation and networks	Low	Medium	Medium	High
Expatriate control	Very high	Very low	High	Medium

Source: Harzing, 1999.

model that sets it clearly apart from MNCs headquartered in other countries. While Japanese MNCs exhibit a very limited use of the four 'classic' control mechanisms, they rely almost exclusively on direct expatriate control. German MNCs, for example, that also rely on expatriates, at the same time employ other means of control, especially personal centralised control and output control as well. US companies generally use an IMC model with a high dependence on bureaucratic, formal control and output control while forgoing the use of expatriates as a means of control. Thus, they constitute the exact opposite of Japanese MNCs. Swedish MNCs fall in between these two extremes, but they too clearly differ from their Japanese counterparts, due to their strong reliance on control by socialisation and networks.

Combining the observations by Tung, Kopp and others, as described before, with these findings of Harzing, we find that Japanese MNCs employ large numbers of expatriates in their overseas subsidiaries *and* strongly rely on them to control and coordinate their overseas activities.[21] Looking at the medium score for personal, centralised control and the low score for control by socialisation and networks, we can further specify: expatriate control by Japanese takes the form of a substitution of personal surveillance by the centre (headquarters in Japan) rather than a facilitation of control and coordination attempts by socialisation and networks.

The main reason for the high degree of centralisation applied by most Japanese MNCs is the so-called 'global' organisational model.[22] Most MNCs in industries such as automobiles and electronics, industries characterised by standardised consumer needs, price competition and economies of scale, follow this model. Hence, these industries emphasise highly integrated and efficient production systems over responsiveness to various local markets. Many Japanese MNCs come from these industries, which partly explains their high degree of centralisation. Interestingly, Japanese companies in other industries have also followed this global business model. This has to be seen as the international extension of a domestic business model that is characterised by centralisation and powerful headquarters.[23]

The high reliance on expatriates can be explained mainly by two factors. First, it reflects the extraordinarily strong personal focus of the Japanese management style at home and thus the influence of the national business system abroad.[24] In

182   *Jochen Legewie*

other words, it is an international extension of the national business system that transfers central decision-making to the international level.[25] At the same time, it reflects an inability to transfer abroad control mechanisms that work at home. This holds especially true for control and coordination by socialisation and networks. This control mechanism is without doubt a specific and important characteristic of the Japanese domestic business system. The very low application abroad, however, suggests major problems with its applicability in Japanese IMC systems in China, as elsewhere overseas, and will receive detailed treatment later.[26]

To sum up, the term 'transplants' – often used to describe Japanese production systems abroad – also seems well suited as a means to characterise the Japanese approach towards control and coordination of their overseas subsidiaries.[27] Japanese MNCs rely on expatriates to facilitate the transfer of their specific ownership advantages abroad. Expatriates have helped in the international extension of efficient production systems, especially in the rather stable environments that characterise most industrialised countries.[28] In the unstable environments of developing countries, expatriates have enabled a flexibility higher than that possible under formal, bureaucratic rules or output control mechanisms.[29]

However, this centralised, expatriate-based approach has its limitations. First, there are industries that mainly require local responsiveness and thus are unsuited to the 'global' business model. This was best demonstrated by the internationalisation failure of branded packaged products leader Kao in the 1980s.[30] Second, the expatriate-based approach can also lead to problems in other fields that require cross-sectional information exchange and horizontal communication flows that go beyond Japanese dominated structures.[31] In broader terms, this relates to the debate over whether or not 'the innovations pioneered by Japanese corporations . . . constitute a discrete package of organisational techniques which can be lifted from its original social and economic context and adopted elsewhere'.[32] This debate raises the question of whether Japanese production and management practices are location-specific or of universal relevance. Amongst others, Dunning[33] suggests that Japanese efficiency is location-specific to Japan. Kenney and Florida argue that an overseas transfer of a wide range of Japanese management practices is possible, but only where 'functional equivalents' to the Japanese socio-economic environment exist.[34] We will return to this point in the discussion on current control and coordination problems of Japanese MNCs in China.

Current business conditions in China

At present, China presents foreign investors with an environment characterised by high complexity and rapid development. Whether we look at the political, legal, economic or social-cultural spheres, all areas display both crude and effective complexity to use the terms of Gell-Mann.[35] By both measures China exhibits one of the most complex business environments, with its large numbers

Managing the global–local dilemma 183

of different actors at the various layers of business and politics. This is combined with huge regional differences and general instability.[36]

At the same time, China has made rapid progress towards clearly defined goals throughout the last twenty years. Economically, China has displayed impressive growth rates and upgraded its technological level. Politically, the situation has stabilised and transparency has increased. In part, this can be attributed to a legal environment that, in anticipation of the introduction of WTO regulations in the near future, promises greater transparency and stability for business. Finally, there have been substantial changes in the social-cultural sphere. One can see the departure from the 'iron rice-bowl' regime to a more individualistic market-based society, at least in the coastal regions.[37]

These trends mean that China will continue to rise in strategic importance for foreign companies. This holds true despite the problems that result from the highly complex and unstable business environment. On the one hand, China obviously presents a huge market potential, an argument that needs no further elaboration here. On the other hand, China will become more important as a link in the global production networks of MNCs. Continuous improvements in technology will allow MNCs to use China both as an inexpensive site for simple production processes and as a site for higher value-added activities that can be integrated on a global scale.

This combination of an unstable business environment and the rapidly developing economy with its promise of a huge future market sets China apart both from developed markets in North America and Europe and from smaller developing economies like Thailand, Poland or Brazil. With regard to international management control, this setting presents a special challenge to foreign MNCs. They have to exhibit a high level of local flexibility in the rapidly changing business environment. At the same time, the cross-border integration of their Chinese operations becomes increasingly important. Ultimately, they must tackle the global–local dilemma and achieve both the ability for a flexible market response and organisational learning and innovation on a global scale.

Problems in international management control by Japanese firms in China

Japanese IMC in China

Since the early 1990s Japanese firms have strongly increased investment in China. As a result, the number of Japanese wholly owned subsidiaries or equity joint ventures in mainland China had risen to more than 1400 by spring 1999 with some of the large multinational companies (MNCs) such as Itochu, Matsushita, or Fujitsu running more than thirty Chinese affiliates each.[38] The control and coordination of these foreign affiliates is a permanent task for Japanese MNCs that seem to rely on expatriates in China in similar ways that they do in other parts of the world.

The mere numbers of Japanese managers in Chinese joint ventures and

184 Jochen Legewie

wholly-owned subsidiaries confirm the well-known picture of an extensive use of expatriates. Larger MNCs like NEC, Mitsubishi Electric, Fujitsu or Matsushita, for example, employ between 100 and 250 expatriates on a permanent basis in China. Data collected by the author show that expatriates on average account for about 2 per cent of the workforce in Chinese subsidiaries of Japanese manufacturers, a figure clearly above that for their Western counterparts, especially US and UK firms.[39]

A large number of these Japanese expatriates (relatively more than in subsidiaries of Western MNCs) are engaged exclusively in technological transfer and the supervision of production techniques and processes.[40] Yet a majority remain in charge of control and coordination of the subsidiary's relations with headquarters. Hence, the IMC model employed by most Japanese MNCs in China follows the general Japanese model described before. Interviews by the author with representatives of twenty large Japanese multinationals regarding the main functions of Japanese expatriates in China confirmed this finding.

Interestingly, these interviews also showed two different patterns of judging the high use of expatriates. One group of Japanese managers did not cite any special IMC problems beside the high costs of sending Japanese employees to China. Most of them belonged to firms with manufacturing operations in China that were highly export-intensive and with only little direct exposure to the Chinese market. Employees of companies or certain division groups with a strong focus on sales to the Chinese market made up the other group. These managers tended to view the relatively high use of expatriates by their firm far more critically and sometimes related concrete labour problems, especially the problem of securing qualified workers, to their expatriates.

Problems of Japanese expatriate control in China

A strong reliance on expatriates in China equips Japanese MNCs with the same advantages and disadvantages in coordinating and controlling their subsidiaries as it does in other parts of the world. This IMC model is especially well suited to the large number of Japanese manufacturers that are heavily engaged in the export-processing trade. Such Chinese plants do not only export most of their output under strict control by Japanese headquarters but are also highly dependent on their headquarters in areas such as inputs, financing, or production technology. In these cases, the typical transplant type of business, the Japanese IMC model still provides an efficient way for many Japanese MNCs to control and coordinate their Chinese operations.

But with an increasing focus toward the Chinese domestic market and improvements in production activities in China, the strong reliance on expatriate control results in a number of problems for Japanese MNCs. Such problems are described by Nakamura, Taylor, Ma, Leung et al. who argue that there are two main troubles with Japanese firms in China:[41]

1   Qualified local workers tend to get frustrated and leave the company

Managing the global–local dilemma 185

because of insufficient participation in decision-making, limited career opportunities and a lack of merit-based appraisal systems.

2 Most firms suffer under an inflexibility in their response to the market because of limited bottom-up information flows. This is due to a missing layer of middle management and a subsequent lack of joint decision-making between expatriates and local employees.

The unpopularity of Japanese firms as employers among Chinese workers as compared to their US and European competitors is described by Ma.[42] This phenomenon is not only based on the higher wages paid by Western firms but also reflects differences in the general systems of appraisal and performance assessment. Nakamura also points to the same dissatisfaction of Chinese employees in Japanese wholly owned subsidiaries around Shenzen.[43] All of his Chinese interviewees complain about not being involved in the decision-making process and are generally pessimistic about their career opportunities. A special problem is the widespread dissatisfaction of Chinese employees with assessments of their performance by their Japanese superiors. Interviews by the author with Japanese managers in China even showed that personnel appraisals sometimes become assessments of language ability, rather than evaluations of work performance.

Leung et al. confirm these observations with a comparative study on job satisfaction in Chinese hotels under Japanese and Western management.[44] They show that employees working under Western expatriates were much more satisfied than those working under Japanese superiors. Those working in Japanese firms perceived that they were rewarded less fairly in relation to their performance and in comparison to other employees in hotels under Chinese or Western management. Finally, the heavy reliance on expatriates also meant limited career opportunities for Chinese managers, constituting the infamous 'rice-paper ceiling' of Japanese companies.[45] In Japanese MNCs, cases of non-Japanese heading a joint venture in China are very rare. A recent survey by JETRO found only about 10 per cent of Japanese joint ventures being headed by a non-Japanese.[46] This contrasts sharply with many US firms and even some German companies (also famous for their high reliance on expatriates). In 1999 for example, out of the heads of nine joint ventures involving the German chemical firm BASF only three were Germans. Managers from Norway, China, Korea, Indonesia and Malaysia held the post of general manager at the other six affiliates.

All these factors hinder Japanese MNCs in China in attracting or keeping qualified personnel. Labour turnover is directly related to job satisfaction and opportunities, as shown by Wong and Law.[47] Fisher and Yuan confirm this view with their study on employee motivation in China.[48] According to their study most Chinese managers prefer salaries and promotions based on individual performance. This requires measurable goals (output control) rather than subjective, personal assessments by expatriates.[49] The seriousness of this labour problem becomes clear in the results of the January 2000 JETRO survey of 674

Japanese firms in China.[50] While 55 per cent of respondents cite 'securing of qualified workers' as the most important success factor for business in China, 35 per cent report problems related to labour and human resources.[51]

The second major problem of Japanese MNCs is their inability to respond flexibly to market changes. Nakamura and Taylor describe this issue well.[52] By dominating decision-making, Japanese managers do more than frustrate Chinese employees. They also hinder a free and constant flow of information from the shop floor to top management. A study of thirty-one Japanese wholly owned and joint venture manufacturing plants in China by Taylor highlights this problem.[53] On the one hand, Taylor finds that some Japanese MNCs have deliberately ceded control of certain organisational functions to Chinese employees, especially in the area of human resource management. On the other hand, however, he detects a 'tendency to dichotomize between either Chinese or Japanese control, with little attempt to make joint decisions'.[54] This reflects language and cultural barriers between Japanese and Chinese managers but also the fact that most Japanese expatriates are sent to China to do a specific job based on their area of expertise.[55] Hence, most focus on their specific jobs rather than seeking to cross-fertilise management knowledge and practice. This results in a striking lack of joint decision-making between locals and expatriates.[56] As a result of the missing middle layer of management Japanese firms often lack a proper system for monitoring the output of local personnel and channelling their market and customer knowledge to the Japanese members of top management.

A study by the Nomura Research Institute reports the same problem for Japanese subsidiaries in Hong Kong, Taiwan, Singapore and the Philippines.[57] It notes a very negative impact on the ability to react to rapid changes in the operating environment. The observations in these four countries also confirm the findings regarding the negative effect of frustrated local employees described earlier. Kawashima and Konomoto find that Japanese subsidiaries in East Asia display a strict top-down structure dominated by senior Japanese management and headquarters.[58] This allows for an organisational structure with a clear goal orientation and a clear and effective chain of command. In this, it is well suited to a stable environment. But, on the other hand, these firms give their local staff little autonomy and opportunity to channel information to their superiors, making a flexible market response under rapidly changing conditions difficult. In China, Japanese operations face exactly the same problem. The complexity of the environment and the speed of changes there are even faster and more unpredictable. Hence the disadvantages of the Japanese expatriate-based IMC system are even stronger in China than they are in Taiwan or Singapore.

Beside the problems that arise from Japanese IMC systems within China, we must also look at the international level. The rising importance of China as both a growing domestic market and an emerging link in the global production networks of MNCs requires that correct information flow quickly from the Japanese subsidiary to the headquarters in Japan as well as between subsidiaries in China and other (especially Asian) countries. Delays and mistakes in generating correct information in China are hence an important problem that extends

Managing the global–local dilemma   187

to the global corporate level. The main trouble lies in the inability of Japanese MNCs to generate a continuous, international exchange of information. And it is here that the Japanese IMC system often fails to provide an adequate structure. By stressing expatriate control over other means, especially control by socialisation and networks, Japanese MNCs restrict the international exchange of information nearly exclusively to Japanese employees. Hence they deny chances for additional and valuable inputs by their non-Japanese colleagues.

Barriers to solutions of control and coordination problems in China

How can Japanese firms solve their IMC problems in China? A reduction in the strong reliance on expatriates and a simultaneous increase in alternative control mechanisms, i.e. formal bureaucratic control, output control and control by socialisation and networks, immediately comes to mind. But such a shift faces several obstacles in Japan and China. Space does not allow for a detailed explanation of why such a shift has to include changes in Japan as well.[59] Here we will focus our discussion on the situation in China.

Among the alternatives to expatriates in China, a stronger emphasis on formal, bureaucratic control might appeal most to Japanese MNCs. This control mechanism is generally suited to complement personal, centralised control already in place in most Japanese subsidiaries. But the high complexity and instability in the Chinese business environment restrict the effective use of this mechanism to limited areas and can lead to an inflexible market response.

An increase in the use of output control combined with more control by socialisation and networks offers an alternative. The combination of these two mechanisms is preferred in situations with high environmental instability and thus seems suited to the current business environment in China. Within such a combination, output control targets areas where outputs are measurable. Control by socialisation and networks targets behaviour that does not lend itself to measurement. Hence, an isolated increase of output control does not fit with a complex environment like China because there are still too many areas that resist any meaningful measuring of numerical goals. This makes control by socialisation and networks the key to a successful coordination of business activities in China. But it is exactly here that the biggest weakness of Japanese firms lies.

Control by socialisation and networks largely takes place through the creation of shared values and goals, through informal, horizontal communication between executives, and through temporarily formalised cross-section relations like task forces or cross-functional teams. Since the functioning of Japanese firms at home is widely based on networks and tacit learning,[60] we might expect them to score highly in these areas at the international level as well. The low significance of control by socialisation and networks, presented in Table 10.2, however, shows the opposite. The reasons for this are numerous.

A high level of shared values and informal communication can be aimed at by expatriate presence but can be better achieved through international training programmes and formal international networks of executives.[61] Such programmes and networks, however, are very rare in Japanese MNCs. If they exist, participation is nearly exclusively Japanese. The same applies to board meetings dealing with global or Asia–Pacific matters and strategies. They usually take place at the Japanese headquarters, not somewhere in the region like China.[62] The fact that foreigners are generally missing on the board of directors at Japanese headquarters adds to the picture.

As a result, chances for socialisation and learning between Japanese and non-Japanese employees at the managerial level are fairly restricted. In any case, they are limited to hierarchical, bilateral exchanges between Japanese and Chinese. They do not allow for a cross-border flow of information between subsidiaries of two different countries that by-pass Japanese headquarters. The same holds true for international task forces and cross-functional teams. They rarely take place in Japanese MNCs involving managers from more than one other country.

One major obstacle to overcoming these barriers is of course, the problem of language. English is the international business language and a prerequisite for all kinds of international networking at the formal and informal level. Since the beginning of international operations, a lack of proficiency in English has put Japanese MNCs in a disadvantageous position versus firms from other industrialised countries. It will continue to do so until the average proficiency level of the international managers at Japanese MNCs improves enough to allow for a smooth international exchange of ideas at the working level.

Another more abstract, though ultimately larger, obstacle to the introduction of effective socialisation and networking at the international level lies in the persistence of ethnocentric elements in Japan that can also be described as an insider–outsider mentality.[63] Such ethnocentric elements can be found at the concrete company level but also within Japanese society itself. Examples of the former include the preference for Japanese-only boards, as described earlier. Examples of ethnocentrism within the society are more difficult to find but probably more important.

One such example is related to the employment of Chinese nationals in Japanese companies. In the early/mid-1990s, larger firms have started to employ Chinese workers in Japan in larger numbers on a permanent basis, offering them regular careers within the mother company. This has increased knowledge about the Chinese market in the head offices of Japanese MNCs. It has also created a pool of 'loyal' Chinese employees who can be sent to overseas postings helping to reduce the problem of over-reliance on Japanese expatriates.

At first sight, this trend seems to constitute a clear example for a shift from ethnocentrism to polycentrism. The author knows, for example, of three cases where native Chinese worked for several years at the head offices of large Japanese MNCs in Tokyo before being promoted to senior positions. One became the head of the China department at headquarters. The two others were sent to China as general managers of existing joint ventures. In all three cases, however, these Chinese took up Japanese nationality during the course of their careers.[64] Such nationality changes have strong repercussions. Even assuming that success in each of these careers is totally unrelated to the switch in

Managing the global–local dilemma   189

nationality, local managers in China might conclude otherwise. With devastating results on their motivation, they might think that such a switch is a prerequisite for promotion or contributes to quick success at those and other Japanese companies.[65]

As such, an indirect form of ethnocentrism or insider–outsider mentality hinders the build-up of truly international operations in Japanese firms. Although this social phenomenon can be partly explained by the relatively late development of Japan within the international environment, it nevertheless influences Japanese MNCs in their current drive to globalise and implement new IMC systems.

Conclusions

The global–local dilemma of MNCs to find an optimal mix between centralised and decentralised decision-making with a suitable employment of control and coordination mechanisms obviously imposes huge problems on Japanese firms in China. The prevailing reliance on expatriates in the IMC system of Japanese companies results in several problems. Most issues are not China-specific by nature. But the unique Chinese business environment is intensifying the problems, and urgency about finding solutions rises with the growing importance of China and its market.

Many Japanese MNCs have already realised the organisational incongruities between their IMC systems and the requirements of the business environment in China and other parts of the world. One indicator here are the numerous plans at headquarters in Japan that call for a reduction in expatriates and numerical targets for localisation of management of overseas subsidiaries. A simple reduction of the number of expatriates would be a radical change in the IMC system. However, such a policy is neither advisable nor to be expected anytime soon. At least three reasons militate against such a scenario in China.

First, a quick shift to one of the various IMC models used by Western firms is not realistic. Japanese MNCs simply cannot develop alternative, effective control mechanisms overnight. The main obstacles are the different domestic business systems and their enduring influence on the organisation of overseas business.[66]

Second, similar to the various problems described for Japanese MNCs, Western competitors face different problems specific to their IMC systems. The low use of expatriates in US overseas operations, for example, might lead to an insufficient international managerial experience in US MNCs in the long run.[67] Another IMC problem, not uncommon among Western firms in China, comes with the employment of overseas Chinese for top-level jobs. These managers speak Chinese and offer familiarity with the local culture. Yet local managers who prefer working under a Western boss often reject them, as stated by many of the author's interviewees.[68]

Third, the choice of an efficient IMC model differs with regard to the type of company. Among Japanese MNCs there are great differences that depend on the type of business in China.[69] Many Japanese plants in China still engage in the

190 *Jochen Legewie*

export-processing trade in which efficient production is more important than market response or organisational learning. For these companies, expatriate-based IMC models have worked fairly well and do not require immediate alteration.

Other Japanese firms, however, have totally different needs, especially with regard to a flexible market response. More than 30 per cent of all Japanese manufacturers in China already sell half or more of their output to the local Chinese market and the numbers of these firms are increasing rapidly.[70] Other companies in fast-moving sectors like information technology and telecommunications equipment are very dependent on quick and comprehensive organisational learning. They embody another example of internationally active MNCs that require fast, cross-border flows of formal and informal information. This is difficult to achieve in an IMC model that is exclusively expatriate-based.

Hence, Japanese MNCs will attempt to implement new IMC models in response to their specific needs and the specific requirements of the business environment in China. The transfer towards learning organisations and transnational companies in the real sense will, however, in any case be a difficult one, be it in China or elsewhere. The various obstacles along the way to solve this global–local dilemma will make the shift from ethnocentric to geocentric firms (or more realistically regiocentric firms) a very 'tortuous evolution', to borrow the term of Perlmutter.[71]

Notes

1 Japan–China Investment Promotion Organisation, *Nikkei kigyō ankieto chōsa shūkei bunseki kekka (Results of the General Analysis of the Questionnaire Survey on Japanese Companies)*, Beijing, JCIPC, 2000.

2 See, for example, J. R. Galbraith and R. K. Kazanjian, 'Organizing to Implement Strategies of Diversity and Globalisation: The Role of Matrix Designs', *Human Resource Management*, 1986, vol. 25 (spring), pp. 37–54; G. Hedlund, 'The Hypermodern MNC – A Heterarchy?', in *Human Resource Management*, 1986, vol. 25, pp. 9–35; M. E. Porter, 'Competition in Global Industries: A Conceptual Framework', in M. E. Porter (ed.) *Competition in Global Industries*, Boston MA, Harvard Business School Press, 1986, pp. 15–56; C. K. Prahalad and Y. L. Doz, *The Multinational Mission*, New York, The Free Press, 1987; R. E. White and T. A. Poynter, 'Organizing for World-wide Advantage', in C. A. Bartlett, Y. Doz and G. Hedlund (eds) *Managing the Global Firm*, London, Routledge, 1990, pp. 95–113.

3 C. A. Bartlett and S. Ghoshal, *Managing Across Borders. The Transnational Solution*, Boston, MA, Harvard Business School Press, 1989.

4 P. A. L. Evans, 'The Strategic Outcomes of Human Resource Management', *Human Resource Management*, 1986, vol. 25, pp. 149–67; J. I. Martinez and J. C. Jarillo, 'The Evolution of Research on Coordination Mechanisms in Multinational Corporations', *Journal of International Business Studies*, 1989, vol. 20, no. 3, pp. 489–514.

5 See, for example, J. Child, *Organization: A Guide to Problems and Practice*, London, Harper and Row, 1984; A. Edström and P. Lorange, 'Matching Strategy and Human Resources in Multinational Corporations', *Journal of International Business Studies*, 1984, vol. 15, pp. 125–37; S. J. Kobrin, 'Expatriate Reduction and Strategic Control in American Multinational Corporations', *Human Resource Management*, 1988, vol. 27,

Managing the global–local dilemma 191

pp. 63–75; J. D. Daniels and L. H. Radebaugh, *International Business. Environment and Operations*, Reading MA, Addison-Wesley, 1989; K. Roth and D. Nigh, 'The Effectiveness of Headquarter Subsidiary Relationships: The Role of Coordination, Control, and Conflict', *Journal of Business Research*, 1992, vol. 25, no. 4, pp. 7–301.

6 A. Edström and J. R. Galbraith, 'Transfer of Managers: A Comparison of Documentary and Interpersonal Methods', *Academy of Management Journal*, 1977, vol. 30, no. 4, pp. 514–39.

7 U. Wiechmann, 'Integrating Multinational Marketing Activities', *Columbia Journal of World Business*, 1974, vol. 9, no. 4, pp. 7–16.

8 For a more detailed introduction to the topic of international management control and the use of various control mechanisms by MNCs from both a theoretical and empirical background, see A. W. Harzing, *Managing the Multinationals – An International Study of Control Mechanisms*, Cheltenham, Edward Elgar, 1999, and G. Reger, *Koordination und strategisches Management internationaler Innovationsprozesse*, Heidelberg, Physica-Verlag, 1997.

9 R. L. Tung, 'Selection and Training Procedures of U. S., European, and Japanese Multinationals', *California Management Review*, 1982, vol. 25, no. 1, pp. 57–71; A. R. Negandhi and M. Welge, *Beyond Theory Z: Global Rationalization Strategies of American, German and Japanese Multinational Companies*, Advances in International Comparative Management, Greenwich CA, JAI Press, 1984; R. Kopp, 'International Human Resource Policies and Practices in Japanese, European, and United States Multinationals', *Human Resource Management*, 1994, vol. 33, no. 4, pp. 581–99.

10 G. L. Harrison et al., 'The Influence of Culture on Organization Design and Planning and Control in Australia and the United States Compared with Singapore and Hong Kong', *Journal of International Financial Management and Accounting*, 1994, October, pp. 242–61; S. C. Jain and L. R. Tucker, 'The Influence of Culture on Strategic Constructs in the Process of Globalization: An Empirical Study of North American and Japanese MNCs', *International Business Review*, 1995, vol. 4, no. 1, pp. 19–37.

11 L. Otterbeck, 'Concluding Remarks – And a Review of Subsidiary Autonomy', in L. Otterbeck (ed.), *The Management of Headquarters Subsidiary Relationships in Multinational Corporations*, Aldershot, Gower, 1981, pp. 337–43; A. R. Negandhi, *International Management*, Newton MA, Allyn and Bacon, 1987; M. P. Kriger and E. E. Solomon, 'Strategic Mindset and Decision-making Autonomy in U.S. and Japanese MNCs', *Management International Review*, 1992, vol. 32, no. 4, pp. 327–43; J. Wolf, *Internationales Personalmanagement. Kontext – Koordination – Erfolg*, Wiesbaden, Gabler, 1994.

12 A. Ferner, 'Country of Origin Effects and Human Resource Management in Multinational Companies', *Human Resource Management*, 1997, vol. 7, no. 1, pp. 19–37.

13 Harzing, op. cit.

14 Martinez and Jarillo, op. cit.; H. Mintzberg, *Structure in Fives. Designing Effective Organizations*, Englewood Cliffs NJ, Prentice-Hall, 1983; W. G. Ouchi, 'A Conceptual Framework for the Design of Organizational Control Mechanisms', *Management Science*, 1979, vol. 25, no. 9, pp. 833–48; Edström and Galbraith, op. cit.; J. R. Galbraith, *Designing Complex Organizations*, Reading MA, Addison-Wesley, 1973; J. W. Lawrence and P. R. Lorsch, *Organization and Environment*, Boston MA, Harvard University Press, 1967; J. G. March and H. A. Simon, *Organizations*, New York, John Wiley and Sons, 1958.

15 Harzing, op. cit., pp. 7–31.

16 Lawrence and Lorsch, op. cit.; Edström and Galbraith, op. cit.; Martinez and Jarillo, op. cit.

17 Child, op. cit., p. 168.

18 There are two other important functions of expatriates. The first is position-filling or the transfer of technical/managerial knowledge to subsidiaries abroad; the second is management development for the people sent abroad, i. e. to give them international

192 *Jochen Legewie*

management experience and thus foster international market experience at the mother company level. See, for example, Edström and Galbraith, op. cit.; S. L. Beechler, *International Management Control in Multinational Corporations: The Case of Japanese Consumer Electronics Subsidiaries in Southeast Asia*, Ann Arbor, UMI, 1993; A. W. Harzing, 'Who's in Charge? An Empirical Study of Executive Staffing Practices in Foreign Subsidiaries', *Human Resource Management*, 2001 (forthcoming).

19 This study covered more than 120 MNCs in eight different industries and with some 1650 subsidiaries in 22 different countries, see Harzing, 1999, op. cit.

20 Harzing, 1999, op. cit.; A. W. Harzing, 'An Empirical Analysis and Extension of the Bartlett and Ghoshal Typology of Multinational Companies', *Journal of International Business Studies*, 2000, vol. 31, no. 1, pp. 101–20.

21 Tung, op. cit.; Kopp, op. cit.

22 Bartlett and Ghoshal, op. cit.

23 W. Hatch and K. Yamamura, *Asia in Japan's Embrace. Building a Regional Production Alliance*, Cambridge and New York, Cambridge University Press, 1996; M. Seki, *Kūdōka o koete – gijutsu to chiiki no saikōchiku*, Tokyo, Nihon Keizai Shinbunsha, 1997.

24 Ferner, op. cit.

25 A. Ferner and J. Quintanilla, 'Multinationals, National Business Systems and HRM: The Enduring Influence of National Identity of a Process of "Anglo-Saxonization"', *The International Journal of Human Resource Management*, 1998, vol. 9, no. 4, pp. 710–31.

26 It can also be argued that expatriate use is cheaper for Japanese firms than it is for US or European MNCs. While Western expatriates tend to bring their spouses and children abroad with them, many more Japanese expatriates go for their overseas secondment alone, leaving their families at home (mainly because of schooling needs). Hence Japanese firms save substantial amounts of money for additional overseas lodging, school fees, and other family-related expenses.

27 M. Kenney and R. Florida, *Beyond Mass Production*, New York and Oxford, Oxford University Press, 1993.

28 A. R. Negandhi and B. R. Belga, 'Multinationals in Industrially Developed Countries: A Comparative Study of American, German, and Japanese Multinationals', in A. R. Negandhi (ed.), *Functioning of the Multinational Corporation – An International Study*, New York, Pergamon Press, 1982, pp. 117–35.

29 A. R. Negandhi, 'Adaptability of American, European, and Japanese Multinational Corporations in Developing Countries', in A. R. Negandhi (ed.), *Functioning of the Multinational Corporation – An International Study*, New York, Pergamon Press, 1982, pp. 136–64.

30 Bartlett and Ghoshal, op. cit.

31 Ferner, op. cit., p. 23.

32 T. Elger and C. Smith, 'Introduction', in T. Elger and C. Smith (ed.), *Global Japanization*, London and New York, Routledge, 1994, p. 2.

33 J. H. Dunning, *Japanese Participation in British Industry*, London, Routledge, 1986.

34 Kenney and Florida, op. cit.; also see B. Taylor, 'Patterns of Control within Japanese Manufacturing Plants in China: Doubts about Japanization in Asia', *Journal of Management Studies*, 1999, vol. 36, no. 6, pp. 853–73.

35 M. Gell-Mann, *The Quark and the Jaguar: Adventures in the Simplex and the Complex*, London, Abacus, 1995. Crude complexity describes the number of elements in a system and the number of connections between them. Effective complexity is the function of the irregularity and unpredictability of a system. See also N. K. Napier and V. T. Vu, 'International Human Resource Management in Developing and Transitional Economy Countries: A Breed Apart?', *Human Resource Management Review*, 1998, vol. 8, no. 1, pp. 50–5.

36 Napier and Vu, op. cit.; J. Child, 'Management and Organizations in China: Key Trends and Issues', in J. T. Li, A. Tsui and E. Weldon (eds), *Management and Organizations in the Chinese Context*, Basingstoke, Macmillan, 2000, pp. 33–62.

Managing the global–local dilemma   193

37 M. Warner, *The Management of Human Resources in Chinese Industry*, London, St Martin's Press, 1995; Child, 2000, op. cit.

38 Tsūshō Sangyōshō, *Kaigai jigyō katsudō dōkō chōsa gaiyō, dai 29-kai*, Tokyo, Sangyō Seisakukyoku Kokusai Kigyōka, 2000, p. 6.

39 Also see *Tōyō Keizai, Kaigai shinshutsu kigyō sōran '00, kigyōbetsu-hen*, Tokyo, Tōyō Keizai Shinpōsha, 2000; JETRO (Results of a survey conducted for the Sanwa Research Institute, internal paper, 2000).

40 Taylor, op. cit., p. 861.

41 A. Nakamura, 'Understanding the Relationships between Japanese Managers and Chinese Employees in Japanese Wholly-Owned Ventures in and around Shenzen' (Paper presented at Thirteenth Annual Conference of the Association of Japanese Business Studies, Oiso, 9–11 June, 2000); Taylor, op. cit.; C. Ma, 'Foreign-Funded Enterprises in China: The Difficult Task of Talent-Keeping and its Impact on the Wage Structure', *JETRO China Newsletter*, 1998, no. 132, pp. 2–9; K. Leung et al., 'Job Satisfaction in Joint Venture Hotels in China – An Organizational Analysis', in P. W. Beamish and P. Killing (eds), *Cooperative Strategies – Asian Pacific Perspectives*, San Francisco, New Lexington Press, 1997, pp. 226–44.

42 Ma, op. cit.

43 Nakamura, op. cit.

44 Leung et al., op. cit.

45 R. Kopp, 'The Rice-Paper Ceiling in Japanese Companies – Why it Exists and Persists', in S. L. Beechler and A. Bird (eds), *Japanese Multinationals Abroad – Individual and Organizational Learning*, New York and Oxford, Oxford University Press, 1999, pp. 107–28.

46 JETRO, op. cit., p. 24.

47 C. S. Wong and K. S. Law, 'Managing Localization of Human Resources in the PRC: A Practical Model', *Journal of World Business*, 1999, vol. 34, no. 1, pp. 26–40.

48 C. D. Fisher and A. X. Yuan, 'What Motivates Employees? A Comparison of US and Chinese Responses', *International Journal of Human Resource Management*, 1998, vol. 9, no. 3, pp. 516–28.

49 Older workers, by contrast, tend to prefer job security and hence do not show any preference for Western over Japanese employers. Interestingly, many Japanese interviewees of the author stressed this fact and suggested an eventual superiority of the Japanese employment system in the long run. Such a view, however, does not help Japanese firms in the current situation in which they compete with other MNCs for young and qualified employees.

50 JETRO, op. cit.

51 The causal relationship between the Japanese IMC system and labour problems becomes even more apparent when we look at the numbers for wholly owned subsidiaries. Without the interference of a local partner, Japanese MNCs are left freely to implement their own systems of labour management and the story becomes even more telling. Among wholly owned subsidiaries, 40 per cent of all respondents cite human-resource-related problems, making them the second largest headache for Japanese MNCs in China after 'tax and legal problems', see JETRO, op. cit., pp. 88–9.

52 Nakamura, op. cit.; Taylor, op. cit.

53 Taylor, op. cit.

54 Taylor, op. cit., p. 864.

55 Language barriers, however, are slowly but gradually being lowered as more and more Japanese expatriates tend to speak Chinese or at least understand a little which was rarely the case ten years ago.

56 Taylor, op. cit., pp. 863–5.

57 I. Kawashima and S. Konomoto, 'Time for More Autonomy: Problems of Japanese Companies in East and Southeast Asia', *NRI Quarterly*, 1999 (autumn), pp. 18–31.

194 *Jochen Legewie*

58 Kawashima and Konomoto, op. cit., p. 21.
59 Such a discussion includes, for example, the current debate on corporate governance in Japan and relates to an eventual shift from the strong personal focus in the Japanese business system towards a more formal and output-based system. Resulting changes in the domestic business system will undoubtedly have important repercussions on international business practices and hence IMC systems. A closer look at these effects, however, requires a study of its own.
60 I. Nonaka and A. Takeuchi, *The Knowledge-Creating Company. How Japanese Companies Create the Dynamics of Innovation*, New York and Oxford, Oxford University Press, 1995.
61 Harzing, 1999, op. cit., p. 318.
62 A rare exception is Sony, which regularly holds board meetings abroad including China.
63 For different states of mind or attitude of international executives, see the models of ethnocentrism (home-country-oriented), polycentrism (host-country-oriented), and geocentrism (world-oriented) as described by H. V. Perlmutter, 'The Tortuous Evolution of the Multinational Company', *Columbia Journal of World Business*, 1969 (Jan/Feb), pp. 9–18. The ethnocentric attitude implies that management style, knowledge, evaluation criteria, and managers from the home country are supposed to be superior to those of the host country. The polycentric attitude takes the opposite point of view, recognising differences between countries and believing that local nationals are in the best position to understand and handle country-specific affairs. The geocentric attitude draws from a worldwide pool of international managers to be appointed regardless of their nationality. See also Harzing, 1999, op. cit., pp. 54–5.
64 Asked for the reasons for the nationality switch, all named, explicitly or implicitly, pressure by Japanese society. While they denied that their Chinese nationality had any influence on their professional careers within the company, they judged it more convenient for their children at school to have a Japanese family name.
65 Also see Nakamura, op. cit.
66 Ferner and Quintanilla, op. cit.
67 Kobrin, op. cit.; Wong and Law, op. cit.
68 Also see Leung et al., op. cit.
69 The three plants of Teijin in Nantong, for example, work de facto as subcontractors for the Teijin headquarters in Japan. These plants receive input materials, engage in the weaving and dying processes and then return 95 per cent of their output to Japan. For this they receive a commission. In other words, because they are (still) not targeting the local market, they have very little need for local feedback.
70 JETRO, op. cit., p. 72.
71 Perlmutter, op. cit.

Index

Note: 'n.' after a page reference indicates the number of a note on that page.

acquisitions 157
Adenauer, Konrad 22
Aegis destroyers 72, 73, 74, 75
agriculture 123
Airborne Warning and Control System
(AWACS) 73, 74
Ando Sadami 90
Annette Lu 90
Anti-Ballistic Missile (ABM) treaty (1972)
71, 72, 80
Asian Monetary Fund 148
Aspin, Les 73
Association of East Asian Relations 94
Association of South-East Asian Nations
(ASEAN) 42
ASEAN Regional Forum (ARF) 61
Athukorala, Prema-chandra 176n.5
Australia 120
Austria 24, 120

background and trend of the partnership
103–4: structure 104–10; future trend
110–13
bacteriological warfare 13: *see also*
chemical weapons
balancing power 63–4, 108
ballistic missile defence (BMD) *see* theatre
missile defence
Ballistic Missile Defence Organisation
(BMDO) 73
BASF 185
battlefield management (BM) systems 72
Beauvoir, Simone de 20
Beijing Electronic Machinery Research
Institute 168
Beijing Nantsune Meat Machinery Joint
Venture Co. Ltd 168–9, 174

Beijing–Tokyo–Washington triangle 32:
East Asia's power relation
configuration 32–6; economic
dimension 36–8; future trend 111;
political dimension 43–7; prospects for
Sino-Japanese relations 47–8; strategic
dimension 38–43
Beijing Urban Railway Construction
Project 122
Beijing Wacoal Co. Ltd 174
Boxer Rebellion 3
Brandt, Willy 24
Brazil 183
Brunei 139
bureaucratic formalised control 179–80,
181, 187
Burma 115
Buruma, Ian 15, 18
Bush, George 72–3
Bush, George W. 83
business environment, Japanese firms in
China 165
Buzan, Barry 25

Cairo Declaration 92
Canada 120, 138, 145
capital formation and FDI 146
carbon dioxide emissions 152
CEC (Commission of European
Communities) 121
centralisation, Japanese companies 166,
178
chemical weapons 24, 112
Chemical Weapons Convention (CWC)
24
Chen Sui-bian 95
Chi Haotian 60, 98

196   *Index*

Chiang Kai-shek: Beijing–Tokyo–
  Washington triangle 39; Taiwan
  question 91, 92, 94, 96, 102n.27
Child, J. 177
China International Trust and
  Investment Corporation (CITIC) 168
China–Japan–Korea Forum 42
Chinese Academy of Sciences (CAS)
  169–70
Chinese Communist Party (CCP):
  Beijing–Tokyo–Washington triangle
  46; Taiwan question 88, 89, 99
Chongqing 123, 125
civil society, China 38
Civil War, China 39, 97
class issues, China 38
Clinton, Bill: Hashimoto–Clinton
  Declaration (1996) 57, 60, 63; Taiwan
  question 40, 95; theatre missile
  defence 83; visit to China 4, 38, 39,
  45, 110
Colombo Plan 115
'comfort women' 13, 17
command, control, communications and
  intelligence (C3¹) systems 72, 73, 77,
  78
communication, Japanese firms in China
  164, 173
communism 3–4: *see also* Chinese
  Communist Party
competitiveness: bilateral trade 139;
  economic relationship 149, 150,
  151–2; Japanese firms in China 172
constitution, Japan 47–8
corruption, China 35, 162, 176n.8
counterfeiting 165
credit problem, Japanese firms in China
  165
crime, China 58
Cronin, Patrick M. 77
cultural issues 3: future trend of the
  relationship 112; history problem
  18–19
Cultural Revolution 4
Cumings, Bruce 91
customs duties 164
Czech Republic 24

Daiichi Pharmaceutical (Beijing) Co. Ltd
  175
Daiichi Pharmaceutical (China) Co. Ltd
  175
Dalian 123, 125, 144
Daniels, J. D. 177

de Beauvoir, Simone 20
debt problem, China 118
defence *see* security issues
Defence Support Programme, US (DSP)
  72, 77
democracy: Beijing–Tokyo–Washington
  triangle 38, 45, 46; and historical
  reconciliation 23–4
Democratic Progressive Party (Taiwan)
  90
Deng Xiao-ping: Beijing–Tokyo–
  Washington triangle 38, 44, 47;
  Diaoyu/Senkaku Islands 54; history
  problem 13, 15; military growth 53
dependency, economic relations 148, 150
Development Assistance Committee
  (DAC) 116, 117
Diaoyu/Senkaku Islands: Beijing–
  Tokyo–Washington triangle 41;
  Defend Diaoyu Islands Movement 14;
  engagement Japanese style 54–5, 62;
  history problem 13, 14
domination, economic relations 148, 150
Dulles, John Foster 92
Dunning, J. H. 182

East China Sea 54–5
economic growth 1, 4, 130–1, 151:
  Beijing–Tokyo–Washington triangle
  33; FDI 146–7; ODA 124; structure of
  China–Japan relationship 105;
  Taiwan 92–3
economic relations: assessment 149–52;
  assumptions 147–8; future trend of the
  relationship 111, 112, 113; history
  problem 14; importance of Sino-
  Japanese relationship 130–2; scenarios
  148–9; *see also* foreign direct
  investment; trade
Edström, A. 177, 179
efficiency wages 165
Eight-Year War of Resistance 16, 28n.3:
  see also history problem
emigration *see* migration patterns
engagement Japanese style 52, 65–7:
  background of security relations in the
  1990s 52–8; liberal element 60–3;
  non-military challenges 58; problems
  59; realist elements 63–5
entrepôt trade through Hong Kong 132–3
Environmental Development Model
  Cities Concept 123, 125
environmental protection 112, 122–3,
  152: *see also* pollution

Index 197

equity participation 157
ethnocentrism, Japanese subsidiaries in China 178, 188–9
Eurasia Bridge 112
European Union (EU) 138, 143–4, 145
Evergreen–Marubeni link 100
exclusive economic zone (EEZ) 54–5, 122
expatriates running Japanese subsidiaries 177–8, 180–2, 184–7, 189
Export Import Bank of Japan (EXIM Bank) 4, 101n.16: ODA 115, 128n.17
exports *see* trade

Falun Gong 122
Ferner, A. 178
Fifteen-Year war *see* Eight-Year War of Resistance
Finland 24
Fisher, C. D. 185
Fishery Agreement (1997) 112
Florida, R. 182
forced labour 13
foreign aid 1, 4; *see also* official development assistance
foreign direct investment (FDI) 124, 131–2, 139–42, 147, 149–51: Beijing–Tokyo–Washington triangle 33–4, 35; economic growth of China 146–7; features 143–4; intensity index 141–2; Japanese firms in China 154, 155–8; motives 144–6; statistical issues 142–3; in Taiwan 91
Foreign Financing Administration, China 119
foreign policy: Beijing–Tokyo–Washington triangle 37, 38, 39, 44–5; history problem 14
France 22, 120
Fuji Bank 168
Fujitsu 183, 184
Fukuyama, Francis 32
Fukuyoshi Shoji 57
Funabashi Yoichi 57
Funada Naka 90
Futemna 57
future trend of the partnership 103–4, 110–13: ODA 126–7

Gaimusho 11, 98; *see also* Ministry of Foreign Affairs, Japan
Galbraith, J. R. 177, 179
gas exploration and production 55
Gell-Mann, M. 182

Germany: and France, relations between 22; MNCs 180, 181, 185; ODA 120; and Poland, accord between 24; World War I 3
Giarra, Paul S. 77
global–local dilemma 177–9, 189–90: current business conditions in China 182–3; international management control of Japanese MNCs in international comparison 180–2; problems in international management control 183–9; typology of international management control systems 179–80
Global Protection Against Limited Strikes (GPALS) 72–3
globalisation: Beijing–Tokyo–Washington triangle 36–7; economic relations 147; history problem 22; Taiwan question 88, 91, 99
Goto Shimpei 90
government administration, China 161–2, 172
Great Britain 120, 184
Great Leap Forward (1958) 92
Green, Michael J. 77
gross domestic product (GDP) 1, 33, 34, 35, 36
Group of Eight (G8) 61
Guangdong Marco Group 166
Guangdong Meizhi Compressor Co. Ltd 166–8, 174
Guangdong Midea Group 166–7
Guidelines for US–Japan Defence Cooperation: Taiwan question 89, 96, 99, 100; theatre missile defence 70, 76, 79, 80
Guiyang 123, 125
Gulf War 52, 53, 73
Guo Moruo 21

Haider, Joerg 24
Hanaoka Incident 27
Harrison, G. L. 178
Harzing, A. W. 179, 180, 181
Hashimoto–Clinton Declaration (1996) 57, 60, 63
Hashimoto Hiroshi 98
Hashimoto Ryutaro: history problem 27; structure of China–Japan relationship 108; Taiwan question 56, 98
Hattori Kenji 176n.6
hedging 64–5
Hill, Hal 176n.5

198 *Index*

Historical Research Committee, Japan 18
history of the relationship 2–4
history problem 10–14, 27–8:
  prescriptions 21–7; sources 15–21;
  structure of China–Japan relationship
  105, 106, 109
Ho Chi-minh 102n.27
Hong Kong: Beijing–Tokyo–Washington
  triangle 36; FDI in China 141, 143,
  155; Japanese subsidiaries in 186;
  trade 132–3, 134, 137
Hong Kong Sanyo 143
Hu Yaobang 44
Huatang Yanghuatang Commercial Co.
  Ltd 173
human resources, and FDI 146
human rights issues: Beijing–Tokyo–
  Washington triangle 41, 44–7;
  engagement Japanese style 61, 64;
  ODA 122
humanitarian considerations, ODA 116,
  120
Hunter, Edward 30n.52
Huntington, Samuel 33, 45

IFAD (International Fund for Agriculture
  Development) 121
Iguchi Sadao 91
Ijiri Hidenori 14, 17
Ikeda Hayato 92
Ikeda Yukihiko 57
illegal immigrants from China 58
imagery intelligence (IMINT) satellites 78
immigration *see* migration patterns
imports *see* trade
income levels 1, 130
Independence, USS 57
India 47, 61
Indonesia: ODA from Japan 62, 115, 116,
  117; trade surplus with Japan 139
infrastructure, Japanese firms in China
  159, 160, 165, 171
insider–outsider mentality, Japanese
  subsidiaries in China 178, 188–9
Institute for Orthodox History 18
Interchange Association 94
intercontinental ballistic missiles (ICBM)
  71–2, 74, 75
intermediate range ballistic missiles
  (IRBM) 75
International Development Association,
  World Bank (IDA) 121, 123, 127
international management control (IMC)
  177–9, 189–90: current business

conditions in China 182–3; of
  Japanese MNC in international
  comparison 180–2; problems 183–9;
  typology of systems 179–80
Iraq 53, 73
Ishihara Shintaro 18, 20, 95
Ishii Mitsujiro 90
Itochu 183

Jain, S. C. 178
Japan Bank of International Cooperation
  (JBIC): FDI 150; Japanese firms in
  China 154, 156, 158, 159; ODA 118,
  119, 123, 125
Japan–China Investment Promotion
  Organisation (JIPO) 154, 156, 160,
  165, 177
Japan Defence Agency (JDA) 69, 81, 83,
  85n.16
Japan External Trade Organisation
  (JETRO) 154, 156, 159, 185
Japan International Cooperation Agency
  (JICA) 118
Japan–ROC Cooperation Committee
  (JRCC) 90
Japan–ROC Dietmembers Consultative
  Committee (Nikkakon) 90, 91, 94
Jarillo, J. C. 179
Jiang Zemin: Beijing–Tokyo–
  Washington triangle 44, 45;
  engagement Japanese style 60; history
  problem 10–11, 13, 15–16, 22–3, 25,
  28; Partnership of Friendship and
  Cooperation for Peace and
  Development 103, 108, 110; Taiwan
  question 95
Johnson, Chalmers 15
Johnstone, Alastair Ian 59, 64
joint ventures 156, 157, 164–5, 172

Kajima Corporation 27
Kajiyama Seiroku 98
Kanemaru Shin 95
Kao 182
Kato Koichi 57, 98
Kawamura Junihiko 95
Kawasaki Heavy Industries 85n.16
Kawashima, I. 186
Kaya Okinori 90–1
Kenney, M. 182
Kim Dae Jung: Beijing–Tokyo–
  Washington triangle 43; history
  problem 10, 22, 23
Kim Il-sung 102n.27

Index   199

Kim Jong Il 43
Kishi Nobusuke: history problem 16, 18; Taiwan question 90, 92
Kissinger, Henry 39
Kobrin, S. J. 177
Koji Kakizawa 113n.2
Kojima Tomoyuki 26
Komori Yoshiki 123
Kono Yohei 122
Konomoto, S. 186
Kopp, R. 181
Korea: annexation 3; Beijing–Tokyo–Washington triangle 42, 43; history problem 17, 22–3; regionalism 148; war 4, 50n.21; *see also* North Korea; South Korea
Kotake Kazuaki 18
Kristof, Nicholas 14
Kuomintang (KMT) 89, 92
Kyuma Fumio 98

labour supply, China 2, 165
language barriers 186, 188
Law, K. S. 185
Lawrence, J. W. 179
Lee Teng-hui: Beijing–Tokyo–Washington triangle 41, 48; engagement Japanese style 58; legacies of colonial period and full diplomatic relations 89, 90; reconciliation through ambiguity 95, 101n.18; security concerns: (re-)emergence of 98; US visit 100
legal system, China 159, 160, 163
Leung, K. 184, 185
Li Peng 98, 108
Li Shengzhi 23
Liberal Democratic Party, Japan (LDP): engagement Japanese style 53, 57; history problem 18, 20, 27; ODA 122, 123; Taiwan question 90, 93; theatre missile defence 78, 80, 83
Liberal Party, Japan 21
localisation, Japanese firms in China 173: *see also* global–local dilemma
logistical problems, Japanese firms in China 165
Lorange, P. 177
Lord, Winston 96
Lorsch, P. R. 179
Lu Xun 25

Ma, C. 184, 185
Mainichi Shimbun 101

Manchuria 3, 28n.3
manufacturing sector, FDI in 143, 146, 155
Mao Zedong: Beijing–Tokyo–Washington triangle 37, 44, 47; nationalism 102n.27; Taiwan question 93
March, J. G. 179
Marco Polo Bridge incident (1937) 28n.3
maritime self-defence force, Japan (MSDF) 54, 56–7
Martinez, J. I. 179
Marubeni–Evergreen link 100
Matsumura Masahiro 77
Matsushita 183, 184
Meiji restoration 3, 90
mergers and acquisitions 157
migration patterns 3, 58
militarism: China 53–4; Japan 10, 17–18, 41, 44; *see also* security issues
Ministry of Finance, China 119, 125
Ministry of Finance, Japan (MOF) 142–3, 154
Ministry of Foreign Affairs, Japan (MOFA): history problem 11; ODA 123; Taiwan question 40, 98; theatre missile defence 69, 79, 80–1, 83; *see also* Gaimucho
Ministry of Foreign Trade and Economic Cooperation, China (MOTFC) 155
Mintzberg, H. 179
Missile Technology Control Regime (MTCR) 84n.6
Mitsubishi Electric 184
Mitsubishi Research Institute (MRI) 155
modernisation 3: Beijing–Tokyo–Washington triangle 38, 44–5, 47
Montaperto, Ronald N. 57
Morishima, M. 153n.16
multilateral forums 1, 61
multinational companies (MNCs) *see* global–local dilemma
Multiple Independently Targetable Re-entry Vehicles (MIRV) 74
Mundell, R. 146
Murayama Tomoichi 27, 56

Nakagane, K. 152–3n.5
Nakajima Mineo 15
Nakamura, A. 184, 185, 186
Nakanishi Keisuke 73
Nakasone Yasuhiro administration 72
Nanjing Massacre: history problem 13, 18, 19, 20, 27; Ishihara 95

200 Index

Nantsune Tekko 168
Nathan, Andrew 41
National Missile Defence (NMD) 80, 83
nationalism 2: Beijing–Tokyo–
    Washington triangle 39, 43; history
    problem 10, 16, 18, 20, 22, 26; ODA
    124; structure of China–Japan
    relationship 105; Taiwan question
    102n.27
natural resources 1, 2
Navy Area Defence (NAD) 71, 72
Navy Theatre Wide Defence (NTWD)
    69, 71–8
NEC 169, 184
NEC–CAS Software Laboratories Co.
    Ltd 169–70, 175
Nie, Minister of Defence 25
Nigh, D. 177
Nikkakon 90, 91, 94
Nish, Ian 20
Nishi, Admiral 60
Nissan Motors 85n.16
Nixon, Richard 39, 96
Nixon–Sato communiqué 96–7
Nomura Research Institute 186
Non-Proliferation Treaty (NPT) 56
Nonaka Hiromu 27, 86n.24
North American Aerospace Command
    (NORAD) 72, 77
North Korea: attack on South Korea
    (1950) 92; Beijing–Tokyo–
    Washington triangle 42, 43, 50n.21;
    nationalism 102n.27; theatre missile
    defence 70, 73–4, 77–83; see also Korea
nuclear weapons, China 19: engagement
    Japanese style 53–4, 56, 61; official
    development assistance 114, 117, 121,
    127; theatre missile defence 74, 76
Numata Sadaaki 95

Observation Island, tracking ship 57
Obuchi Keizo: Beijing–Tokyo–
    Washington triangle 44; engagement
    Japanese style 61; history problem 11,
    22; Taiwan question 95
Office for Abandoned Chemical
    Weapons 113n.9
official development assistance (ODA)
    114–15, 147: Beijing–Tokyo–
    Washington triangle 37, 38;
    characteristics of China as recipient
    118–19; characteristics of Japanese aid
    115–18; Charter 117, 121, 122, 124;
    development of relationship 119–22;

engagement Japanese style 56, 57, 61,
    62, 66; environmental protection 112;
    future relationship 126–7; history
    problem 14; present situation 122–4;
    suggested policy changes 124–6
Ogawa Akira 23
Ohira Masayoshi 62, 120
oil crisis 116
oil exploration and production 55
Okazaki Hisahiko 24
Okinawa 54, 55, 56, 57
Omron (China) Co. Ltd 174–5
Ouchi, W. G. 179
output control 179–80, 181, 187
Overseas Economic Cooperation Fund
    (OECF) 116, 128n.17
Ozawa Ichiro 26–7

PAC-2 system 71, 73
PAC-3 system 71, 72
Pakistan 61
Park Chung-Hee 102n.27
partnership, Japanese firms in China
    164–5, 171, 172
Partnership of Friendship and
    Cooperation for Peace and
    Development 103, 108–9, 111
Patriot system 73, 85n.12
patriotism, China 16
Peace and Friendship Treaty 19
People's Liberation Army (PLA) 61
Perlmutter, H. V. 190
permanent normal trading relations
    (PNTR) status, China 38
personal centralised control 179–80, 181,
    187
Philippines 115, 186
Phillips, Ann 24
piracy 58
Plaza Accord (1985) 4
Poland 24, 183
policy issues, Japanese firms in China
    163–4
pollution 58, 123
polycentrism 188, 194n.63
population levels 1
Primakov, Yevgeny 50n.22
private sector 154–5, 171–6: background
    155–8; engagement Japanese style 62;
    future trend of the relationship 112;
    global–local dilemma *see* global–local
    dilemma; history problem 27;
    import–export programme 4; ODA
    from Japan 117; problems and

difficulties 158–66; successful cases 166–71
profitability of Japanese firms in China 156, 157, 159

Qian Qichen 57

Radebaugh, L. H. 177
Reagan administration 72
real estate markets, FDI in 143
refugees from China 58
regional disparities, China 35: FDI 144, 145, 155; Japanese firms 163; ODA 122, 123, 124
regionalism, economic relations 147, 148, 150, 152
rivalry between China and Japan 2: economic relations 148, 150–1
Robinson, Mary 46
Roh Tae Woo 22
Ross, Robert S. 41, 59, 64
Roth, K. 177
Russia: future trend of the China–Japan partnership 111; theatre missile defence 71, 80
Russo-Japanese War 3, 10

San Francisco Peace Treaty (1951) 57
Sankei Shimbun 99
Sanyo Japan 143
Sato Eisaku: Nixon–Sato communiqué 96–7; Taiwan question 90, 93
security issues 3, 4: Beijing–Tokyo–Washington triangle 39, 40, 41–2; engagement Japanese style 52–8, 60, 63–4; future trend of the relationship 112, 113; history problem 12, 19; Taiwan question 39, 40, 96–8; theatre missile defence see theatre missile defence
Security Subcommittee (SSC) 73
Segal, George 97
Self-Defence Force, Japan 12, 84n.6
self-reliance policy, China 118, 140
Senkaku Islands see Diaoyu/Senkaku Islands
service sector, FDI in 143
Shanghai Friendship Seiyu Co. Ltd 173
Shanghai ZODOS CITIC Cosmetics Co. Ltd 174
Shiina Etsusaburo 90
Shimonoseki Treaty (1895) 90
Shizuka Kamei 123
short range ballistic missiles (SRBM) 75

Simon, H. A. 179
Singapore 186
Sino-Japanese War: 1894–5: 3, 10; 1937–45 see Eight-Year War of Resistance
size of firms, and FDI 144
smuggling 58
Social Democratic Party, Japan 105
socialisation and networks, control by 179–80, 181, 187
Soeya Yoshihide 79, 81
Sony 194n.62
South China Sea 55
South Korea: attack by North Korea (1950) 92; Beijing–Tokyo–Washington triangle 50n.21; confidence building measures 61; domestic abuses 23; history problem 25; nationalism 102n.27
Soviet Union 4, 19, 32, 105–6
Spain 120
Star Wars see Strategic Defence Initiative
State Council, China 119
state-owned enterprises (SOEs), China 35
State Planning Commission, China 119
State Science and Technology Commission, China 119
Strategic Defence Initiative (SDI) 72–3, 81
Strategic Defence Initiative Office, US (SDIO) 73
structure of the partnership 103, 104–10
Sumitomo Chemical Co. Ltd 174
Sweden 180, 181
Syngman Rhee 102n.27
synthetic aperture radar (SAR) systems 78

Tahara Soichiro 13
Taipei Economic and Cultural Representative Office (TECRO) 94
Taiwan 88, 98–100: Beijing–Tokyo–Washington triangle 39–41, 44, 47, 48; engagement Japanese style 56–8, 63–4, 66; FDI in China 141, 155; gained by Japan 3, 10; history problem 14; Japanese subsidiaries in 186; legacies of colonial period and full diplomatic relations 88–93; ODA 119–20; reconciliation through ambiguity 93–5; regionalism 148; security concerns, (re-)emergence of 96–8; structure of China–Japan relationship 105, 106, 109, 110; theatre missile defence 4, 74, 75–6, 77, 78, 80, 82, 83; trade 134

202　*Index*

Taiwan Relations Act (USA, 1979) 40, 95
Taiwan Security Enhancement Act (USA, 2000) 40
Tanaka Akihiko 113n.1
Tanaka Kakuei 19, 90
Tanino Sakutaro 11–12, 17, 19, 25
taxation 159, 160, 163
Taylor, B. 184, 186
technology 2: FDI 146; Japanese companies in China 166; multinational companies 183; transfers 38, 184
Teijin 194n.69
textbook controversy *see* history problem
textile industry, Japan 3
TF Tianjin Industrial Co. Ltd 170–1, 175–6
Thailand 183
Theatre High Altitude Defence (THAAD) 71, 72, 73, 85n.12
theatre missile defence (TMD)/ballistic missile defence (BMD) 4, 69–70, 82–3: Beijing–Tokyo–Washington triangle 42, 43, 48; development 72–4; engagement Japanese style 57, 61, 64, 65, 66; 'escape routes' 78–9; impact on security relations 74–6; potential security tensions with US 76–8; strategic considerations 79–82; systems 71–2
Tiananmen Square incident 4: Japanese response 14, 19, 37, 44, 52, 61, 120; ODA 118, 120
Tibet 64
Tong Zeng 21
Toshiba 166–7
Toynbee, Arnold 20
trade 4, 131–2, 147, 149: Beijing–Tokyo–Washington triangle 33, 34, 36–7; dynamics 138–40; through Hong Kong 132–3; interdependence 134–8; ODA from Japan 116; shares 133–4; Taiwan 91; volumes 132, 133; *see also* economic relations
trade intensity indices 134–8
transnational companies 177: *see also* global–local dilemma
transport 116, 120
Tucker, L. R. 178
Tung, R. L. 181

UNICEF (United Nations Children's Fund) 121

Union of Soviet Socialist Republics *see* Soviet Union
United Kingdom 120, 184
United Nations (UN): Charter 46; Development Programme (UNDP) 118, 121; future trend for the relationship 113; Security Council 4, 61
US–Japan Security Treaties 39, 40, 43
United States of America: anti-communism 4; cooperation with Japan 4; engagement Japanese style 52, 53–4, 55, 56–8, 60, 63–6; firms in China 173, 180, 181, 184, 185, 189; FDI in China 141, 143–4, 145, 146, 155; history problem 15, 19; *rapprochement* with China 4, 39; structure of China–Japan relationship 105–6; Taiwan question 91–3, 95, 96–100; theatre missile defence 69, 70–83; trade 133, 134, 138, 139; World War II 3; *see also* Beijing–Tokyo–Washington triangle
US Space Command (USSPACECOM) 72
university proposal 50n.27
Uno Sosuke 14

Versailles Treaty 3
Vietnam 47, 102n.27

wages: efficiency 165; FDI 146, 149
Waldheim, Kurt 24
Western Pacific Missile Architecture (WESTPAC) 73
WFP (World Food Program) 121
Wiechmann, U. 177
Wong, C. S. 185
World Bank 116, 118, 120, 121, 127
World Trade Organisation (WTO): China's entry 37, 62, 113, 147, 183; Taiwan question 99
World War I 3
World War II 3, 25, 27, 115

Xi'an Xianyang International Airport Terminal Expansion Project 122

Yaji Kazuo 16
Yasukuni Shrine 13, 16, 18, 19
Yellow River Delta Comprehensive Agricultural Development Project 123
Yoshida Doctrine 96
Yuan, A. X. 185

Zhang Ming 57
Zhao, Suisheng 99
Zhou Enlai: foreign policy 37; history problem 15–16; Taiwan question 93

Zhou Hongjing 101n.16
Zhu Jianrong 27–8
Zhu Rongji 28, 45, 122
Zhuge Liang 41
Zipingpu Dam 123